THE PHILIPPINES

WHAT EVERYONE NEEDS TO KNOW®

THE PHILIPPINES
WHAT EVERYONE NEEDS TO KNOW®

STEVEN ROOD

OXFORD
UNIVERSITY PRESS

OXFORD
UNIVERSITY PRESS

Oxford University Press is a department of the University of Oxford. It furthers the University's objective of excellence in research, scholarship, and education by publishing worldwide. Oxford is a registered trade mark of Oxford University Press in the UK and certain other countries.

What Everyone Needs to Know" is a registered trademark of Oxford University Press

Published in the United States of America by Oxford University Press 198 Madison Avenue, New York, NY 10016, United States of America.

© Oxford University Press 2019

CIP data is on file at the Library of Congress
ISBN 978–0–19–092061–6 (pbk.)
ISBN 978–0–19–092060–9 (hbk.)

CONTENTS

2 History: "300 Years in a Convent, 50 Years in Hollywood," Then on Its Own   35

6 Geopolitics and the Future: The Philippines in the World   207

ACKNOWLEDGMENTS

In 2014, the Ateneo de Zamboanga University was gracious enough to give me a Peace Award for my work in the Bangsamoro Peace Process. My award lecture was entitled "I Remember Being Ignorant," and I concluded with "I remember being ignorant . . . because I still am, and learn something new always." Writing this book certainly proved this all over again—and I look forward to continued learning.

It was Paul Rodell who first suggested that the 101 blogs I had written over the years for The Asia Foundation might make the good start for a book. As I began work, the expanse of literature that confronted me made it clear that this was not as easy as it might have seemed, but I had help along the way. The Department of Political and Social Change of the Bell School, College of Asia and the Pacific (CAP) at the Australian National University (ANU) has provided me with a visiting fellowship since 2017. When I returned to the Philippines in 2018, the Social Weather Stations (SWS) provided me an office as fellow-in-residence. I am grateful to Veronica Taylor and her successor as dean of the CAP, Michael Wesley, as well as to Mahar Mangahas and Linda Guerrero, president and vice president, respectively, of SWS, for their generosity and goodwill.

The two institutions that defined my career in the Philippines were the University of the Philippines (1981–1999) and The Asia Foundation (1999–2017). The number of people to thank is beyond the scope what I can offer here, but I must mention Sophie Catbagan (now Cannon) and the late Edgardo J. Angara, who as dean of the University of the Philippines Baguio and president of the university, respectively, made it possible for me to settle into the faculty permanently. I have friends and colleagues in universities throughout the country and abroad, but the University of the Philippines is my intellectual home.

In 1999 Richard Fuller was in charge of the hiring process that brought me into The Asia Foundation, and at the end Vice President Gordon Hein and President David Arnold were generous in their support of my 2017 residential visiting fellowship at the ANU. In Washington, D.C., Vice President Nancy Yuan joined the late James J. Dalton in supporting my stint at the Foundation. My successor as Philippine country representative, Sam Chittick, has been interested in and made suggestions about this text.

During 2018 I had the opportunity to present the approach in this book at two academic conferences. I would like to thank Jowel Canuday and Enrique Niño Leviste for the invitation to present to the Ateneo School of Social Sciences, and Bernadette Churchill and Clem Camposano for the invitation to present to the Philippine Studies Association.

Bernadette Churchill and Patricio Abinales were both very complimentary about this project and the book draft. David Dutton of Australia's Department of Foreign Affairs and Trade was always supportive of my ideas. Anonymous reviewers for the Oxford University Press helped improve the thrust of the overall outline as I wrestled it into text. Athena Lydia Casambre read the entire work and edited it closely. The next pass through the text was undertaken by OUP's Holly Mitchell while David McBride, editor in chief of social sciences, was from my first inquiry a constantly enthusiastic proponent of the project.

Gabriela Casambre Rood helped decipher a particularly dense piece of postmodern scholarship, and then worked over the entire draft. Leah Aldave was an invaluable research assistant in the last months of completing the first draft. At the risk of omitting somebody, I'd like to thank several people for specific help: Teresita Ang See, Peter Bellwood, Kit Collier, Jayell Cornelio, Elyon Mondia Divina, Robin Hemley, Iramae Lacubay, Vlad Licudine, Carolyn Mercado, Emma Porio, P. J. Punla, Manuel L. Quezon III, Mary Racelis, Lawrence A. Reid, and Carlos P. Tatel Jr. Of course, any remaining mistakes are on my head.

For my part, all I needed to know about the Philippines is that it is where Athena Lydia Casambre wanted to live out our lives after we got our PhDs. All the rest is detail that I picked up along the way.

INTRODUCTION

The Philippines is an endlessly fascinating country, full of contradictions. Book titles include David Joel Steinberg's "A Singular and a Plural Place" and Alfred McCoy's "An Anarchy of Families" (see Bibliographic Essay). After Filipinos ousted Ferdinand Marcos (who ruled from 1965 to 1972 as an elected president, thereafter in an authoritarian manner until the "People Power" Revolution of 1986), Benedict Anderson wrote of the new regime as a "cacique democracy," while James Fallows declared that the country suffered from a "damaged culture."[*]

In the 1950s, the country was the third most prosperous in Asia, after Japan and Malaysia. By the turn of the century, so many countries had surpassed the Philippines that it was called the "Sick Man of Asia." Yet since the Asian financial crisis in 1997, there has not been a recession in the Philippines, not even during the 2008 global financial crisis, and in recent years the country's economic growth rate has been one of the highest in the world. A recent economics volume is subtitled "No Longer the East Asian Exception?" Still, the poverty rate remains stubbornly high.

---

[*] See section "Is the Philippines a 'cacique democracy'?" for discussion of "cacique democracy" and for "damaged culture."

When the Spanish arrived in the islands that they called *Las Islas Filipinas* (The Philippine Islands, later just the Philippines) (after King Philip II of Spain), the inhabitants mainly lived in autonomous villages that had relations with other villages. The only larger political entities were sultanates in some localities, introduced less than two hundred years before, as Islam spread through the Malay Archipelago and provided a cultural template for larger political units. Subsequent history has been described as "300 years in a convent, and then 50 years in Hollywood" after the Americans acquired the islands in the 1898 Spanish-American War. Muslims in the south and animists in highland areas largely remained "un-Hispanized," but the American colonial regime managed political control over these areas and enacted limited social change in the archipelago, particularly through education.

World War II devastated Manila, but still the country achieved full independence, on July 4, 1946. In the postwar period, two political parties alternated in power (while individual politicians did considerable party switching) until Ferdinand Marcos consolidated power, first by being the first president to win re-election, in 1969, and then by declaring martial law in 1972. When he was ousted in the peaceful "People Power" Revolution in 1986, electoral democracy was restored and the economy finally began to recover after years of crisis. Since that time, elections have been held regularly (even after President Joseph Estrada was ousted in early 2001 in "People Power II"), administrative authority has decentralized to the local government level, and social indicators have improved.

With the May 2016 election of Rodrigo Roa Duterte as president, the Philippines became more visible on the international scene, often for unfortunate reasons. Duterte's "war on drugs" has caused thousands of casualties, violent extremists managed to take over the Islamic City of Marawi in May 2017 for five months before being overcome, and the Philippines's July 2016 legal victory at the Arbitral Tribunal in the South China Sea case was not exploited; rather, President Duterte announced a shift away from longtime ally America and toward China and Russia.

Culturally, the Philippines mixes Eastern and Western influences and shares traits with developed and developing countries. English is widely spoken; the main cities have modern shopping centers, with three of the largest malls in the world in Manila; and Filipinos tend to be knowledgeable about Western (particularly American) culture. Outside the major metropolitan areas, though, it quickly becomes obvious that the Philippines is a tropical Asian country, with sometimes distressingly high rates of poverty. Modern politics is carried out on social media but still involves levels of violence that would never be found in advanced countries.

An symbol of the Philippines that embodies many contradictions is the unique jeepney, which occupies a strategic spot in Philippine ground transportation between neighborhood tricycles (either motorized or pedal powered) and larger buses. They developed from World War II surplus jeeps left behind by the American forces,[†] which were then modified locally by stretching to accommodate 16 to 20 people on facing benches in the back—while there is a roof there are no windows. Almost 200,000 have fixed-route franchises nationwide; estimates in Manila are that forty percent of all transport rides involve them. Many are very colorfully decorated based on the taste of the owner. While often cited as a cultural icon, many feel the fact that they continue to be hand-built (and continuously repaired through the years) with second-hand drive trains makes them rickety and polluting. The government for years has planned a comprehensive modernization program, phasing out the current vehicles (beginning with those more than 15 years old) in favor of purpose-built, even electric vehicles as per trends in more developed countries. However, the

---

† "Jeepney" is a portmanteau of "jeep" and "jitney." This is the point at which the Phililppines switched to drive on the right-hand side of the road, American style.

operators resist the more expensive replacements, commuters fear that the cheap fares ($0.15 to $0.60) would subsequently rise, and the everyman status of a jeepney driver provides legitimacy to resistance to this disruption of a key component of the transportation mix.

The Philippines has long been open to global influences; evidence of trading with China and India stretches back into prehistory. Under the Spanish colonial regime, the "Galleon Trade" brought silver from the colonies in Latin America to China in exchange for Chinese goods, with Manila being the entrepôt. In the contemporary world, geopolitical challenges are stark as the Philippines, long a treaty ally of the United States, "pivots" toward China under the Duterte administration. Less controversial and publicized is the Philippines's influence on the rest of the world, from the mundane (overseas workers) to the sacred (religious organizations and practices).

This volume aims to provide a general overview of the Philippines—its geography, history, culture, economy, politics, government, and prospects for the future. The question-and-answer organization of the book is meant to make it easy for readers to locate topics that are of interest to them. The main audience for this book are those interested in learning about the Philippines; however, I hope that Filipinos (and long-term residents) will feel that the portrait of the country is credible, and that the nuances of the analysis are correct.

The first chapter canvasses the diverse geography and demography of the archipelago. The second traces the history from precolonial times, through the Spanish and American colonial experiences, to independence after World War II. In recent years there have been persistent insurgencies, military adventurism, and political changes. The third chapter discusses the economy: the country's recovery from being the "sick man of Asia" but also some continuing challenges. The fourth chapter revisits the theme of diversity in society, culture, and religion. The fifth chapter discusses government and the turbulent politics of the country. The final chapter looks into the future, given the geopolitical situation the Philippines finds itself in.

In this book, I discuss things that Filipinos "know" but that are not true (such as the wave theory of migration); to this end I occasionally cite what is in school texts to illustrate what Filipinos generally would know. As someone who has worked for years both in the Cordillera of northern Luzon and in Muslim Mindanao, I try to avoid a Manila-centric viewpoint.

1

GEOGRAPHY, DEMOGRAPHY, AND CLIMATE

How many islands does the Philippines have?

When at the 1994 Miss Universe pageant (being held in the Philippines), Philippine contestant Charlene Gonzales was asked, "How many islands does the Philippines have?," she quipped, "High tide or low tide?" Filipinos loved the insouciance, though later she admitted that she was basically stalling for time to recall the answer, and in any case a feature in the sea that disappears at high tide does not qualify as an "island" (an important distinction for disputes in the South China Sea). The correct answer was thought to be 7,107 islands, but in 2016 the official count from the National Mapping and Resource Information Authority was updated to 7,641, though fewer than 3,000 have a name and only some 2,000 are inhabited.

One new element of discussion on the number of islands is the possible effect of global warming and sea rise—that the number would decrease as islands are submerged. While there are no serious estimates of how many might disappear, it has been estimated that more than 167,000 hectares of coastland—about 0.6 percent of the country's total area—are projected to go underwater in the Philippines by the end of the century.

There were fewer islands during the last period of maximum glaciation, when sea levels fell because so much water was locked in ice—perhaps 120 meters below the current level. As seen in figure 1.1, the southern island of "Greater" Mindanao was connected with Samar, Leyte, and Bohol, and with Basilan in the period when the shallow seas receded. "Greater" Luzon connected to such islands as Marinduque and Catanduanes, while the central islands of Panay, Negros, and Cebu became one. "Greater" Sulu was connected to some of the islands in the province of Tawi-Tawi. Palawan was separated from the rest of the Philippine islands by a deep trench; in the distant past it was connected to Borneo and to the Asian landmass that paleontologists have dubbed "Sundaland," but never to the rest of the Philippines.

Figure 1.1 illustrates that some of the seas around and among the current islands of the archipelago are shallow, while there are some deep dividing trenches. On the east there is the Philippine Trench, the third deepest trench in the world. On the west of Luzon there is the Manila Trench, which helps to separate Palawan from Mindoro. The center of the Philippines is called by geologists the "Philippine Mobile Belt," which is an indication (along with many identified fault lines throughout the country) of just how seismically active the country is, producing earthquakes and underlying the volcanoes.

Of the currently existing islands, eleven have 94 percent of the land mass (and 96 percent of the population). Luzon in the north is the largest (fifteenth largest in the world), covering one-third of the country's land area and stretching 740 kilometers from north to south. Metro Manila (comprising sixteen cities and one municipality) is on Luzon and has Manila City itself as the "capital city," but the entire metropolis is the seat of government because many government offices are scattered among other cities of the metro area.

The southern island of Mindanao, the second largest in the country (nineteenth largest in the world), includes the heartland of Muslims in the Philippines because the associated islands of the Sulu Archipelago stretch out toward the island of Borneo, making sea communication with the Malay Archipelago quite easy. These are among the trading routes

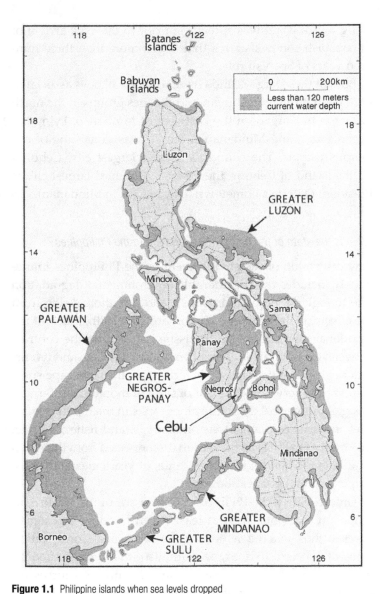

Figure 1.1 Philippine islands when sea levels dropped

Source: Darin A. Croft, Lawrence R. Heaney, John J. Flynn, Angel P. Bautista, *Journal of Mammalogy* 87, no. 5 (October 2006): 1037–1051, figure 1, p. 1038

along which Islam was spreading prior to the 1565 arrival of the Spanish conquistadores that began more than three hundred years of Spanish rule.

Both of these large islands have some small ones associated with them, from the Babuyan and Batanes groups in the north of Luzon to Siargao on the east side of Mindanao. Lying between Luzon and Mindanao is the Visayas, consisting of numerous islands. The country's second largest city, Cebu, is on the island of Cebu in the Visayas (the third largest city is President Duterte's hometown, Davao City, in Mindanao).

What is the state of the natural environment in the Philippines?

Any discussion of the environment in the Philippines immediately includes the considerable environmental degradation due to logging, population stress, and pollution. Aside from the effects on the economy and on human health, much of the emotional tone relating to the issue is based on the contrast between the natural biodiversity of the archipelago and its current degraded state. The soil is fertile and the landscape spectacular (it is very rare to be out of sight of mountains). Termed "mega-biodiverse," the Philippines ranks in the top five countries in terms of plants, trees, mammals, and fishes; the fact that most of the islands have been disconnected from the Asian mainland for hundreds of thousands of years means that endemic (unique) species abound.

Unfortunately, the Philippines is also one of the world's biodiversity hotspots, with at least seven hundred threatened species, thus making it one of the top global conservation areas of concern. In 2007, an administrative order issued by the Department of Environment and Natural Resources established a national list of threatened plant species, indicating that 99 species were critically endangered, 187 were endangered, 176 were vulnerable, and 64 were threatened.

It is estimated that 90 percent of the islands were covered by forests at the beginning of the Spanish colonial period, and

70 percent at the end. By the middle of the twentieth century, shortly after independence from the American colonial administration, approximately 55 percent remained, whereas by now it is estimated that only 3 percent of the Philippines land area is covered by primary virgin forest, the lowest among Conservation International's biodiversity hotspots. At least the rate of destruction has eased; over the last twenty-five years various government policies (including the National Greening Program begun in 2011) have led to a slow (0.7 percent per year) increase in forest cover.

A similar assessment could be made of fisheries resources. Visitors to the Philippines in the mid-nineteenth century were struck by the fact that fishers would start cooking the rice before they set off to catch fish for the meal; it was faster to land a catch than to the few minutes it takes to cook rice. The Philippines still is a major fishing ground, ranking tenth in the world in terms of fish catch. Some 90 percent of this is consumed in the country, with Filipinos consuming an average thirty-three kilos of fish per person each year (ranking thirteenth in the world). Given the population increase, it is unsurprising that there is pressure on fish stocks, with some 70 percent of fish populations overfished. Thus, in recent years fish catch has stagnated (though total marine production has increased due to farmed fish in aquaculture).

Pressure is increased by the use of destructive fishing methods, such as dynamite or poison to stun fish, with obvious implications for the health of coral reefs. The Philippines is part of the incredibly biodiverse Coral Triangle, but only 5 percent of the country's coral reefs are in excellent condition. Considerable effort has been expended over the years to institute marine protected areas to preserve the habitat (and increase yields). The reefs of Apo Island off the coast of Negros Oriental in the Visayas remain in excellent condition after more than thirty-five years of preservation (initiated by Silliman University in Dumaguete City), and many local efforts around the country hope to emulate that success.

Solid waste and water pollution remain persistent problems. A law passed in 2000 was intended to regulate solid waste management, including the phaseout of open dumpsites. Unfortunately, the cost to localities and the rapid turnover of local officials (who have three-year terms, with a maximum of three consecutive terms) means that over half of localities still have open dumpsites. Downstream, the Philippines is ranked third in the world (after China and Indonesia) for plastic debris that washes into the ocean marine environment.

Water pollution is an increasing problem, with only half of freshwater bodies in the country rated by the Environmental Management Bureau as having good water quality (40 percent fair, and the rest poor). The problem is most widespread in the area in and around Metro Manila, with its concentration of population and industrial production. But the problem can be severe elsewhere, as evidenced by the six-month total shutdown in 2018 of the Philippines's foremost seaside destination, Boracay Island, due to long-standing concerns about the contamination of the waters at the beach. Many establishments on the resort island were not connected to any sewage system but discharged wastewater directly into the sea.

It can be said that the issue of air pollution is not quite as dire as for other forms of pollution. Urban air pollution from vehicular traffic has been slowly improving, beginning with the elimination of lead from gasoline in 2000. Emissions testing has been stepped up, and the result is that pollution by small particulate matter (PM2.5) in Metro Manila has come down to levels much below cities in India and China and comparable to Bangkok and Kuala Lumpur—though at 17 micrograms per cubic meter of air ($\mu g/m^3$) per year, it is still above the World Health Organization's recommended safe level of 10 $\mu g/m^3$. The majority of the remaining pollution comes from public transportation (jeepneys and buses) with poorly maintained diesel engines.

There is considerable citizen and civil society activism around environmental issues, and over the years policy improvements have been enacted. Governance weaknesses tend to reduce the impact of environmental remediation efforts, however. The Pasig River, biologically dead despite sporadic rehabilitation efforts over the years, runs through the heart of Metro Manila through nine different local government jurisdictions that are all mandated to protect the environment. The appearance of many stretches of the river has improved, but it remains unable to sustain healthy aquatic life.

The Philippines does have "charismatic megafauna" such as the majestic "monkey-eating" Philippine eagle (critically endangered, with only some six hundred in the wild) and the shy nocturnal Philippine tarsier (classified as "threatened" in 2015 by the International Union for the Conservation of Nature). For these animals, as well as for less visible cases in air, land, and sea, the main danger comes from habitat loss. Thus, the news that forest cover is slowly recovering is welcome. In general, there is some evidence that "conservation in the Philippines, against many odds, shows signs of success."[1]

What is the weather like in the Philippines?

In a word, the weather is tropical, with frequent storms. This is unsurprising because the archipelago lies entirely in the tropics, in latitudes between the equator and the Tropic of Cancer (4° to 21° north).

One peculiarity of the widespread use of English in the Philippines is the mismatch between seasonal names and the months of the year. The Philippine term for the long, hot, dry days of April and May is literally "the time of heat," but among English speakers this is referred to as "summer," rather to the bemusement of Americans who associate that term with June through August. Hence the label "summer brownouts" for the possible power shortages feared to occur in May, the hottest month overall in the country. ("Brownouts" is a Filipinism;

rather than referring to voltage reductions, it means power outages or "blackouts.")

However, truly scorching temperatures are not encountered; 42.2 degrees Celsius (107.96 degrees Fahrenheit) is the highest, recorded in northern Luzon in the Cagayan Valley. The lowest officially recorded temperature was 6.3 degrees in Baguio City on Luzon, the "summer capital" at an altitude of 1,700 meters, which was established in the early twentieth century by the American colonial power. The temperatures in the rural hinterlands of this Cordillera Mountain range sometimes allow frost to form and threaten the commercial vegetable crops. But there is no snow, though hail is far from unknown.

The seasonality of the weather is often characterized in a Manila-centric way as being dry and cool from November to March, hot in April and May, with a rainy season that begins in June. In truth, seasonality of weather depends where one is in the Philippines (e.g., the eastern Pacific coast versus the coast facing the West Philippine/South China Sea), but without north-south distinctions since the entire country lies in the tropics. For most of the country, outside of Mindanao, weather is driven by the shifting seasonal prevailing winds. The effect of these monsoons is different for different locations (see figure 1.2).

The west coast of the Philippines, including the sociopolitical center Metro Manila, tends to have one wet and one dry season: rains brought on by the southwest monsoon (*habagat* in Filipino) from May through November, then a dry period December through April (at first cool, then increasingly hotter). Of course "cool" is relative, since the average low temperature is still above 20 degrees C in January, while the high temperature during the hottest month (May) is only an average of 5 degrees more than in January. In short, temperature variation is low.

The eastern coast of Bicol (in southern Luzon) and eastern Visayas and Mindanao tend to have rain year-round (though

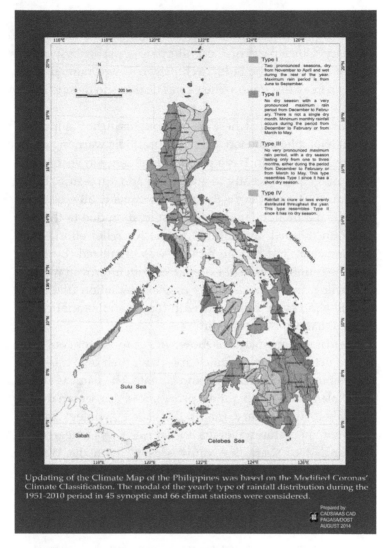

Updating of the Climate Map of the Philippines was based on the Modified Coronas'
Climate Classification. The modal of the yearly type of rainfall distribution during the
1951-2010 period in 45 synoptic and 66 climat stations were considered.

Figure 1.2 Climate map of the Philippines (1951–2010)

Source: Philippine Atmospheric, Geophysical and Astronomical Services Administration
(PAGASA)

they are driest from March to May) and one very wet season during the northeast monsoon (*amihan*) from December to February. Other parts of the Philippines—particularly much of Mindanao and the Sulu Archipelago—have rainfall more evenly spread throughout the year. There are no deserts in the Philippines!

That's not to say that there are no droughts in the Philippines. The El Niño phenomenon, driven by periodic warming of the eastern Pacific Ocean, has a profound influence in years when it is strong, most recently in 1997–1998 and 2015–2016. In the subsequent drought in 1998, before the rains finally returned, more than a million families faced starvation due to their reliance on rain-fed agriculture. A massive relief effort—both governmental and private sector—was organized. By 2015–2016 the country was better prepared, with improved weather forecasting and a much better financial situation (the 1997–1998 El Niño event coincided with the Asian financial crisis), so the situation was not so dire.

There is one anomaly not shown in figure 1.2: the cool areas of Benguet—including Baguio City—have their own classification: subtropical oceanic highland climate. The name is almost self-explanatory—with quite a pronounced dry season during December and January (naturally, called "winter" though the low temperatures average 13 degrees C, 55.4 degrees F). This area does share the "rainy season" with the Western Philippines, and then some; Baguio gets 50 percent more rain than does Manila, with more than two meters per year falling.

Why is the Philippines labeled disaster prone?

Heavy seasonal tropical monsoon rains cause floods and landslides; typhoons are frequent; and the Philippines is located along the Pacific "Ring of Fire," which produces earthquakes and volcanic eruptions. "Natural disasters" are exacerbated by societal conditions and the poor quality of physical infrastructure in the country. Taking both sets of factors into account, the Philippines typically ranks third most vulnerable in the world—after the Pacific Island nations of Vanuatu and Tonga—and more vulnerable than Guatemala and Bangladesh.

An average of ten destructive storms make landfall per year, with another ten entering the Philippine Area of Responsibility. The Philippines takes the unusual step of giving storms a local name, sometimes causing confusion since the rest of the world uses just the international name. Since the weather phenomenon is caused by warm water in the Pacific, typhoons are rarest from December through March and most frequent from June through October. But typhoons can happen any time of year. One of the strongest on record, typhoon Haiyan (local name Yolanda), hit in November 2013 and caused some seven thousand deaths due to flooding and a storm surge.

Typhoons can bring enormous amounts of rain; the Philippine record is over 2,200 mm in Baguio City in 1911 (the second highest is more than 1,800 mm in 2009, also in Baguio City). But the southwest monsoon can be intensified by weather patterns to also bring destructive amounts of rain— particularly to western Luzon—ranging from 450 to 600 mm in only twenty-four hours. Given that this area includes Metro Manila and the most industrialized areas of the country, such rainfall can cause considerable damage. This regular occurrence exceeds any twenty-four-hour record in the United Kingdom, matches the all-time record in Sydney, and is over three times the record for rainfall in a day in Washington, D.C.

Local weather forecasting has dramatically improved in recent years, with the Philippine Atmospheric, Geophysical, and Astronomical Services Administration (PAGASA; "hope" in Filipino) acquiring equipment and expertise that allow it to more accurately predict not only storm tracks but also the possibility of storm surges and, more generally, forecast the intensity of rainfall. Local government officials have become more proactive about closing schools and offices in line with forecasts, so that stories of children being stuck in flood-impeded traffic have declined.

As for earthquakes, mild tremors are frequently felt throughout the country, and destructive earthquakes occur. The deadliest was in 1976 when a quake in the Moro Gulf hit at midnight and caused a tsunami (reaching an estimated 9 meters in height) that swept southwestern Mindanao and parts of the Sulu Archipelago, leaving some 10,000 killed or missing. The earthquake on July 16, 1990, in northern Luzon caused 2,500 casualties; it is sometimes called the Baguio earthquake because that city in the mountainous Cordillera region sustained the most damage. One-third of the structures in the city were damaged.

The other recent earthquake that caused extensive damage occurred in October 2013 in the center of the country, most severely affecting the islands of Bohol and Cebu. Some 230 persons were killed or remain missing, and a number of centuries-old historic churches were destroyed. Residents of the Greater Manila Area have been warned about the "Big One" from the Marikina Valley fault System, expected to be 7.2 on the Richter scale, which could kill 50,000 persons and injure more than 100,000. Recently, periodic earthquake drills ("drop, cover, and hold on") have been instituted to prepare residents.

The Philippine Institute of Volcanology and Seismology (PHIVOLCS) lists twenty-four active volcanos, so catastrophic volcanic eruptions are a constant possibility, though considerably rarer than earthquakes. Most famous is the June 1991 eruption of Mt. Pinatubo, the second largest in the twentieth century. Volcanologists successfully warned residents in the weeks ahead of the eruption, and tens of thousands evacuated. In the event, fewer than one thousand persons were killed, many by roofs collapsing under the weight of volcanic ash. Volcanic ash deposits and flows of lahar (volcanic ash and rock carried by water) remade the landscape of Central Luzon, with normal land travel routes taking a decade to be completely rehabilitated. An immediate consequence was the closure of the nearby US facility Clark Air Base, due to heavy ash fall—a prelude to the closure of all US bases in the Philippines after the

Philippine Senate rejected an agreement that would have allowed their continuation.

At the other end of the volcanic spectrum, Mt. Mayon frequently erupts, and produces lava flows, leading to formation of an almost perfect steep cone. Its most destructive eruption was in 1814, when more than one thousand people were killed in the nearby town of Cagsawa; the ruins of the church still stand as a tourist attraction (see figure 1.3). And Mayon remains the most active of Philippine volcanos, with alert levels being raised and evacuations ordered several times each decade, but no casualties have been recorded since the early 1990s.

Other notable volcanos include Taal, only 50 kilometers from Manila and the site of the booming city of Tagaytay, which is much prized for its cooler temperatures (some 5 degrees lower than in Manila), as it is at 600 meters altitude, on a ridge overlooking the volcano. Its most recent deadly eruption was in 1911, when more than one thousand people died. There was an impressive eruption in 1754, documented by fleeing

Figure 1.3 Mt. Mayon and ruined Cagsawa church
Source: © iStock/gionnixxx

Spanish clergy. Taal's proximity to densely populated areas increases concern about what might happen.

Where did inhabitants of the Philippines come from?

In 2018, an exciting archaeological discovery was reported in the journal *Nature*, revealing evidence for early human occupation in the Philippines 709,000 years ago. While hominid remains were not found, a nearly complete skeleton of a rhinoceros that had been butchered and some stone tools were unearthed. It is not clear how these early humans (or the rhinoceros, for that matter) got to the island of Luzon, which has been separate from the Asian mainland for millions of years (see figure 1.1).

The earliest hominid remains have been found in Callao Cave in the nearby Cagayan Valley and are sixty-seven thousand years old. Thirteen bones and teeth were enough for the researchers to argue in 2019 that these are from a previously unknown species they dubbed *Homo Luzonensis*. As with the discovery from the much earlier era, there are remains of butchered animals present, though no tools.

Skipping ahead several tens of thousands of years, more extensive remains from the Tabon Cave complex in Palawan have been positively identified as *Homo sapiens* and dated to thirty thousand to forty-five thousand years ago. Here, we can begin to speculate on where these inhabitants came from, since Palawan during periods of maximum glaciation (meaning, minimum sea levels) was part of "Sundaland" and thus connected to mainland Asia. This cave complex has materials covering tens of thousands of years, with burial jars, human remains, and tools, possibly until seven hundred years ago, including trade goods from China. Thus, we can turn our attention to the current population of the Philippines: Where did it come from?

Land migration from mainland Asia was never possible (see figure 1.1). The long-dominant "wave theory" of migration, which claims that three different groups came to the Philippines over the years by sea, is usually attributed to H. Otley Beyer, but it in fact predates him. An Austrian anthropologist who became a close friend of José Rizal, Ferdinand Blumentritt, hypothesized such waves in 1882, and this influenced Rizal and other *ilustrados* (secular intellectuals) in the late nineteenth century. A University of Michigan scholar, Dean C. Worcester, then took up the idea, writing "The Native Peoples of the Philippines" for the 1900 report of the Philippine Commission, newly installed by the American conquerors, in which he enumerated Negritos, and then Indonesians, followed by Malays, with increasing levels of technological sophistication.

Most Philippine adults were taught this description of the populating of the country by successive waves; the durability of this theory is seen in its inclusion in the 2013 redesign of the public school curriculum as a "theory" to be discussed along with more recent theories.

In any case, there is virtually no evidence for the wave theory. It now seems clear that "Australo-Papuan" or "Sundalanders" migrated from mainland Asia through Southeast Asia and beyond and are the ancestors of Aetas and Negritos in the Philippines and Southeast Asia, Papuans in the highlands of New Guinea, and Aboriginal Australians. Given that the most recent estimates are that humans reached Australia sixty-eight thousand years ago, it certainly is possible that the archaeological evidence from Callao Cave and the Tabon Caves originates with these people.

Who came next is expounded in a widely accepted model: the influx of Austronesian-speaking immigrants from Taiwan. This group presumably originated from southern China, although Austronesian languages no longer exist on the mainland. Austronesian is the language family with the greatest global spread—all the way to Madagascar off the coast of Africa and Hawai'i in the Pacific. This model was labeled "The Express Train to Polynesia" by Jared Diamond in 1988. Genetic evidence for this migration into the Philippines is strong, but it is disputed whether there was further move-ment of people on an "express train" or a diffusion of lan-guages over the extended geographic space.

As noted, there are descendants of the original population still in the Philippines. Indeed, the fact that Negritos and Aetas are found in several places throughout the islands bolsters the case that a considerable number of them were already pre-sent upon the arrival of Austronesian migrants. Austronesian speakers did not wipe out their predecessors, but their use of domesticated plants and animals in agricultural production allowed them to out-produce and out-reproduce the hunter-gatherers, spread throughout the lowlands, and influence the culture of the previous inhabitants.

Linguistic and archaeological evidence helps unravel what the Austronesians brought that made them so successful and widespread. Certainly they had boats and sails, knew about the monsoon winds, and knew how to fish. Crucially, they grew rice, probably initially in coastal or lowland marshy areas. They domesticated pigs and dogs and brought along red-slipped pottery, wherein a thin mixture of clay was put on top of the basic pottery before firing.

Thus, there do seem to have been two "waves" of human migration to the islands that came to be known as the Philippines (hominids presumably butchered the rhinoc-eros). But the second migration came from the north rather than other parts of the Malay Archipelago. This second wave may have continued through archipelagic Southeast Asia and far afield to Hawai'i and Madagascar. This is not to say that the Philippines was not influenced by mainland countries. There is clear evidence of the cultural impact of India and China over the centuries, and certainly Islam came to the Philippines via the Malay Archipelago. But the basic population flow was of Austronesian speakers coming from the north.

What are the size, trajectory, and distribution of the population of the Philippines?

In terms of size, the Philippines has now passed 100 million persons (104 million estimated for 2018), making it the thirteenth largest country in the world by population. The growth rate has been slowly declining over the decades and is now at 1.6 percent per year, versus 1.1 percent in Indonesia and 0.3 percent in Thailand. A comparison with Thailand is an apt illustration of the effect of declining birth rates. In 1970, Thailand and the Philippines had roughly the same population, 36 or 37 million people. By 2015, the Philippines had grown to 101 million, while Thailand had only 68 million.

Population control advocates claim that reducing birth rates would make it easier to reduce pressure on natural resources and provide social services for citizens. Opponents point to the possibility that a drastic reduction in population growth—as in Thailand, as well as richer countries such as Japan, Korea, and Germany—can lead to an "old age" burden of fewer persons of working age supporting the retired segment of the population (a particular problem for retirement schemes such as the Social Security System in the Philippines).

This is a long-running argument, fueled in part by the Roman Catholic Church's official opposition to artificial methods of birth control. It is not, however, the religious belief of the average Filipino that keeps the rate of births high; repeated surveys have demonstrated approval for government-sponsored family planning programs. Rather, there is a considerable unmet need for contraception since the government was not providing family planning materials. In 2013, the percentage of married women of child-bearing age using modern methods of contraception was only 37 percent, compared to 58 percent in Indonesia. Only the passage of the Reproductive Health Act in December 2012 finally involved the national government in provision of reproductive health services.

Aside from the issue of using contraception to avoid unwanted births, there is a general decline in the number of children desired. Planning for a smaller family is often connected to the education of women (who in the Philippines are better educated than the men). In the 2013 Demographic and Health Survey, women who had been to college had a total fertility rate (TFR) of 2.1, which is generally described as the "replacement rate" (if all women had 2.1 children, the population would stabilize). Those who only studied through elementary school had a TFR of 4.6.

The Reproductive Health Law, passed in 2012, more than a decade after it was first introduced in the Philippine Congress, reframed the population growth issue in broader health terms. The fight over the law included a court challenge and a ruling by the Philippines Food and Drug Agency that available contraceptive methods are safe and not abortifacients, abortion being absolutely banned in the Philippines. The law was only fully implemented in November 2017.

Geographically, the island of Luzon is the fourth most populous in the world, though it is only the fifteenth largest in area. Greater Metro Manila is estimated in 2015 have twenty-four million people. The southern area of Mindanao and associated islands account for about one-fourth of the Philippine population, with the Davao metropolitan area estimated at 2.5 million, while the central island cluster of the Visayas has about one-fifth. In the Visayas, Cebu styles itself the "Queen City of the South," with the second largest metropolitan population, about three million.

Internal migration over the years has filled up what were previously sparsely populated rural areas, such as Cagayan Valley in the north and large areas of Mindanao in the south. Spontaneous migration of rural peasants from the northwestern Ilocos region, with its narrow coastal plain, made Ilocano the language of two-thirds of current residents of the Cagayan Valley (on the other side of the rugged Cordillera mountain range). A similar migration from the Visayas to the broad plains of Mindanao led to Cebuano being the most widely spoken language in that region, though Ilonggos also came from the Visayas, and Ilocanos from the far north. By the late 1950s, though, these "frontiers" had closed, with available land already taken.

Of course, many moved to the bright lights of the cities instead of to agricultural areas, but the Philippines is not a particularly urbanized country by world standards. Leaving aside advanced economies, the Philippines has 44 percent of its population in urban areas, less than Indonesia and Thailand (55 percent and 53 percent, respectively) but more than Vietnam, Myanmar, and India (35 percent, 35 percent, and 31 percent, respectively).

Finally, as might be guessed from a look at a map of the more than seven thousand islands in the Philippine archipelago, the Philippines has an extraordinarily long coastline. It is the fifth longest in the world, at 36,000 kilometers (Canada is number one with 202,000 km, and Indonesia is number two at 55,000 km). This means that a majority of cities and municipalities are along the coast, and these contain 62 percent of the population.

What languages are spoken in the Philippines?

While counts differ from various sources, a common estimate is 183 different languages are still in use. Filipinos, particularly those proficient in English, often refer to Philippine languages as "dialects," but in fact they are mutually unintelligible languages. Despite continuing complaints about the decline of English proficiency, it is widely spoken; in any gathering foreigners will find somebody who understands English. Spanish was never widespread and faded away under the impact of general education in English introduced by the American colonial administration. As the twentieth century wore on, English became dominant because it was the language of instruction at all levels and thus needed for entry into the professions or the elite. The place of English in the Philippines can be a fraught topic, as some stigmatize it as a colonial language, but for decades the Philippines managed to avoid some of the language divisions that exist elsewhere; all Filipino languages were equally disadvantaged when English was necessary for social advancement.

Beginning in the Commonwealth period, efforts were made to promote a national language, "Filipino," with a "language week" each August, expanded to a month in 1997. In 1937, the Commonwealth government officially adopted Tagalog as the basis for a national language now known as Filipino. In the American period, students were fined if they spoke any Philippine language in school. For a long period after World War II, students were fined if they spoke any language other than the Tagalog-based "Filipino" (generally their mother tongue: Cebuano, Ilocano, Bicolano, etc.). After the overthrow of President Marcos in 1986 a nationalist reaction ensued, and Philippine languages became much more emphasized. Naturally, these kinds of shifts concerned those who wanted to maintain a comparative advantage in English-language competency, as well as those who resented the dominance of a "Filipino" that at its core is Tagalog, the language of the National Capital Region.

In 2012, the Department of Education began full implementation of a mother-tongue-based multilingual education; through the third grade, instruction would be in the mother tongue, with English and Filipino as subjects. Of course, instructional materials cannot be produced in 183 different languages, but the Department of Education strives to provide 19 different languages. From grades 4 to 6, there is a graduated transition, so that from grades 7 to 12 instruction is in English and Filipino.

Among Filipino languages, the two most widespread are Tagalog-based Filipino (originally spoken in the area around Manila, now the language with the most native speakers, with roughly one-third of the population conversant) and Cebuano (originally from the area around the second most populated city, Cebu; roughly one-fourth of the population cites it as a mother tongue). Both languages are now routinely utilized far outside their region of origin. Given that much of the media (particularly television and cinema) is in Filipino, it is not surprising that over half of the country speaks it as a second language. As a result of the extensive migration from the central Philippines to Mindanao, Cebuano (sometimes misleadingly called "Bisaya") is a lingua franca in that region and is dominant on the streets of Davao, the third largest city in the country, where President Duterte was previously city mayor. Besides Filipino and Cebuano, Ilocano is politically important given that the late president Marcos (in office 1965–1986) was from the Ilocos. Also, Ilocanos often migrated to other parts of Luzon and Mindanao because the Ilocos region is quite mountainous and thus not very suitable for agriculture.

Eleven additional languages have a million or more native speakers, so that a total of fourteen major languages cover some 87 percent of the population, and the nineteen adopted by the Department of Education (including four spoken by predominantly Muslim populations—Maranao, Maguindanao, Tausug, and Yakan) accommodate over 90 percent of students.

All of the languages native to the Philippine archipelago are Austronesian. Interestingly, even descendants of the preexisting Australo-Papuan population, the Aetas and Negritos, have adopted Austronesian languages. Presumably, hunter-gatherers who are surrounded by larger numbers of farmers and fisherfolk, with whom they interact, gradually undergo a language shift.

The far-flung influence of Austronesian is seen in the fact that the language of the Sama-Badjaw (generally styled "Badjao" in the Philippines) is related to Malagasy, the Austronesian indigenous language of Madagascar. Otherwise, it only resembles Yakan, the indigenous language of Basilan in the Sulu Archipelago of the Philippines. Sama-Badjaw are often called "sea gypsies" based on their traditional seaborne lifestyle. These nomads were probably part of the spice trade before the arrival of Europeans, and genetic evidence tends to suggest they were part of the Austronesian migration across the Indian Ocean, though this is not certain.

Another outlier among major Philippine languages is Chavacano, spoken in Zamboanga City. Linguists refer to this as "Mindanao Creole Spanish."[2] Zamboanga was a Spanish outpost among the Muslims of Mindanao and the Sulu Archipelago continuously from 1718. Over the years the Spanish garrison and administration obviously influenced the local language, while later the administrative importance of Chavacano meant that it can be heard elsewhere in Mindanao. Linguists say that the underlying grammar and structure is influenced by Austronesian languages such as Tagalog, Ilonggo, and Cebuano, but much of the vocabulary comes from Spanish or even central American languages, since the Philippines was administered as part of the Viceroyalty of New Spain (Mexico) until Mexico gained its independence in 1821.

Is Manila a "primate city"?

In geographical discussions, a "primate city" in a country is twice as populous as its second largest city. Bangkok, Jakarta, and Dhaka, where economic activity and political power coalesce in one locale, are widely recognized as primate cities, with the rest of the country focused on the capital city. Manila has qualified as one since it became the entrepôt for the Galleon Trade between New Spain (Mexico) and China, and it had a monopoly on all foreign trade under the Spanish colonial system until 1834. Throughout the history of the Philippine archipelago, Manila has loomed large.

Lists of primate cities tend not to include Manila, despite considerable complaints in the country about the dominance of "Imperial Manila." Manila is also frequently characterized as "the most densely populated city in the world." The root of both of these observations lies in the confusion between "Manila" as a concept and the administrative unit "Manila City."

When people speak of "Manila" in the more generic sense, they are thinking of the dominance of media outlets (which tend to be in Quezon City), education (Manila City, Quezon City), finance (Makati and Taguig), and national government agencies (Quezon City, Pasig, Makati, Manila City). In short, they are thinking of Metro Manila. The city of Manila is only one of sixteen cities (plus Pateros, a geographically small municipality) that make up the National Capital Region. Metro Manila, as the capital region is often called (e.g., the Metro Manila Development Authority), is indeed more than twice as populous (at 13 million) as the second largest metropolitan area, Metro Cebu (3 million) and the third largest, Metro Davao (2.5 million).

The urban agglomeration radiating out from the historic capital on Manila Bay extends beyond the formal administrative boundaries of Metro Manila into the nearby provinces of Cavite, Laguna, Bulacan, and Rizal. In this Greater Manila Area there are some twenty-four million people, and this built-up area is the second most densely populated in the world (after Mumbai, just ahead of Greater Delhi). The Greater Manila Area comprises over half of the Philippine economy and has about one-fourth of the country's population.

Everything outside of the Greater Manila Area is called "the provinces," often with a derogatory connotation of lack of sophistication. But life in the big city itself can be quite grim. It may not be the "Gates of Hell" portrayed in one of Dan Brown's novels, but there are less spectacular aspersions cast at it. Some 24 percent of the population of Metro Manila is informal settlers, with perhaps 100,000 living in dangerous circumstances such as along waterways that flood, under road bridges, and along railways. Filipinos of all strata recognize that Manila is one of the worst cities in the world for traffic, as measured by driving app Waze.

Striking contrasts abound between modern buildings and informal settlements. Economic opportunities also abound: Metro Manila has three of the twelve largest shopping malls in the world; both formal and informal services provide employment opportunities; and the National Capital Region has the lowest poverty incidence, in both official statistics from the National Statistics Coordination Board and in survey-based "self-rated poverty" from the Social Weather Stations.

The dominance of Manila has contributed to the spread of the Tagalog-derived Filipino language, as television and cinema production are overwhelmingly concentrated in the area. Even as new technology has allowed local outlets of national broadcast networks to offer news in more local languages, Tagalog media dominate. National government offices are in the Greater Manila Area, and national officials who do not use English speak in Filipino. President Duterte is a striking exception, regularly slipping colloquially into the Cebuano of his hometown, Davao City.

During the martial law years an attempt was made to govern Metro Manila as a whole, with President Marcos's wife Imelda being made governor of Metro Manila. After the 1986 ouster of President Marcos, there was no longer a governor, but an appointed "chairman" of the Metropolitan Manila Development Authority. The sixteen cities and one municipality (Pateros, being too small in area to qualify as a "city") all retain their powers under the 1991 Local Government Code. This means that there are seventeen mayors with control and supervision of their local police, each local government operates its own solid waste management system, and traffic rules (particularly vehicle reduction schemes banning cars on certain roads on certain days) vary from jurisdiction to jurisdiction. In short, Metro Manila is similar to the eighteen other administrative regions of the country, with no overarching government.

Under the administration of President Duterte (2016–) there has been a push toward a federal system of government, instituting federal states across the country. In that constitutional change, questions of how to govern Metro Manila—Will it still be the national capital? Will it have a similar (though contentious) status as New Delhi, a federal capital?—are certain to arise.

How far is it "from Aparri to Jolo" (and what is in between)?

"From Aparri to Jolo" is the iconic way to say "from one end of the Philippines to the other." In a straight line, the distance from Aparri on the north coast of the island of Luzon to Jolo in the Sulu Archipelago is 1,371 kilometers. Should one try to do it by land, the journey would cover 2,134 kilometers, with the last leg from Zamboanga City (at the western tip of the island of Mindanao) to Jolo having to be made by ferry.

However, this is a restricted view of "one end to the other." From the capital of the northernmost province, Batanes, to the capital of the southernmost province, Tawi-Tawi—that is, from Basco to Bongao—is 1,710 kilometers as the crow flies. And from the northernmost island municipality in Batanes, Itbayat, to the southernmost island municipality in Tawi-Tawi, Sitangkay, is 1,906 kilometers. This is roughly the distance from the Canadian to the Mexican borders of the West Coast of the United States.

The Philippines is not as wide east to west as it is long north to south; the distance from the eastern shore of Mindanao to the westernmost part of Palawan is some 1,060 kilometers. Subduction zones in the east and the west, associated with the Philippine and Manila Trenches, push most of the archipelago (on the Philippine Mobile Belt) into a general north-south orientation. The Philippines covers some 300,000 square kilometers, roughly the same size as Italy or the US state of Arizona. With 183 different languages, though, diversity is a key feature. A quick scan of localities from north to south yields an overall idea of the variety found throughout the Philippines.

In the north of the main island of Luzon, there are two mountain ranges, the Cordillera Central and the Sierra Madre, extending along the eastern Pacific coast. The Ilocos coast, Ferdinand Marcos's home region, lies to the west of the Cordillera. Since the coast is narrow, land-hungry Ilocanos filled the broad Cagayan Valley between the two mountain ranges. Both highlands are home to numerous indigenous communities; these ethnolinguistic groups remained un-Hispanized because of the difficult terrain, and in fact may originate from those who fled from the Spanish-controlled lowlands. In the Cordillera, there is Baguio City, the "Summer Capital" that was established by the American colonial administration at the beginning of its occupation because the city's 1,700-meter altitude provides a respite from the hot season of April and May.

By far the largest contiguous area of plains in the Philippines is that of Central Luzon. The Luzon plains stretch all the way from the Lingayen Gulf to Tagaytay and Los Baños south of Metro Manila. This has long been a rich agricultural area, but as modernization progresses, this area is increasingly urbanized.

This brings us to "Manila"—the city of Manila, Metro Manila, or Greater Manila. For centuries the Chinese traded with Manila, and there was a Muslim ruler connected with the Sultanate of Brunei when the Spanish arrived in 1571. Thereafter, it was the center of the Spanish colonial administration, and the Galleon Trade between New Spain (Mexico) and China, with Manila as the entrepôt, was the economic lifeblood of the colony.

The southern stretch of Luzon is the Bicol Peninsula, one of the poorest regions of the country, as it is often the entry point for typhoons. Bicol includes Mount Mayon, a perfectly conical volcano with lava flows that often provide a nighttime light show. Mt. Mayon is a magnificent sight but also the most active volcano in the country (see figure 1.3).

In the center of the country are the many islands collectively known as the Visayas, which have multiple languages and heritages. Two main islands, Samar and Leyte, are connected by the beautiful, 2.2-kilometer San Juanico Bridge. The bridge was inaugurated early in the long administration of Ferdinand Marcos and was touted as a "birthday present" for Marcos's wife Imelda, who is from Leyte.

Cebu City is the second most populous city in the country and was the center of trade throughout the Visayas even after Manila became the capital (in 1571). Before the advent of mass media, Cebuano was the language with the largest number of speakers, and it is still in second place. The influence of Cebuano extends throughout the southern Philippines, so that it is generally the lingua franca. South of the Visayas, Mindanao is the second largest island in the Philippines. The third most populous metropolitan area in the country is centered on Davao City in southern Mindanao, where President Duterte was over thirty years sequentially vice mayor, mayor, representative, mayor, vice mayor, and then mayor again. As the largest city in Mindanao and the largest in the country in land area, Davao is sometimes accused of being "Imperial Davao" by those in other areas of Mindanao (much as Manila is dubbed "Imperial Manila"). While the population is predominantly of Visayan heritage (Cebuano and secondarily Ilonggo), emphasis is on the multicultural heritage. An innovation of then mayor Duterte was the appointment of eleven "deputy mayors" to serve as links to eleven "tribes": six Moro ethnicities and five Lumad (indigenous peoples).

In the Muslim Mindanao, Lanao del Sur and Maguindanao are on the mainland, along with the Islamic City of Marawi (whose business district was destroyed in the May October 2017 occupation by militants associated with the Islamic State). Lanao del Sur and Maguindanao are home to the Meranao and Maguindano ethnic groups, respectively. The island provinces, stretching out toward Malaysia from the tip of the Zamboanga Peninsula, are collectively known as the Sulu Archipelago. Zamboanga City was a bastion of Spanish power in a hostile Moro environment and still sees itself as different from its surroundings. Styling itself "Asia's Latin city," its local lingua franca is a Spanish creole known as Chavacano. The Sulu Archipelago is comprised of Basilan, Sulu, and Tawi-Tawi. Notably, Sulu was the seat of the Sultanate of Sulu for more than five hundred years, and its Tausug ethnic group prides itself on its warrior tradition. Tawi-Tawi is where the Philippines's first mosque was built.

What is the role of Chinese in the Philippines?

The history of the Chinese in the Spanish colony of the Philippines was often fraught, with a number of massacres in early decades, restrictions, and banning, but in the end they were considered "necessary outsiders" or "pariah entrepreneurs." Over the years, missionary efforts to convert the predominantly male Chinese immigrants to Catholicism and intermarriage with Indio (Malayan native born) women produced a Hispanized class of Chinese mestizos numbering in the hundreds of thousands. Immigration from China surged in the late 1800s, so that there were perhaps 100,000 Chinese immigrants in the Philippines by the 1890s.

The 1882 Chinese Exclusion Act enacted by the United States applied to the Philippines while the country was under American administration, causing something of a lull in immigration. But immigration picked up again after World War II, as the Philippines gained independence and unrest in China encouraged outflow. It is at this point that a local-born second Chinese generation began to emerge. Previously, male Chinese immigrants had tended either to return to their families back in China or to marry local Filipinas and start Chinese mestizo families. In reaction to this influx of immigrants, the 1954 Retail Trade Nationalization Act insisted that only Philippine citizens could engage in retail trade.

By this time, after more than a century of cultural and social assimilation, the Chinese mestizo community that had originated during the Spanish era was often indistinguishable from other Hispanized Filipinos—except sometimes, though not always, by their names. During the Spanish era Chinese often adopted multisyllabic surnames composed of a transliteration of the family patriarch's full name joined together, and many prominent family names survive: Consunji, Gokongwei, Gosiengfiao, Gotianun, Locsin, Ongpin, Quisumbing, Sycip, Tambunting, Teehankee, and Uytengsu. Other Filipinos with Chinese ancestry may have Hispanic surnames, either because their ancestors deliberately adopted them or because of a decree in 1849 issued by Governor General Narciso Claveria that required adoption of surnames from *Catalogo alfabetico de apellidos* (the alphabetical catalog of surnames). Twentieth-century immigrants often kept their original Chinese family names, so that the phrase "people with short names" may be an allusion to Chinese. Tan is the most common Chinese surname among Filipinos but is only fifty-fifth among all surnames in the Philippines. Other short names include Ang, Chan, Chua, Dee, Lee, Lim, Ong, Sy, Ty, and Yap.

Citizenship debates on the 1935 Constitution for the Republic of the Philippines were spirited, with some arguing that *jus sanguinis* (right of blood) would prevent those born in the Philippines of foreign parentage from stealing the "national patrimony." In 1947, the Philippine Supreme Court ruled that the American principle of *jus soli* (right of soil) never applied to the Philippines, causing considerable doubt about the citizenship of those born in the American period (1902–1935). Instead, the court applied *jus sanguinis*, invalidating the citizenship claims of those who had not undergone naturalization through a tedious judicial process or by act of Congress.

This had two consequences. First, long-running disputes about whether a particular person was a natural-born citizen would erupt in business (in areas of the economy reserved for citizens) or political cases. For instance, Jesse Robredo was elected mayor of Naga City six times, but because one of his grandfathers had come to the Philippines early in the twentieth century, a protracted legal battle was waged by his opponents, alleging Robredo was not a natural-born Philippine citizen. The dispute was settled with finality in his favor four weeks before the end of his sixth term as mayor, on June 2, 2010.[3]

The second consequence was that there were a growing number of Chinese nationals who found it difficult to acquire citizenship. As part of the opening of the Philippines to China, the citizenship issue had to be settled before diplomatic relations could be established. Thus, in April 1975 President Marcos used his martial law powers to convert the tedious legal procedure to a simplified administrative one. Tens of thousands of Chinese nationals availed themselves of this opportunity to become Philippine citizens.

Filipinos of Chinese descent are found in all sectors: media, culture and the arts, sports, and politics and governance. There are still some indicators of discrimination, of treating them as "others," such as when an outstanding academic achiever is criticized for not being a "real Filipino," or when a list of "Chinese" businessmen includes both those from mainland China and citizens of the Philippines. The latter retort that they are an integral part of the Philippines and should be celebrated as such. The standard Filipino word "Intsik" for Chinese (derived from the Malay honorific for males, *encik*) is often regarded as derogatory. Currently, "Chinoy" (a portmanteau of Chinese *Pinoy*, Filipino) is the preferred term.

Perhaps the most common stereotype is that Chinoys are rich. Indeed, seven of the ten richest Filipinos, ranked by Forbes in 2018, are of Chinese descent (Sy, Gokongwei, Lucio Tan, Ty, Tan Caktiong, Andrew Tan, Ang), and only three are of Spanish descent (Villar, Razon, Zobel de Ayala). Chinoys are often businessmen and professionals in the upper income strata. This has had the unfortunate, and occasionally truly horrific, consequence of making them the targets for kidnapping. An estimated 70 percent of all kidnap-for-ransom victims are Chinoy despite the group making up only 5 percent of the population. In the late 1990s, the number of such kidnappings rose to over one hundred per year. The risk was reduced through concerted efforts by Chinoy civil society, especially the Movement for the Restoration of Peace and Order, and a special task force known as PACER (President's Anti-Crime and Emergency Response). Still, there are several dozen such kidnappings each year, with ransoms ranging up to US$500,000.

Where in the world are Filipinos found?

One indicator of just how dispersed Filipinos are is how the Philippine press covers calamities, disasters, or incidents causing deaths across the globe. One of the facts that is generally noted is whether or not a Filipino (or somebody of Philippine extraction) was caught up in the event. No matter what part of the world the news report covers, whether a Filipino was affected is a plausible question.

Persons from the Philippines have long been prolific travelers, dating back to seamen on the first galleon heading from the islands to Nueva España (New Spain [Mexico]) in 1565. In fact, a plausible case can be made that the first person to sail around the world came from the Philippine Islands. "Enrique de Malacca" was a slave owned by Ferdinand Magellan, labeled as "from Malacca" because he was acquired in Malacca during a previous voyage. There was a trading colony of people from Luzon in Malacca, and Enrique served as Magellan's translator when the circumnavigation voyage reached the Philippines in 1521. That said, some other accounts make Enrique a native of Sumatra or Malacca, and it is possible that as a translator he spoke Malay as a trade language rather than a Philippine tongue. In any case, Enrique stayed in Cebu after Magellan's death in battle with the warrior Lapu-Lapu of Mactan Island.

Philippine wanderlust has continued throughout history. Some "Manilamen" who jumped ship from the Galleon Trade in the New World made their way to Louisiana, which was a Spanish possession until 1803, settling in Saint Malo in approximately 1763. This Filipino settlement was destroyed in a hurricane in 1915, but descendants still reside in New Orleans, taking pride in being the first Filipinos in the United States.

Entry into the United States accelerated after the Philippines became a colony, with more than 100,000 agricultural workers (*sacada*) flocking to the West Coast and Hawai'i. So many migrated from the impoverished region of the Ilocos that Ilocano is widely spoken in Hawai'i. Along with Tagalog, Ilocano is the most widely spoken language other than English in that state—ahead of Japanese, Chinese, and Hawaiian. The flow from the Philippines to the United States was severely restricted, however, when the Philippines became a Commonwealth in 1936.

There are more than ten million Filipinos living outside the country—roughly 10 percent of the population—about half of them permanent migrants. The remittances from these overseas Filipino workers (OFWs) make up about 10 percent of the gross national product (GNP), providing automatic stabilization during economic crises. Protecting OFWs is a foreign policy priority. For instance, the Philippines had a diplomatic spat with Qatar in 2018 over the treatment of workers there. And there is considerable sensitivity to slights or stereotypes in foreign media or elsewhere. There was a furor when "Filipina" was defined in a Greek dictionary as "maid," for example.

Filipinos abroad are spread out in 221 countries, of which the top ten destinations are the United States, Saudi Arabia, the United Arab Emirates, Malaysia, Canada, Australia, Italy, the United Kingdom, Qatar, and Singapore. In the United States, Canada, and the United Kingdom, most are permanent migrants; in many other places they are on temporary contracts, with more than half signing multiple contracts during their careers.

Half of the temporary migrants are found in the Middle East: Saudi Arabia, the United Arab Emirates, and Qatar. The 1970s kicked off the Filipino diaspora to the Middle East when a 1974 Martial Law Labor Code tried to meet domestic challenges of high unemployment and low wages by sending workers into the oil-rich Gulf region.

One of the more prominent OFW categories is nursing; hundreds of thousands of Filipino nurses are found in healthcare facilities around the world. In fact, the majority of nurses trained in the Philippines leave the country; on average, almost twenty thousand depart yearly. Like many OFWs, their English-language skills are generally welcomed, though those hoping to stay in Japan need to pass a Japanese language exam.

The Philippines is second only to China in supplying officers to the international shipping industry and leads the world in non-officers in this sector. Recently, Filipino mariners have struggled with accreditation due to the non-compliance of some of the sixty Philippine maritime schools with the international standards for seafarers. The Maritime Industry Authority (Marina) works with the Commission on Higher Education to try to upgrade curricula and facilities to meet European Maritime Safety Agency (EMSA) standards, but progress has been slow.

In the Filipino entertainment industry, particularly the music industry, performing abroad is frequently the goal. Filipino performing artists abroad include actors, dancers, singers, musicians, choreographers, composers, stage directors, circus performers, and producers, working in restaurants, clubs, hotels, casinos such as in Las Vegas and Macau, theme parks such as Disneyland and Universal Studios in Asia, and Caribbean cruise liners. Proud of their musicality, Filipinos note that their countrymen who have won Tony Awards on Broadway and been nominated for Olivier Awards in London. Unfortunately, entertainers are often subject to exploitation.

Over the years, overseas work has become "feminized" such that more than half of the workers are female. The greatest concentrations of OFWs are in "elementary occupations"—that is, they are domestic helpers—in Hong Kong, Singapore, and Kuwait. Such workers are often college graduates, with trained teachers being the stereotypical source, but they are able to earn more abroad than in the Philippines. Domestic workers are some of the most vulnerable to abuse among OFWs and are repeatedly the subject of highly publicized horror stories. That said, the feminization of overseas work is not always detrimental. It is worth noting that women outnumber men in the professions, especially nursing, and represent about 40 percent of managers—reflecting the fact that in the Philippines women are more educated than men.

Worries have been expressed about the social effects of such large numbers of adults being away from their families as OFWs. There have been considerable anecdotal and ethnographic studies of marital strain, infidelity, and adverse consequences for the well-being of the children. On the other hand, the extended Filipino family allows other relations to fulfill some of the parenting responsibilities that may be left behind by an OFW. Quantitative evidence is difficult to find, except with respect to children's educational achievement, which is highly valued by Filipinos. At least in this domain, there is no evidence for adverse consequences and some evidence for positive educational outcomes, particularly if the mother is the one remaining in the country. Given that beyond everyday expenses, OFW remittances go toward educational and medical expenses as well as paying off debts, the ability to financially support children's education does seem to imply social as well as economic benefits to working overseas.

2

HISTORY

"300 YEARS IN A CONVENT, 50 YEARS IN HOLLYWOOD," THEN ON ITS OWN

History wars in the Philippines seem never-ending. How should the nation view Spain, which created the concept of "the Philippines" and brought Christianity to its shores—at the same time attacking traditional cultures in the Philippines and exercising widespread oppression? Who are the Filipino heroes and who the Filipino villains in the revolution against the Spanish (1896–1898) and the subsequent (1898–1902) Philippine-American War? How do we judge the American colonial experience, from its bloody beginning in war through the establishment of public education and electoral democracy, which formally ended after the horrors of World War II? What should we think about the vicissitudes of the postwar republic prior to the 1972 declaration of martial law by Ferdinand Marcos?

The debate over the legacy of that authoritarian period is a current topic in Philippine politics, given the prominence in national and local politics of Marcos's children and the admiration for him that President Rodrigo Duterte has expressed. And disputes about governance since the restoration of electoral democracy in 1987 underlie much of current politics. Lest this portrayal of historical discussion come across as exceedingly grim and determined, it is good to remember Filipino humor. For instance, during food shortages toward the end of the Japanese occupation in World War II, Filipinos summarized history thus:

The Spanish gave us Religion
The Americans gave us Education
The Japanese gave us Ration

How does the Philippines compare to its neighbors in the precolonial era?

The stereotype that the Philippines spent three hundred years in a convent and then fifty years in Hollywood refers to the Spanish and American colonial experiences. But of course, people have been living in the islands that came to be known as the Philippines for tens of thousands of years. It is important to realize that the Philippines was unlike other areas of Southeast Asia. When the Spanish arrived at the beginning of the colonial era, there were no large "Indianized" states comparable to Kampuchea in Cambodia or Majapahit in Indonesia. There are no ancient monuments in the Philippines like Cambodia's Angkor Wat or Indonesia's Borobudur.

This is not to say that the islands consisted only of isolated small villages; interaction among settlements in the archipelago, and with the larger maritime region, had been going on for more than a thousand years. Archaeological finds, such as locally traded earthenware and metalware and "Indo-Pacific" beads, date back perhaps to the first century AD, and mention of trade with the Philippines in Chinese chronicles dates back to AD 971. Astonishing archaeological finds include a number of well-preserved ancient boats called *balangays* preserved in wetlands at the mouth of the Agusan River in Butuan. Dating of the boats thus far ranges from AD 320 to AD 1250. Pigafetta, Magellan's chronicler in 1521, described seafarers and river travelers and mentioned these outrigger boats, which could be quite large. Filipinos have been able to visit Southeast Asia and China using twenty-first century reconstructions of the *balangays*.

Spectacular gold finds in Butuan include an almost two kilogram, twenty-one-carat Hindu statue known as *Golden Tara*.

A local Manobo tribeswoman discovered the statue in 1918, and it was sold to the Field Museum in Chicago in 1922. There are other hints of influence from South Asia; for example, more than 150 words in Philippine languages can be traced definitely to Sanskrit. Another archaeological find is the oldest document in the Philippines, the "Laguna Copperplate," dating perhaps to AD 900, which was found near Manila in 1989.* The copperplate documented the forgiving of a debt and was written in script and language that reflected Sanskrit influences via Old Malay and Old Javanese. The place names in the document are speculative but clearly reflect a number of different communities with their own headmen. These villages would have been typical throughout most of the Philippines. It has long been thought that these entities reflected a group of settlers who came on one *balangay*, but this misrepresents the peopling of the Philippines—that the successors to Negritos were from Indonesia or the Malay Peninsula. Rather, the Austronesians moved to the archipelago from Taiwan some four thousand years ago, and though they clearly traveled by sea to cross the Bashi Channel, there is no evidence about their boat technology.

The leaders were generally termed *datus*, and the communities interacted with each other in constantly shifting ways. Relationships, and hierarchy, were personal, and so the influence of a particular community or *datu* could expand or contract. In a sparsely populated geography, control of people was more important than territory; with people, a society could engage in agriculture, trade along river or sea routes, and conduct raids and capture of slaves. Debt bondage of various sorts was also a way of controlling labor. Perhaps more important, though, was the ability to attract followers through kinship,

---

* This document is to be distinguished from the nonexistent "Code of Kalantiaw," supposedly consisting of eighteen articles. Despite being exposed as a fraud fifty years ago, the Code persists into the twenty-first century in school texts. Thus many Filipinos are unaware that it is fictitious.

deeds, or exchange of gifts—demonstrations of prowess. Alliances could be built up through marriage or kinship-like arrangements ("fictive kinship"), but as these were based on personal relationships, they could be unstable.

The evidence seems to indicate that the processes of trade and social stratification intensified in the 1300s and 1400s, as places such as Manila, Cebu, and Jolo (Sulu) evolved into trading hubs. There is evidence of increasing warfare, such as walls, moats, and watchtowers around communities. In various burial sites there are signs of wounds and decapitation on the remains. This was not a tranquil set of communities, but a dynamic, evolving situation in which local elites and their followers absorbed influences from the outside, but in their own way.

Then, at the beginning of the historical period, two monotheistic religions with their own styles of governance arrived. Islam spread from the Malay Archipelago into what is now the southern Philippines;, the Sultanate of Sulu was established circa 1450 and that of Maguindanao circa 1525. Catholicism came with the conquistadores and friars, briefly in 1521 and then permanently in 1565.

How did Islam arrive and survive in the Philippines?

Islam moved through the Malay Archipelago in Southeast Asia from the 1200s onward "like a slow, giant wave."[1] Muslim traders from the Middle East, South Asia, and even China plied the waters, settling in port cities where they married locals and sometimes brought their own religious teachers. On occasion the local rulers converted to Islam, whether from conviction or for practical advantages, and gradually the populace began to adhere. From an early period, the Hanafi school of Islamic jurisprudence was prevalent, and the influence of Sufis (Islamic mystics), whether as individuals or organized groups, allowed for locals to adopt and adapt a syncretic approach to Islam.

The "slow giant wave" met the more rapid influx of Europeans as the Portuguese entered the Indian Ocean beginning in 1498. By 1511, the Portuguese had captured the key trading center of Malacca on the Malay peninsula, with Ferdinand Magellan taking part in this effort. They massacred Muslims and disrupted the trading network in the area. Thus began the clash between Islam and Christianity in insular Southeast Asia (the Malay Archipelago), which led the Spanish to call the Muslims they found in the islands they conquered "Moros," after the Moors they had long fought against in the Iberian Peninsula.

The oldest mosque in the Philippines is found on Simunul Island in Tawi-Tawi (the province closest to the border with Malaysia). Sheikh Makhdum Karim, or Karim ul-Makhdum, described both as a trader and a missionary, erected a mosque traditionally dated to 1380. On the site, there is now a renovated mosque with four pillars once thought to be original but now dated to a 1700s reconstruction.

In the island chain, the province of Sulu is next nearest to Malaysia. In the mid-fifteenth century, Sayyid Abu Bakr, whose name indicates descent from the Prophet Mohammad, came to Sulu from Johore. He became the first sultan of Sulu using the royal name Sultan Sharif ul-Hashim, again indicating that the Prophet Mohammad was his ancestor. The sultanate still exists, though in 1936 the Commonwealth government, wishing to extinguish royal titles, did not recognize a successor to the thirty-second sultan. In the early 1960s the Philippine government once again recognized a sultanate, though there are currently rival claimants to the title. The Philippine government, at least nominally, continues to maintain a claim on the Malaysian state of Sabah, based on the sultanate's claim (see "What is the Sabah claim?" in Chapter 6).

Besides spirituality, Islam brought with it an idiom for state-building that was utilized by sultans. This was spread to mainland Mindanao in about 1515 by Sharif Kabungsuwan, from whom the Sultanates of Maguindanao and Buayan derive. The most powerful individual Muslim ruler was the long-ruling sultan of Maguindanao, Muhammad Dipatuan Kudarat, who ruled from 1619 to 1671 and alternately fought and reached agreements with the Spanish.

Muslims in Southeast Asia were certainly aware of the dangers brought by the Europeans. When Magellan reached Cebu, which was not Islamized, a Muslim trader warned against trusting the "Franks" (a term dating back to the Crusades). After the Spanish came to stay, in 1569, the sultan of Brunei ordered "Moros" (as the Spanish called them) to destroy the Spanish outposts in Cebu. By 1571, the Spanish had conquered Manila, ruled by Rajah Sulayman (a relative of the sultan of Brunei) with the aid of Visayan troops. Thus ended the existence of Islam in colonial Luzon or Visayas.

The Spanish felt strong enough to go on the offensive in 1578, capturing the capital of Brunei, burning down its large mosque, and briefly occupying Jolo. Sulu continued its role as a sea power and trading entrepôt for several centuries and was the strongest of the Muslim polities. By the mid-1700s, Sulu welcomed British ships to trade with China, a full century before ports throughout the Philippines were opened to foreign trade by the Spanish colonial administration.

The centuries that followed continued the hostilities between Spain and the Moros. Despite having settlements in northern and eastern Mindanao, Spain only established a permanent presence in Zamboanga City, which is centrally situated between Maguindanao and Sulu, in 1718. The Moros, for their part, launched raids throughout the archipelago, resulting in colonial-era churches in the Philippines erecting fortress-like walls behind which residents could retreat during raids. It is estimated that 300,000 slaves were seized by the Sultanate of Sulu. Throughout sparsely populated Southeast Asia, control over persons was more important than control over particular geographic areas.

This centuries-long conflict still resonates in the Philippines. In Philippine languages, "Moro-Moro" refers to a widely performed theatrical presentation about Christians defeating Moros and metaphorically means "a show put on for the public," as in "during the 1986 People Power Revolution, Defense Minister Enrile admitted that the ambush of his car in 1972, which was used to justify the imposition of Martial Law, was a Moro-Moro."[2†] There is considerable concern about long-standing anti-Muslim prejudice, such as that given full rein during media coverage of the January 2015 Mamasapano incident, when forty-four members of the Special Action Force died in a botched police operation to arrest a wanted terrorist in a Muslim community. Still, most Christians express a favorable attitude toward Muslims on surveys, as do Muslims toward Christians.

In the mid-nineteenth century, the Spanish colonial government acquired steam-powered gunboats, which finally gave them an advantage in Muslim areas in the South. In 1878, the efforts to pacify the archipelago resulted in a treaty of pacification and capitulation with the sultan of Sulu. In this instance, there is little doubt about the substantive intent, as the Tausug version of the treaty states:

> Article I. All the people of Sulu and its Archipelago shall obey only the King of Spain, Alfonso XII, or whosoever shall succeed him. This being our wish, we will not change or turn away to any other nation.
>
> Still, controversy is possible about precise terms, as the Spanish version says:
> Article 1. We declare that the sovereignty to Spain over all the Archipelago of Sulu and its dependencies is indisputable.

Muslims in the Sulu Archipelago point out that "sovereignty" is not in the Tausug text and dispute the right of Spain

† In his 2012 memoir, Enrile asserted that the ambush had not been staged.

to sign away "sovereignty" to the United States in the 1898 Treaty of Paris ending the Spanish-American War.

How did the Spanish arrive in the Philippines?

The Spanish arrived in the Philippines as part of their competition with the Portuguese over the spice trade from Asia. The Portuguese controlled the routes via the Indian Ocean under the 1494 Treaty of Tordesillas, so traveling to the "East" by going west around the American continent made sense. Magellan's voyage around South America was a difficult feat, and crossing the vast Pacific Ocean was a journey almost twice as long as the transatlantic voyages undertaken by Columbus. Magellan reached land in several places in the archipelago and docked in Cebu, already a major trading site, only to die on a neighboring island in the Battle of Mactan. He had been welcomed in Cebu, utilizing his slave Enrique (de Malacca) as an interpreter, and looked to establish trading relations. There were apparently mass conversions (estimates range up to two thousand people) undertaken in the three weeks that Magellan was there. One of the first converts, the Cebu native Rajah Humabon, was christened Carlos, after the king of Spain, and his wife Juana, after the king's mother. Magellan gave Juana a statue of the infant Jesus that has survived the vicissitudes of history, is still enshrined in Cebu, and is the focus of the Santo Niño festival (also called Sinulog, named for the dance movement devotees perform).

In the first foreign interference in the domestic politics of the Philippines, Magellan tried to get other *datus* in the area to pay homage to Don Carlos (Humabon). When Lapu-Lapu, on the nearby island of Mactan, declined to do so, Magellan personally led an attack on Lapu-Lapu and was killed. After Magellan's death in 1521, his expedition struggled on. By the end of 1521, the two remaining ships had reached Tidore in the Moluccas and managed to refit. The two ships split up, with the *Victoria*, commanded by Juan Sebastian Elcano, making it back to Spain by September 1522 (having violated the Treaty of Tordesillas by continuing across the Indian Ocean and rounding the Cape of Good Hope). The *Victoria* had a cargo of spices, and the profit from this one galleon meant that the entire Magellan expedition was a financial success. The other ship, the *Trinidad*, tried to return eastward across the Pacific to New Spain (Mexico), failed, and after seven months ended up in Portuguese custody in the Moluccas.

Encouraged by the spice profits, the second Armada de Molucca set off in 1525 under Juan Sebastian Elcano and Garcia Jofre de Loaisa, both of whom died while their one remaining ship was crossing the Pacific. That ship made it to Tidore (in Indonesia), which was at war with the Portuguese, but never returned. Another expedition set out, this time commissioned by Cortes in New Spain, and managed to reach Tidore in early 1528. This expedition, sailing on the *Florida*, tried twice to get back to New Spain with its cargo of cloves and eventually joined the other Spanish seamen in the Moluccas. This ordeal only came to an end in 1534 when, as part of a settlement between the kings of Spain and Portugal, the Spaniards were given safe passage home. Eventually, in 1536, seventeen Spaniards made it back home; the most well-known to history was the explorer Andres de Urdeneta, who returned to the Philippines on the expedition in 1565 that established a permanent Spanish presence in the archipelago.

Another expedition that sailed from New Spain in 1542, headed by Ruy Lopez de Villalobos, aimed to colonize "The Western Isles." But Villalobos's crew also ended up in the Moluccas, having failed to settle what this expedition called Las Islas Filipinas in honor of then prince (later king) Philip II. There was some argument about whether the archipelago was covered by the Treaty of Zaragoza, which extended the

Treaty of Tordesillas to the other side of the globe. This was at a time when longitude was difficult to establish—a reliable sea-borne method based on chronometers was some 250 years in the future—so disputes were inevitable. The Philippines is in fact on the "Portuguese" side of the line. But since there seemed to be few spices on the islands, the Portuguese ceded the Philippines to Spain, albeit after inconclusive confrontations with the Spanish in Cebu in 1567–1568 and during a period when the two kingdoms were united from 1580 to 1640.

This sporadic interaction finally came to an end in 1565, when Miguel López de Legazpi was charged with "the conversion of the natives and the discovery of a safe route back to Nueva España (New Spain), that the kingdom may increase and profit from trade." Legazpi, like Magellan, arrived in Cebu, but this time the Spanish were met with hostility. They bombarded the town, and it burned down—but in the ashes was the statue of the child Jesus that Magellan had left more than forty years earlier. The statue's survival was and has been ever since considered an indication of divine favor for the religious aspirations of Catholics and an indication of religious idolatry for those less inclined to believe.

The Augustinian friars on the expedition began "conversion of the natives," while the "discovery of a safe route back to Nueva España" was in the hands of Andrés de Urdeneta, who had joined the Augustinian order in Mexico after having survived the Loaisa expedition some forty years before.

He made the return trip in the latter half of 1565 trip and kept careful charts, initiating the use of Acapulco as the eastern terminus of the Manila Galleon Trade (see figure 2.1).

As for the conversion of the natives, the Augustinians were followed by the Franciscan order in 1578, Jesuits in 1581, Dominicans in 1587, and Recollects in 1606. By 1595, there were fewer than three hundred missionaries operating in the archipelago, but they recorded approximately 288,000 baptisms (out of a population of 667,000–905,000).

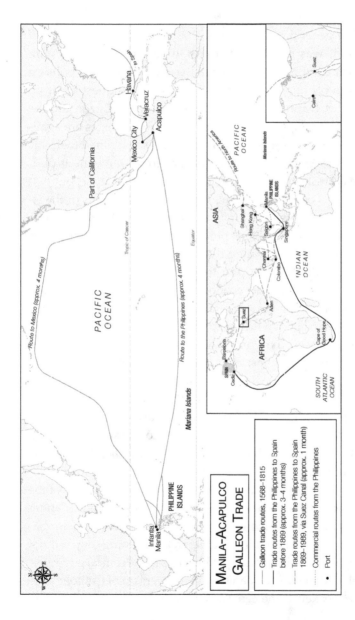

Figure 2.1 Galleon Trade route

Source: Philippine Presidential Museum and Library. Redrawn from Map 7 of the "Historical Atlas of the Republic: Charting the History of the Philippines" (Presidential Communications Development and Strategic Planning Office, 2016)

How did Spain impact Filipinos?

We can begin with an effect that is rarely cited: depopulation. The general impression is that the Spanish conquest of the islands was relatively peaceful, except for hostilities with the Muslims of Mindanao. Since there were no large political entities to conquer in one blow, piecemeal conquest went on for decades. Estimates are that the population of Luzon and the Visayas declined by 36 percent by 1600. No estimates are available for Mindanao, inasmuch as the Spanish only had toeholds there. In the Americas, a similar decline in the indigenous population is attributed to the spread of infectious disease, but that seems not to be the case in the Philippines. Residents of the islands did have some immunity to so-called Old World diseases (e.g., smallpox, measles, typhus, and cholera), so epidemics were much less devastating than in the Americas. The loss of life was predominantly due to warfare and the consequent disruption of social and economic life. Mortalities continued with warfare after the conquest, such as the Spanish-Dutch War (1609–1648), in which ships operating out of Batavia (now Jakarta) harassed the Philippines. Moro raids from the south caused further fatalities; Bicol, Leyte, and Samar suffered repeatedly, and occasional raids occurred all the way north to the Ilocos.

The Spanish method of rule largely turned colonial power over to the friars in all the towns, with the cooperation of the local elite (the *datu* class, which became the *principalia*). Given how thinly spread Spaniards were—in 1810, there were four thousand located across the more than seven thousand islands of the Philippines—usually the only Spaniard that the average islander saw was the friar in the local parish. These friars were in religious "orders," with their own hierarchy meaning they did not even report to the local bishop, much less to the central governor-general in Manila. The Spanish-colonial version of Catholic governance weakened the central state apparatus in Manila. In an

Figure 2.2 Rice terraces in Banaue
Source: © IStock/tropicalpixsingapore

extreme example, Governor-General Fernando Bustamante was assassinated in a dispute with the clergy in 1719.[‡]

Under a control policy called *reducción*, Spanish colonists persuaded or forced scattered villages to join into towns, which were organized around a church in the central *población* (town center) that had a resident friar. Naturally, some did not want to live in these towns, pay tribute to the Spanish, or become Christian, and they tended to gather in interiors of islands or up in the mountains (thus known as *remontado*). We know little about what happened to them because they escaped the record-keeping of the Spanish, but the famous wet-rice terraces of Banaue date from this time rather than being ancient, as is often assumed (see figure 2.2). An entirely new socioeconomic

[‡] The incident was immortalized in 1884 by a painting by Felix Resurreccion Hidalgo, one of the *ilustrados* residing in Spain (the iconic artwork is currently on display at the National Art Gallery).

system of extensive irrigation sprang up as refugees settled in, beyond Spanish control.

The "Hispanization" of the Philippines began with conversion to Catholicism, though how the religion was perceived by the residents of the islands was different from what was preached by the friars. Religious texts were translated into local languages—beginning in 1593 with the *Doctrina Christiana*, the first book published in the Philippines, which was offered in Tagalog in both Roman script and the indigenous Baybayin. This catechism aimed to make the doctrine understandable in local conditions, and it is often remarked how baroque Roman Catholicism, with its panoply of saints and its various images and statues, was compatible with the preexisting animism of the islands. Spirits, sacred objects, and feasts became fiestas for the parish's patron saint in a process that scholars call "enculturation."

Under the Spanish system, the *datu* class became much less fluid than before, solidifying into the *principalia*, an aristocracy of those who could become *cabeza de barangay* (village heads) or *gobernadorcillo* (little governor) of the town. Whereas in pre-Spanish times a *datu* needed the support of followers for economic and military purposes, under the colonial state, tribute and forced labor were required of all ordinary subjects. This more formalized system, and the collaboration between friars and *principalia*, widened the difference between the classes.

Since the economic life of the colony revolved around the Galleon Trade, economic change was slow. Crops introduced from Spanish America included corn and camote, and varied irrigation techniques increased rice production for the growing population (e.g., in Cebu). A tobacco monopoly was introduced in 1781, and the revenues began to offset the cost of administering the colony. Then in the 1800s, Spain's loss of the American colonies, the opening of Philippine ports to international trade, the development of export crops, and the increasing impact of the cash economy began to induce wider social change.

There are many markers of the Spanish colonial era still evident in the Philippines. For instance, Dominicans founded the oldest university in Asia, the University of Santo Tomas, in 1611. Other educational institutions were established, generally focusing on religion, so that by the nineteenth century both "native priests" and an educated secular class known as *ilustrados* were part of the burgeoning struggle against Spain.

A particularly obvious legacy of Spain is the widespread use of Spanish surnames. The Christianized population began adopting suitable surnames such as Santos, de la Cruz, and de los Reyes. To standardize this and systematize tax collection and census, Governor General Narciso Claveria required adoption of surnames from the *Catalogo alfabetico de apellidos* (Alphabetical catalog of surnames) in 1849. While the majority of the names in the catalog were Spanish, some were from the archipelago (e.g., Sicat, Magsaysay, Panganiban).

In the middle of the nineteenth century, the colonial administration tried to modernize and bureaucratize. More provinces were created; a majority of them were military as the Spanish authorities tried to exert control over all the territory. Steam-powered gunboats finally made a difference in the politics of the south, where Muslims had been able to resist Christianization and keep their political institutions. As noted in the section on Islam ("How did Islam arrive and survive in the Philippines?"), Spain and the sultan of Sulu, who represented a prominent southern island, entered a treaty of pacification in 1878.

What is the history of Chinese in the Philippines through the nineteenth century?

When the Spanish first sailed into Manila Bay in 1570, there were four Chinese vessels there for trade. When Manila was conquered in the next year by forces under Legazpi, there were 150 Chinese residents in the country; thus began the long, fraught relationship between the Spanish authorities and the Chinese residing in the Philippines.

The basic fact was that there were few Spanish, and large numbers of Chinese. For instance, by 1586 there were some ten thousand Sangleys (from a Hokkien term meaning "traveling merchants" or "businessmen," though many of the Chinese were laborers and craftsmen) in the area but only eight hundred Spanish and mestizos (mixed-race persons). In response to suspicions exacerbated by some resident Chinese joining in when the Chinese pirate Limahong raided Manila in 1575, the Spanish took steps to control the Chinese population. Their efforts included the establishment of the world's first "Chinatown" in 1581; called the Parian ("Marketplace" [Malay]), it was located outside of the defensive walls of Intramuros ("Inside the Walls"), where the Spanish resided. The area of Manila named Binondo was set up as another Chinatown with a land grant in perpetuity, limited self-governance, and no taxes. Today, the Binondo Chinatown still exists, though it is no longer tax-free.

Cycles of expulsion or massacre of Chinese, followed by renewed influxes, went on for almost two hundred years. For instance, in 1603, when the Spanish authorities began preparing for an invasion, the Chinese feared a massacre and rose in a preemptive revolt, killing about half of the Spanish. The Spanish, aided by Tagalogs and Japanese settlers, went on to massacre some twenty-three thousand Chinese, while some Spanish elites fled on the Manila galleon *San Antonio*, which disappeared somewhere in the Pacific on the way to Acapulco. The estimate in the early seventeenth century was that there were only five hundred Chinese left; as Antonio de Morga said in his 1609 *Sucesos de las Islas Filipinas* (*Events in the Philippine Isles*): "The city found itself in distress, for since there were no Sangleys there was nothing to eat and no shoes to wear."

By 1621, there was once again a large Chinese population, estimated at twenty thousand. Not only was trade with China integral to the galleon exchange with New Spain (Mexico), but practically all of the food for the Spanish colony had to be imported; it is estimated that only five Spaniards were farmers in 1600. The Spanish focused on profiting from the Galleon Trade and left it to Chinese to work as artisans, craftsman, and laborers. So the cycle continued; in 1662, the Chinese warlord Koxinga, who had recently taken over Taiwan from the Dutch, sent a messenger demanding tribute. An action-reaction sequence followed, with once again some twenty thousand Chinese being massacred. There were perhaps fourteen Chinese uprisings and subsequent massacres by the 1760s. The British, as part of the Seven Years' War (1756–1763), occupied Manila from 1762 to 1764. The Chinese sided with the British, and in 1766 once again an order was issued expelling many Chinese from the colony and confining the rest to Manila. Shortly thereafter, the Philippines made efforts to get the Chinese to come back.

Over time, Chinese males married Indio women and had mixed-race children who were classified as Chinese mestizo. Even in times of trouble, Chinese could flee into the Philippine countryside and settle there. The extent of Chinese-Filipino integration can be seen in the adoption of Hokkien kinship terms into Tagalog—*kuya* ("elder brother") and *ate/atchi* ("elder sister"), among others. Thus originated the segment of society generally thought of as Filipino in culture, but with Chinese ancestry. Their status was recognized in 1741 when Chinese mestizos were recognized as a class, with a head tax twice that of Indios (Malayan native born residents) but half that of Chinese immigrants.

When the Chinese were expelled in the late eighteenth century, the Chinese mestizos were able to occupy the entrepreneurial economic niche and spread around the country (there were previously Chinese-dominated markets in Cebu and Iloilo, for instance), including obtaining connections to land. As the economy opened up in the mid-nineteenth century, restrictions on Chinese immigration were once again lifted, and Chinese began to reoccupy their niches. The Chinese mestizos began to move out of retail and wholesale commerce and into managing the export industries of textile weaving and sugar. Over several decades, a prosperous Chinese mestizo community was established, and their access to education and travel during the second half of the nineteenth century meant that they were central to the growth of a domestic intelligentsia known as the *ilustrados* (see the next section).

What was the course of the struggle against Spain?

Change came to the Philippines beginning in the nineteenth century, partly as a consequence of Mexico's gaining independence from Spain. The Galleon Trade, which had slowly been tapering off, came to an end in 1815. In economic matters, Manila opened up to international trade in 1834, followed by ports in the provinces opening in 1855. Agricultural exports—sugar, abaca, indigo, cotton, coffee, and tobacco became important, and the government monopoly on tobacco made the colonial government self-sufficient. The *principalia* (the local and provincial authorities) began to expand their economic horizons, joined by Chinese mestizos, who moved into these new economic activities while immigrant Chinese returned to the retail trade.

Social unrest became more widespread, with localized revolts occurring in Luzon and the Visayas. In 1841, the Cofradia de San Jose (the Confraternity of St. Joseph) was led by Apolinario de la Cruz (known as "Hermano Pule" [Brother Pule]). An Indio (native born), he was disappointed at not being allowed to join a religious order because of his race and became the most famous of a series of religious leaders who mixed heterodox devotions with aspirations for *kalayaan* (freedom). The Cofridia's armed uprising was crushed by the Spanish authorities, but confirmed their suspicions of such men. In the aftermath of an 1872 anti-tax mutiny by Filipino military personnel in Cavite, the Spanish implicated and executed a prominent Filipino priest, Jose Burgos, and two associates, Fathers Mariano Gomez and Jacinto Zamora, collectively known as

"Gomburza." This execution and the Cavite mutiny are often seen as the opening round of the 1896 revolt against Spain. The three "native" priests executed in 1872 all had Chinese ancestry, yet they were seen as representing Indio interests. This is a prime example of the historical blurring between Indio and Chinese mestizo culture. Another example is how the grandfather of José Rizal, the most famous of the *ilustrados*, moved from the Chinese mestizo tax register to the Indio one, so that legally speaking he was an Indio. In short, by this time revolutionaries with Chinese ancestry, such as Emilio Aguinaldo (president of the 1898 Philippine Republic) participated as Filipinos, a nascent identity.

As education began to spread in the Philippines and it became easier to travel to Europe via the Suez Canal (opened in 1869), a new group of secular intellectuals arose, known as the *ilustrados*. They had illustrious careers and often colorful lives. Targeting the Spanish government and popular opinion, the Propaganda Movement in the 1880s and early 1890s published for a few years a periodical, *La Solidaridad*, in Spain. But most important in the eyes of the Spanish colonial authorities, and in the hindsight of history, were the novels of José Rizal.

While in Europe in 1887, Rizal published the first of his two famous novels, *Noli me Tangere* (*Touch Me Not*). The book was banned in the Philippines for its biting social criticism of the realities of being a colony of Spain. Rizal briefly returned to the Philippines but departed again, and in 1891 he published *El Filibusterismo* (*Subversion*), a much darker portrayal of revolutionary efforts. When he returned to Manila in 1892 he organized La Liga Filipina, a moderate social reform movement, but the government banned it and exiled Rizal to Dapitan in northern Mindanao.

On the day Rizal's exile was announced, Andrés Bonifacio and others founded the organization generally known as the Katipunan (Kataas-taasan Kagalang-galangang na Katipunan ng mga Anak ng Bayan—the highest most respected society of the children of the nation), a secret revolutionary society.

Bonifacio is sometimes called the "Great Plebeian," though his being working class is somewhat overblown; he had a white-collar job and was a skilled writer. The Katipunan nonetheless resonated with ordinary Filipinos in its language and imagery, including blood oaths and interpreting membership as a redemptive act. The Spanish moved to arrest members of the growing movement in August 1896, and the Katipunan launched an armed revolt with some success in areas surrounding Manila (Cavite, Bulacan, and Morong). That same year, Rizal was arrested and executed by the Spanish authorities in Manila on December 30, 1896.

Herein lies one front of the history wars. Early on, the American authorities and, later, Filipino governing elites found Rizal to be an acceptable heroic figure as he did not advocate violence. Today, Rizal is generally considered, though never officially proclaimed, the Philippine national hero. More militant leftists, however, prefer Bonifacio due to his working-class image and his willingness to engage in armed insurrection.

The progress of the uprising against the Spanish opened up another front of the history wars regarding the fate of Bonifacio. As the insurrection went badly near Manila, Bonifacio moved to Cavite, and in March 1897 the Tejeros Convention met to elect the leadership of the revolutionary republic. There were two main, but unstable, factions: Magdiwang, largely allied with Bonifacio, and Magdalo, largely associated with Emilio Aguinaldo, a member of the local upper class. There were accusations of electoral fraud, and there was bad blood. Aguinaldo was elected president, and Bonifacio was executed on what are generally agreed to be trumped-up charges on May 10, 1897.

The insurrection continued to struggle, and in December 1897 Aguinaldo, as leader of the revolution, accepted a Spanish offer of amnesty and exile to Hong Kong. Abroad, he continued to organize a "Supreme Council of the Nation" for the Philippines. Then the Americans arrived in Manila Bay, and on May 1, 1898, destroyed the Spanish fleet as part of the

Spanish-American War. Weeks after the defeat of the Spanish, Aguinaldo was transported back to Manila on an American ship. On June 12, 1898, the Act of Proclamation of Independence of the Filipino People was delivered in Cavite; it included the pious claim that independence was "under the protection of the Powerful and Humanitarian Nation, the United States of America." The Americans, however, had other plans.

How did the Americans arrive in the Philippines?

By the mid-1890s, American expansion had moved beyond the North American continent into the Pacific. Hawai'i became a territory of the United States in July 1898, by which time the Battle of Manila Bay (May 1898) had occurred as part of the Spanish-American War. After having destroyed the Spanish fleet in the Battle of Manila Bay, Admiral George Dewey ordered that the Filipino revolutionary Emilio Aguinaldo be brought back from his brief exile in Hong Kong.

Aguinaldo's forces on land bottled up the Spanish in Manila with a long line of trenches as the Americans blockaded by sea. Aguinaldo proclaimed Philippine independence on June 12, 1898, but when the United States and Spain signed the 1898 Treaty of Paris, neither country recognized the sovereignty of the Filipinos. Instead, Spain ceded sovereignty over the islands to the United States for US$20 million. In the same period, the Filipinos convened a congress in Malolos, Bulacan, and established the First Philippine Republic when the Malolos Constitution was ratified in January 1899. On February 4 of that year, hostilities broke out between American forces, which had occupied Manila upon the surrender of the Spanish, and the surrounding Filipino forces. In the ensuing Philippine-American War, Aguinaldo was captured in March 1901 and issued a proclamation of formal surrender in April. Aguinaldo's last general, Miguel Malvar, was forced to surrender in April 1902, and the war was officially declared over in July 1902.

The Philippine-American War, like the Philippine Revolution, is still being fought in popular culture, political rhetoric, and academic discourse. It was a brutal affair; the US lost over 4,200 soldiers, while the Filipinos lost 20,000 combatants by American estimates. Noncombatant deaths were countless, in the sense that no good data exist for civilian deaths by violence. In the end, the exact count matters less than the overall demographic catastrophe that occurred due to violence, famine, and disease. It is estimated that there were 775,000 excess deaths from 1899 to 1902 and a smaller cohort of newborns immediately after the war, amounting to a further population deficit of 400,000. This was especially devastating given that the population of the Philippines was about 7 million at the start of the war.

One particular incident in the war still resonates. In September 1901, villagers and insurgents in Balangiga on Samar Island surprised a company of American soldiers at breakfast. More than half of the seventy-four Americans were killed and most of the rest wounded, while Filipinos suffered fifty casualties. General Jacob Smith ordered a fierce retaliation, declaring that "the interior of Samar must be made a howling wilderness," and ordered the killing of everyone over the age of ten years who was fighting Americans. Though his subordinates countermanded the details of this order, deaths were widespread; at least two thousand people were killed. When Smith's order became known in the United States, it created a firestorm of controversy; he was court-martialed, convicted, and forced to retire.

The issue continued to be contentious because the US Army took the three church bells that had been rung as a signal to the Filipinos to attack. The bells of Balangiga were displayed as war booty at US bases in Korea and Wyoming and long proved an irritant in US-Philippine relations. But in December 2018, the United States returned the bells to the Philippines as part of a stepped-up effort to counter the country's possible pivot to China under President Duterte (see figure 6.1).

A pair of blockbuster movies demonstrates how controversies from the Philippine-American War persist. First, *Heneral Luna* (General Luna, 2015) covers the assassination of Antonio Luna, chief of staff of the Philippine Armed Forces, allegedly on the orders of President Emilio Aguinaldo, who strenuously denied this until the end of his life. Second, *Goyo: Ang Batang Heneral* (Goyo: The boy general, 2018) follows the story of Gregorio "Goyo" del Pilar, who at the age of twenty-four was one of Aguinaldo's favorites. He died in December 1899 in the Battle of Tirad Pass, which allowed Aguinaldo to continue retreating from the Americans. A third movie has been mooted but not yet formalized; it takes up the story of Manuel Quezon, who served under Miguel Malvar at the end of the war in 1902 and went on to win election in 1935 as president of the Commonwealth, defeating, among others, Aguinaldo.

There were certainly hostilities after 1902 (see "What are the roots of the Muslim separatist insurgency?" in this chapter). Notably, Macario Sakay operated as a guerrilla commander and self-styled president of the Tagalog Republic until his capture and execution for "brigandage" in 1906. He has also been the subject of a number of films and other artistic works, and in 2016 an existing Philippine Army camp in Los Baños, Laguna, was named Camp General Macario Sakay to honor him as a Filipino patriot rather than the bandit that the colonizers alleged he was.

The United States established an appointive advisory civilian Philippine Commission in 1899. In 1900, the commission was headed by Judge (later President) William Howard Taft and exercised legislative powers. It began establishing civilian provinces in 1901, and the first municipal elections (with a severely restricted franchise) and indirect provincial elections were held. Posts in the civilian government were a strong inducement for the Filipino elite, and thus many cooperated with the US governance efforts. In 1907, the Philippine Assembly was elected as the lower house of a national legislature, and the Philippine Commission became the upper house. Sergio Osmeña was elected speaker of the eighty-man body, and Manuel L. Quezon the majority floor leader. In the Assembly, the Philippine elite reconciled themselves to temporary American rule; all agreed that their country should gain independence, but argued about how short the timetable should be.

What was the impact of the American period?

Despite the positive contemporary view of the United States by the average Filipino citizen, many in the intellectual, policy, and official elite—including President Duterte—express resentment over the colonial experience. The Americans crushed Filipino aspirations for independence in a brutal counterinsurgency war. Official American rhetoric, though, tends to talk about the "special relationship" that began in 1898, glossing over the fact that the colonial period began with a counterinsurgency campaign.[3]

The American mission of "benevolent assimilation" was articulated by President William McKinley at the end of 1898. Almost immediately, plans for mass education in English in the Philippines were put in motion. In August 1901, 509 American teachers arrived in the American transport ship *Thomas*; hence they and other American teachers who followed up until 1921 were known as "Thomasites." They were spread thinly throughout the country and acted as mentors to the Filipino teachers (who were always in the majority) in addition to teaching in the classroom. Also in 1901, the Philippine Commission established a teacher training institute (now Philippine Normal University) and a technical school (now Technological University of the Philippines). Such institutions were instrumental in spreading a cadre of educated Filipinos literate in English, the new language of power and governance.

Another mechanism for "benevolent assimilation," the *pensionado* ("pensioner") program, sent government-supported students to the United States for advanced education. A total of 218 were sent by 1915, when the program lapsed, since the University of the Philippines, having been founded 1908, was available for advanced study. The *pensionados* became part of the elite when they returned, but they originated from a broader set of social backgrounds than did the *ilustrados* of the late Spanish era, since the colonial government selected them and financed their education. Some came back convinced of the virtues of American governance, and others of the need for independence.

In 1913 the American governor-general, Francis Burton Harrison, launched a program of "Filipinization" of the colonial bureaucracy. As a result, the number of Americans in the colonial state apparatus declined rapidly, from 29 to 6 percent of all positions. This process was ratified in the 1916 "Jones Act," the Philippine Autonomy Act, aiming to place "in the hands of the people of the Philippines as large a control of their domestic affairs as can be given them."

Having an elective Philippine Assembly before Filipinizing the bureaucracy had the lasting effect of subordinating the civil service to political control. Governor-General Harrison was a classic urban American machine politician from New York and thought it natural that the Nacionalista Party members of the Assembly should have a free hand in appointments and in budgetary matters. This American style of colonial control meant that it was difficult to develop a professional civil service. To the present day, senators and representatives regularly try to influence the bureaucracy, particularly during the annual budgetary process. The Filipino political elite quickly adapted to the American political structures that had been introduced.

During the American period, the population began to grow at an increasing rate, which demographers attribute to control of infectious diseases such as smallpox; the reduction of cholera due to better sanitation; and improved information on nutrition, childbirth, and other areas of healthcare. Scholars of public health point out that racism and a desire to discipline a subjugated population were part of these efforts, but the upshot was the improved health of the citizenry.

Population increase led to growing pressure on agriculture as the smallholdings of peasants were fragmented and a class of landless tenants emerged. This pressure interacted with a political-economic situation that was created in Central Luzon as the American administration sold off Spanish friar lands acquired during the colonial changeover. The haciendas were acquired by the elite, who could buy the lands. Here, and in the central Visayas, a landed class developed, particularly the sugar bloc that became powerful in the postwar independent Philippines. This change laid the groundwork for agrarian unrest led by the postwar Huks (politically organized peasant farmers originally formed as anti-Japanese forces) and later by the communist New People's Army (NPA), which originated in Central Luzon then spread nationwide. However, the effective pacification of Mindanao provided something of a safety valve by opening up new lands for migration—some sponsored by the state, but mostly spontaneous.

In popular culture, the legacy of the American period can be seen in the Philippine mania for basketball. Despite Filipinos being on average among the shortest people in the world, basketball is a favorite pastime. Sports were one of the core elements of American presence in the archipelago, and the fairly new game of basketball was promoted by the Young Men's Christian Association (YMCA) and in schools. Unlike baseball, which largely faded away after the American period, basketball requires little space or equipment and has thus flourished. Every neighborhood boasts half-courts with a hoop, often utilizing the road itself, whether paved or dirt. Almost three-fourths of the population say they follow the game, and stories from the (American) National

Basketball Association are in the newspapers and on television every day.

What were the special provinces (Moro, Mountain) at the beginning of the American period?

At the beginning of the American civil administration, several "special provinces" were set up; initially, they were not under civil authorities but rather had army officers as their local district governors and vice governors. The most important of these were Moro Province—with five districts covering most of Mindanao: Cotabato, Davao, Lanao, Jolo, and Zamboanga—and Mountain Province—with seven subprovinces covering roughly the current Cordillera Administrative Region but not including the province of Abra at that time. These areas were largely un-Hispanized at the beginning of the US colonial enterprise. Moro Province was divided into regular provinces in 1913, while Mountain Province remained whole until 1966, when subprovinces became provinces: Benguet, Mountain Province (Bontok), Ifugao, and Kalinga-Apayao (which further split into two provinces in 1995). Another special province in Mindanao, Agusan, was sparsely populated, largely by shifting cultivators, but soon became two regular provinces (Bukidnon and Agusan) with a large influx of Hispanized Filipinos (mostly Visayan and Ilocanos).

In the martial law period, both the Cordillera and Muslim Mindanao were hotbeds of insurgency. The two regions' desire for autonomy was subsequently recognized in the 1987 Constitution because activists lobbied the Constitutional Commission. (The Moro province is dealt with in "What are the roots of the Muslim separatist insurgency?" in this chapter.)

Mountain Province was populated by a number of different ethnolinguistic groups speaking mutually unintelligible languages: Ibaloy, Kankanaey, Bontok, Ifugao, Kalinga, Itneg, and Isnag, among others. The sociopolitical organization was by autonomous village, as each village tried to maintain control over its irrigation system and rice paddies, swidden fields, orchards, and other forest resources. This led to a considerable amount of inter-village warfare to maintain both resources and fierce reputations, but that was somewhat kept in check by "peace pacts" (*bodong* in Kalinga and *pechen* in Bontok). Such villages were run by councils of elders, typically men chosen for their record as warriors, knowledge of customs, and judgment in resolving disputes, or in some cases for their wealth, especially in cattle in southern areas among the slightly more dispersed Ibaloy. The Spanish had penetrated the mountains somewhat and carried out missionary work, but by and large the region had preserved its indigenous culture.

The American military appointed officers to run the various subprovinces and districts. With very few coercive resources at their disposal, these officers tended to utilize means that were seen as locally legitimate. In a dispute, the American officer would often merely ratify the decision of the council of elders. Given these non-disruptive techniques, it is not surprising that some American officers became known as "White Apo," "apo" being a term of respect.

It has been argued that the American administrative grid, imposed on Mountain Province by the military and continued by the civilian administration, led to region-wide consciousness-raising. For instance, the Trinidad Agricultural School (now Benguet State University) in La Trinidad (adjacent to Baguio City) was a place where students from all over Mountain Province could continue their education beyond elementary school and interact with and begin to understand their peers from other villages or ethnolinguistic groups for the first time. English was the classroom language, and Ilocano the common language among peers.

A region-wide consciousness was indeed being formed; whether locals used the term Cordillerans, Highlanders, or Igorots, there was a felt difference from the lowlanders. "Igorot" is in fact a derogatory term that outsiders, beginning with the Spanish, used for the people of the Cordillera. In 1943,

Filipino statesman Carolos P. Romulo wrote, "The fact remains that the Igorot is not Filipino," and this slight is still remembered in the region.

Over the following decades, the term "Igorot" was reclaimed with pride. Thus, the post-1986 push for an autonomous region was often based on an imagined "Ka-Igorotan" (Igorot collectivity). Reaching for indigenous authenticity was a form of political struggle for the Cordillera Bodong Association, a 1986 breakaway from the communist movement in the region. The association asserted that an authentic version of autonomy should be based on indigenous institutions, like the peace pact among villages. This position led anthropologist William Henry Scott to wryly suggest that trying to organize an autonomous region on the basis of the *bodong* would be like trying to organize the European Union along the lines of the Hitler-Stalin nonaggression pact.

In the event, an autonomous region for the Cordillera was never established. Two unsuccessful plebiscites were held in which only one province (Ifugao in 1990; Apayao in 1998) voted in favor of ratifying organic acts drafted by the Philippine Congress, and the Philippine Supreme Court ruled that an autonomous region needs more than one province. Thus, the Cordillera remains an administrative region similar to all other regions of the country (except the autonomous region in Muslim Mindanao), a venue for planning and consultation among local officials and regional heads of national line agencies.

In recent years, regional government agency heads and local government officials throughout the Cordillera have embarked on a new effort to be recognized as a region. Encouraged both by progress toward a new organic law for Muslim Mindanao and initiatives toward federalism, they have submitted a draft law to Congress for its consideration. In that law, "Cordilleran" is defined as anybody living within the regional boundaries, obscuring the historical distinction between lowlanders and highlanders. The 1987 Constitution specifies that the rationale for autonomy is "sharing common and distinctive historical and cultural heritage, economic and social structures," and the question of what Cordilleran identity is still remains.

How did the "Commonwealth period" (1935–1946) emerge?

The United States quite soon began to take up the issue of whether, how, or when the Philippines might become independent. Domestic national politics were beginning among Filipinos, with some resistance from Muslims in particular to the notion of an independent Philippines. But the United States eventually granted "commonwealth" status to the Philippines in 1935 and independence a decade later.

Manuel L. Quezon emerged as the paramount leader, rising from the provincial ranks to national prominence by 1907 and to clear dominance by 1922. He successfully exercised and maintained dominance until his death in 1944, during World War II. The passage from commonwealth status into independence can be told through the lens of his career and how events surrounded and influenced him.

The Philippine Organic Act of 1902, passed by the US Congress, called for the establishment of a bicameral legislature. Once peace had been established and a census taken, the appointed Philippine Commission, the lawmaking body at the beginning of the colonial enterprise, was paired with an elected National Assembly. The first election was held in 1907. Quezon, governor of Tayabas Province (now Quezon Province), and Sergio Osmeña, governor of Cebu Province, led the Nacionalista Party to overwhelming victory by calling for independence for the Philippines and wielding the power of their local networks. Osmeña became speaker of the Assembly, and Quezon was initially majority leader. In 1909, he left to become one of two Philippine commissioners whose job it was to inform the US Congress about the situation in the Philippines. Quezon held this position for four terms, until he was elected to the new Senate in 1916.

The "Jones Act"—the Philippine Autonomy Act of 1916—called for an elected Senate to replace the Philippine Commission as the upper house of the legislature. In that Act, the American government stated that its intention was to "withdraw . . . sovereignty over the Philippine Islands as soon as a stable government can be established therein." Filipinos took up the promise by sending an "independence mission" to the United States in early 1919, after the end of World War I. Headed by Quezon, the mission reported receiving a sympathetic hearing from the Democratic administration of Woodrow Wilson. However, the Republicans won the US election of 1920 and were much less sympathetic to the Philippine appeal for independence. A 1921 fact-finding mission led by US generals Leonard Wood and Cameron Forbes concluded that the islands were not prepared for independence. The Philippine legislature kept sending "independence missions" almost every year—nine more until 1933.

During this period, Quezon was getting restive as Senate president, irritated by the political prominence of Osmeña as speaker of the Assembly. Executive department heads, by now all Filipinos, were said to clear everything with Osmeña. So, for the 1922 Senate elections, which Osmeña also joined, Quezon split the Nacionalista Party, and his faction won overwhelmingly. The factions reunited with Quezon as Senate president; Osmeña as president pro tempore; and Manuel Roxas, who had been governor of Capiz Province, as speaker of the House of Representatives.

A similar exercise of dominance occurred in 1933 when Osmeña and Roxas (together known as "OsRox") returned from their independence mission with the Hare-Hawes-Cutting Act, granting the Philippines independence by July 4, 1946. Quezon led an "anti" campaign—anti-Philippines independence—out of both substantive disagreement (e.g., about American military bases) and personal political interest. Once again, Quezon triumphed in the legislature; he went to Washington and obtained a similar independence bill, the Tydings-McDuffie

Act, that he could claim as his own. Quezon's supporters won overwhelmingly in the 1934 elections.

This set the stage for a constitutional convention; 202 delegates were elected, including some Muslims from the south. During the American period, petitions from Muslims asked not to be included in the new country, but to be considered separately. While these sentiments were heard by some members of the US Congress, splitting the Philippine Islands was never seriously considered.

The convention met in July 1934 and resulted in the 1935 Constitution. It provided for a presidential system of government, with a 120-member unicameral National Assembly. But in 1940, the constitution was amended so that there would be a House of Representatives and a nationally elected Senate. In response to rural unrest, manifested by Sakdalista (a peasant-based party) electoral victories and Communist Party organizing, the constitution declared it a principle that "social justice to insure the well-being and economic security of all the people should be the concern of the State." One reason for the adoption of a nationally elected Senate was to dilute the impact of particular localities that might be dominated by social unrest.

Quezon continued to dominate the political scene and was elected president in 1935, with Osmeña as his vice president. Quezon won 68 percent of the vote, while Aguinaldo (president during the Philippine Revolution) got 17.5 percent and Gregorio Aglipay (head of Iglesia Filipina Independiente— Philippine Independent Church) got 14.5 percent.

Quezon continued to lead Philippine politics until his death in 1944. The 1940 amendments allowed him to run for re-election, and remained head of state even from his World War II–era exile in the United States. Upon his death from tuberculosis, he was succeeded by Osmeña. In the end, despite the disruption of World War II, the Philippines was declared independent on July 4, 1946, as previously scheduled.

What was the course of World War II in the Philippines?

Commonwealth Act No. 1, the first law passed by the new Philippine Commonwealth, was the National Defense Act of 1935; the new state was going to begin by constructing its own armed forces. President Quezon asked former US Army chief of staff Douglas MacArthur, whom he had known since they were young men at the beginning of the American period, to be military adviser to the Philippines and gave him a "Field Marshal" rank with permission from the US Army. With inadequate funding, MacArthur tried to build a military force and was mobilizing by September 1941 in view of increasing tensions with Japan, but this nascent effort was interrupted by the beginning of US involvement in World War II.

Douglas MacArthur was recalled to service in the US armed forces. After the Japanese invasion of the Philippines in December 1941, he ordered Filipino and American troops to retreat to the Bataan peninsula to await a chimerical relief force from across the Pacific. Manila was declared an open city on December 24, and MacArthur hunkered down on Corregidor Island at the mouth of Manila Bay while US and Philippine troops defended Bataan Peninsula. As no relief force was coming, MacArthur was ordered to leave the Philippines, and he departed for Australia in March, promising in a broadcast, "I shall return."

After five months of fighting, Bataan fell to Japan on April 9, 1942, and the Bataan Death March of surrendered American and Filipino troops began. Estimates of how many died in the six-day, 106-kilometer ordeal vary because it is not clear how many troops surrendered and how many faded into the countryside, many to join the resistance. Some fifty-four thousand reached Camp O'Donnell in Tarlac, but there were perhaps three thousand deaths en route and thousands of deaths in the camp. Eventually, Filipino prisoners were paroled, promising not to become guerrillas—a promise often violated—and American prisoners were shifted to other camps.

Guerrilla warfare occurred throughout the country, as Filipino and American troops resisted the Japanese occupation. Many myths and controversies stem from this period of resistance—perhaps the most fiercely contested one being the story of heroism by Ferdinand Marcos. A 1964 campaign biography proclaimed him the most decorated soldier of World War II, a controversial statement not laid to rest by his being buried in August 2016 in Libingan ng mga Bayani (the Heroes' Cemetery) despite the National Historical Commission having concluded that the "military record is fraught with myths, factual inconsistencies, and lies." Another lingering question is how the service of Filipinos in the resistance should be recognized. Philippine World War II veterans are continually lobbying the US Congress for recognition and compensation. An estimated 225,000 Filipinos joined the armed forces or guerrilla movements, but chaotic record-keeping in the aftermath of the war and concerns over fraudulent claims has drawn out the process of honoring those who fought. Most recently, approximately 19,000 veterans availed themselves of lump-sum benefits authorized in 2008, and in 2017 a US Congressional Gold Medal of Honor was presented to Filipino veterans of World War II, of whom 10,000 to 20,000 remain.

During World War II, some Filipinos welcomed Japan, as happened elsewhere in Southeast Asia, but a majority backed the United States instead of the "puppet government" of "collaborators" established in October 1943 by the Japanese. Jose P. Laurel, a prewar senator and justice of the Supreme Court, was the head of this government until he dissolved it, while taking refuge in Japan, on August 17, 1945. As the war continued, hyperinflation ravaged the economy, leading to hunger, bartering, and printing of "Mickey Mouse" money, a paper currency in enormous denominations that was worth very little—a sack of bills for one loaf of bread.

On October 24, 1944, MacArthur made good on his promise to return to the Philippines by wading ashore in Leyte, in the southern Philippines—and he was photographed doing so.

There is a widespread myth that the iconic image was staged, but it is candid, though often misread. In fact, MacArthur's expression was not determination but irritation with the "beachmaster," who was in charge of the logistics of the amphibious landing, for not sending out a boat. With MacArthur was Philippine president Sergio Osmeña (far left in figure 2.3) and in the rear of the group was Carlos P. Romulo, an aide to MacArthur at the time (subsequently signatory of the UN Charter, president of the General Assembly, and later foreign minister of the Philippines).

Beginning in February 1945, the one-month Battle of Manila took place. Surrounded, the 17,000 Japanese military personnel fought to the last man, and in the process 100,000 to 240,000 civilians were killed. Estimates are of course speculative, but perhaps one-third of the casualties were collateral

Figure 2.3 MacArthur lands in Leyte, 1944
Source: Department of Defense, Department of the Army, Office of the Chief Signal Officer (09181947-02281964)

damage from American shelling and two-thirds due to delib-
erate Japanese massacres. By the end on March 3, Manila was
the second most devastated city in World War II, after Warsaw.
The old city of Manila, Intramuros, was almost entirely destroyed and was reconstructed in late colonial Spanish style in
the late 1970s.

An issue that continues to linger in the Philippines, as elsewhere in Asia, is that of "comfort women"—those forced into
sexual slavery by the Japanese Army. There were an estimated
one thousand victims in the Philippines, with fewer than one
hundred surviving. Their cause has been taken up by the Liga
ng mga Lolang Pilipina (League of Filipino Grandmothers; Lila
Pilipina), made up of survivors and their advocates. Though
the Japanese government offered apologies and compensation
in the 1990s, discontent remains over the form: moral, rather
than legal responsibility, and indirect (often private) compensation instead of official government funding. In 2017, the
National Historical Commission of the Philippines erected
a commemorative statue for comfort women, but in the face
of an expression of Japanese government displeasure, it was
removed.

What was the postwar period (1946–1965) like in the Philippines?

Manuel L. Quezon, who had been president of the Philippine
Commonwealth since 1935, passed away in exile in August
1944, shortly before MacArthur's Leyte landing in October. He
was succeeded by his vice president, Sergio Osmeña, who then
accompanied MacArthur in the landing.

The last elections under the Commonwealth were held in
April 1946, and Osmeña was defeated by Manuel Roxas with
the newly established Liberal Party. Thus began two decades of alternating party rule between the long-established
Nacionalista Party and the new Liberal Party. Roxas was the
last president of the Commonwealth, and when independence
was granted by the United States as scheduled on July 4, 1946,

he became the first president of what is known as the Third Philippine Republic. The First Republic was the short-lived Malolos Republic during the Philippine Revolution, and the Second Republic was that established by the Japanese. The controversial issue of the "collaborationist" nature of this Second Republic was laid to rest, legally at least, when Roxas issued an amnesty proclamation in January 1948, ending the prosecution of former president Laurel and others, including Benigno S. Aquino Sr., father of Ninoy Aquino (martyred on August 21, 1983) and grandfather of Noynoy Aquino (president 2010–2016).

Reconstruction after the war was a controversial issue; Manila was devastated and the rest of the country had suffered both economic and physical damage. The Bell Trade Act was passed in 1946 by the US Congress, providing $800 million with the condition that US citizens and entities would have the same rights to natural resources as did Filipinos. This required an amendment to the 1935 Constitution, the "Parity Amendment," which was duly passed in a plebiscite in March 1947. Shortly thereafter the Philippine Senate ratified a bases agreement that gave the United States bases on the islands for ninety-nine years. Both of these moves provided fodder for accusations of violations of Philippine sovereignty, and while the Parity Amendment lapsed as scheduled in 1974, American military presence and exercises in the Philippines continue to be a live issue to this day despite the closure of permanent bases by 1992.

A looming threat to the stability of postwar Philippines was the insurgency based in the plains of Central Luzon. The Hukbong Mapagpalaya ng Bayan (Huks) were the People's Liberation Army and the successors to the Hukbong Bayan Laban sa Hapon (People's Anti-Japanese Army, Hukbalahap), a group of communist-led anti-Japanese guerrillas. Agrarian unrest predated the war, but the armed mobilization and social disruption of the war provided ideal circumstances for a rural insurgency. A Huk offensive alarmed the United States in 1949 in the wake of the communist victory in China. But the attacks damaged the Huks in the public eye when the late President Quezon's widow Aurora was killed in an ambush. American military assistance increased, and the Philippine military expanded in response. Ramon Magsaysay was appointed defense secretary and formed a close friendship with an American adviser, Edward Lansdale. By 1954, an increasingly effective Philippine security apparatus had crushed the Huk rebellion, with most of its leadership captured or surrendered. Lansdale went on to ply his counterinsurgency strategies less successfully in Vietnam, while Magsaysay joined the Nacionalista Party in 1953 and successfully ran against Roxas's successor in the Liberal Party, Elpidio Quirino.

Thus the stage was set for a stable postwar social, political, and economic arrangement. While there were some "new men" in the Philippine political elite, such as Magsaysay and Marcos, there was considerable stability. Electoral politics were based on pyramids of patron-client relations in which locally influential individuals received benefits in return for political support and were happy to switch allegiance. Generally, this fragile patron-client system manifested at the top levels in party switching and in the inability of presidents to win re-election after a full term. Both Magsaysay and Marcos switched to the Nacionalista Party in their successful runs for the presidency in 1953 and 1965, for instance. In 1969, Marcos was the first president to win re-election.

The Philippines's relationship with the United States remained close but contested. Philippine troops served in the Korean War, and there was a Philippine civic action group in the early stages of the Vietnam War, until 1969. American use of Subic Naval Base and Clark Air Base caused friction between the two countries, due to concerns about both the social ills surrounding the bases and the limits on Philippine sovereignty. The Central Intelligence Agency (CIA) had helped Magsaysay win the presidency in 1954, believing his victory crucial for continued success against the Huks. The agency was involved in designing the government's community development schemes, helped instigate the National Movement for Free Elections (NAMFREL) in the early 1950s, and supported other organizations such as The Asia Foundation and the National Union of Students of the Philippines. Records show that such support ceased in 1967, but despite over five decades of disassociation from their CIA connections, Filipinos occasionally still voice suspicions about NAMFREL (reconstituted in the 1980s) and The Asia Foundation.

Economic relations between the Philippines and the United States were quite close under the Parity Amendment. Initial postwar recovery, particularly as the Huk threat receded, was brisk. Thereafter growth slowed, as the Philippines failed to undertake structural transformation of the stagnant and oppressive agricultural sector, and as the limits to import substitution industrialization and capital controls constricted economic modernization. Exports tended to be in primary industries, with sugar going to the United States comprising up to 25 percent of exports. The "Sugar Bloc" grew rich and powerful as witness the two-time vice presidency of Fernando Lopez from the sugar planting elite, who served from 1949 to 1953 under the Liberal president Quirino and from 1965 to 1972 under the Nacionalista president Marcos.

Nationalism was gradually emphasized more and more as the 1950s wore on. For instance, the Retail Trade Nationalization Act in 1954 restricted retail business to Philippine and American citizens, as opposed to Chinese "aliens." In 1956, Senator Claro M. Recto sponsored a law that aimed to promote nationalism by mandating the teaching of Rizal and his works in all schools. This effort succeeded despite fierce opposition from the Catholic Church, which disliked the depiction of friars in Rizal's novels. President Carlos P. Garcia, who succeeded Magsaysay after his death in a plane crash in March 1957 and won his own term in November 1957, formulated a "Filipino First" policy. In 1959, he renegotiated the bases agreement to shorten the term of US occupancy and to share criminal jurisdiction between the two countries. Before that, in the two decades after the bases were established, some thirty Filipinos had been killed on or near the bases without any cases being tried in Philippine courts. Garcia lost the 1961 contest to his vice president, Diosdado Macapagal, who moved the celebration of Independence Day from July 4 to June 12 in 1962, thus recognizing the date in 1898 when Emilio Aguinaldo proclaimed the independence of the Philippines.

How did Ferdinand Marcos serve two terms as elected president?

Given that Imelda Marcos, wife of the late president Ferdinand Marcos, is still on the public scene fifty years later, running for public office, it can be difficult to imagine how in the mid-1960s she and her husband were regarded as breaths of fresh air, the "Asian Kennedys." The Marcos legacy is one of the most hotly contested issues in Philippine history and politics.

Ferdinand Marcos led, at the very least, a colorful life. In December 1938, while in law school at the University of the Philippines, he was convicted of the assassination of a political opponent of his father. But he managed to pass the bar exam in 1939 and won his appeal in 1940 by arguing his own case in front of the Supreme Court. As a Reserve Officers' Training Corps graduate, he was called into service in 1941 and survived the Death March in 1942. He claimed that after his release he commanded a guerrilla force, but this claim was not accepted by the US military. He officially rejoined the United States Armed Forces in the Philippines in December 1944, six weeks after MacArthur waded ashore in Leyte. In his campaign biographies, he persistently claimed that he was awarded many medals, and the claims have just as persistently been disputed, including by the National Historical Commission of the Philippines in August 2016.

Marcos began his political career as a congressman in his home province of Ilocos Norte, serving from 1949 until his election in 1959 to the Senate. He eventually became Senate president and was president of the Liberal Party. But he switched parties to run for president against Macapagal in 1965, and he won the election by a 52–43 percent margin.

He married Imelda Romualdez, a beauty queen from a political family in the central Philippines, after a whirlwind courtship in 1954. As he himself admitted, she was an enormous asset on the campaign trail—glamorous and always ready to entertain the crowd by singing. She was criticized for her lavish lifestyle, but never apologized. Of the famous shoe collection discovered in the presidential palace after their 1986 ouster she said, "They went into my closets looking for skeletons, but thank God, all they found were shoes, beautiful shoes."[4] Her role in Marcos's long administration is disputed, with some dubbing it "The Conjugal Dictatorship" and others dismissing the idea that Imelda was influential. She often represented Marcos diplomatically, was governor of Metro Manila, and oversaw such projects as the Manila Film Center, the Cultural Center of the Philippines, and hospitals for advanced care (cardiac, kidney, etc.).

Marcos promised, "This nation can be great again." One of his thrusts was rural development; he increased spending on rural infrastructure such as roads, irrigation, and schools. The impact was increased by the 1968 release of an improved rice variety (IR-8) by the International Rice Research Institute, which doubled the average per hectare yields in the coming decades. Marcos reinvigorated community development schemes under the Presidential Arm for Community Development, along with the Barrio (village) Development Fund, which provided 2,000 pesos to every barrio captain, not coincidentally beginning just before the 1969 election, in which Marcos was the only Philippine president to win a second full four-year term. His 1969 campaign was several times as expensive as the one in 1965, and he won an overwhelming victory of more than 61 percent of the vote.

Marcos ran government deficits, and in 1970 the peso plunged 50 percent, to six to the US dollar, touching off inflation. Student unrest grew, partly to protest Philippine participation in Vietnam and in sympathy with growing unionization. Anger had already flared when the Philippines hosted the 1966 SEATO Manila Conference of nations involved in the Vietnam War. When Marcos delivered his post-election State of the Nation Address to Congress in January 1970, students gathered outside, and while Marcos and Imelda exited the event, the protesters jostled people and threw rocks. Four days later, in another protest a fire engine was rammed into the gates of the Presidential Palace (Malacañang), and then four student protesters were killed by live fire. Protests continued for months in what has come to be called the "First Quarter Storm."

In view of political unrest and economic problems, a constitutional convention was called to consider changes to the 1935 Constitution. Delegates were elected in November 1970, it convened in June 1971, and considerable controversy ensued about a possible third term for Marcos and alleged bribery attempts. In the run-up to the November 1971 midterm elections, a Liberal Party rally was bombed, killing five persons and injuring several candidates. At the time, many suspected Marcos had a hand in it, but later evidence points to the communists. Marcos briefly suspended the writ of habeas corpus; in retrospect this is seen as a rehearsal for martial law, declared in September 1972.

How did the authoritarian interlude (1972–1986) unfold?

In September 1972, the justifications for martial law in Decree 1081 ran to dozens of paragraphs on the communist insurgency, with four paragraphs mentioning unrest in Mindanao. (See "What is the course of fighting and numerous peace settlements with Muslim separatist fronts?" and "What lies behind the long-running communist insurgency and failure to reach a peace agreement?" in this chapter.) But the immediate effect was on above-ground political actors. Congress was closed, political opponents arrested, the constitutional convention suspended, and media outlets shuttered. In the event, many in the Philippines welcomed the imposition of martial law after years of turmoil. The American Chamber of Commerce sent a telegram pledging cooperation, the United States doubled military assistance to help with counterinsurgency operations, and in the early years both commercial banks and development agencies such as the World Bank and the Asian Development Bank (ADB) and lent the Philippines funds for ambitious projects.

This economic growth spurt was somewhat lessened by the oil crisis of 1973–1974, but foreign borrowing helped to finance infrastructure and other government projects. Marcos's first decree was to reorganize the executive branch, and his second was to declare the entire country a land reform area (followed by Presidential Decree 27, "Operation Land Transfer"). This was in effect "Revolution from the Center: How the Philippines Is Using Martial Law to Build a New Society," to quote a book published under Marcos's name. Marcos recruited technocrats to fill the reorganized government, had a vision of a "New Filipino," and mandated that "For the Development of the Nation, Discipline is Needed." Aside from counterinsurgency efforts, "discipline included press censorship, 'Arrest Search and Seizure Orders' (ASSO) issued by the military," and even cutting the long hair of young males on the street. The general estimate of noncombat extrajudicial killings that occurred is 3,740.

Marcos claimed to be moving against oligarchs to restructure the Philippines as part of his "revolution from the center." For instance, the family of his estranged vice president, Fernando Lopez, was forced out of its conglomerate interests in media, the power sector, and industry. However, what increasingly happened was that Marcos's associates gained monopoly power over key sectors of the economy, such as Roberto Benedicto over sugar and Eduardo Cojuangco over coconut. This is what came to be known as "crony capitalism."

By the early 1980s, economic growth was running out of steam, and foreign debt tripled in the years between 1977 and 1982. In January 1981, Marcos formally lifted martial law, but he retained the ability to rule by decree, and many presidential decrees are still the law of the land. Marcos hoped that lifting martial law would reduce the Catholic Church's criticism of his regime before Pope John Paul II's February 1981 visit to the Philippines. In June 1981, Marcos staged a presidential election against Alejo Santos, a former secretary of national defense and much-decorated war hero, of the moribund Nacionalista Party. Marcos duly won 88 percent of the vote, and at his July inauguration, then vice president George H. W. Bush proclaimed, "We love your adherence to democratic principle and to the democratic processes."

This fragile situation was cracked wide open when former senator and Marcos opponent Benigno S. "Ninoy" Aquino Jr. returned from the United States. He had been allowed to leave political detention to go to the United States for a heart operation. On August 21, 1983, he arrived in Manila, was escorted off the plane by soldiers, and was immediately assassinated on the tarmac. While the government blamed an alleged communist hitman, the man, Rolando Galman, was also immediately killed, and few believed the story. Galman was known by neighbors in Bulacan as a rice farmer and pig farmer and had had a run-in with the law in 1982; his children testified that he had been fetched by a military man days before the assassination, and the accusation was that he was merely a fall guy.[5] The public blamed the Marcoses, mass demonstrations were held in the following months, and perhaps most damaging, the Philippines lost access to international finance, declaring a moratorium on debt payments in October 1983 and only reaching an agreement with creditors in May 1985.

The inflation rate hit 50 percent in 1984, while real per capita income fell 18 percent by 1986. The communist insurgency increased in strength, and the middle classes and business community began openly to mobilize against the regime. In late

1983, the Makati Business Club and other businessmen backed the re-establishment of NAMFREL, which promised that it would receive no foreign funding, unlike its 1950s namesake. Marcos called for legislative elections (Batasang Pambansa) for May 1984, as the legislature had been styled "interim" since the 1978 elections. NAMFREL mobilized 150,000 volunteers to cover 85 percent of all precincts in these legislative elections. The united opposition (UNIDO) won one-third of the vote and one-third of the elected seats; political commentators mused that Marcos's people had taken him too seriously when he publicly called for an honest election.

What is the story of the 1986 "People Power" (or EDSA) Revolution?

Pressure continued on Marcos as the crisis following the 1983 assassination of Ninoy Aquino unfolded. For instance, the US Congress voted to delay military assistance while continuing economic assistance, in order to watch for progress toward democracy. During a live interview on American television in November 1985, Marcos announced that he would call a "snap" election to demonstrate his democratic bona fides. The opposition presented a united ticket, with Salvador Laurel (son of Jose P. Laurel, former senator and president of the Japanese-sponsored republic during World War II) running as vice president and Corazon Cojuangco Aquino (widow of the martyred Ninoy) as the presidential candidate. The surging Communist Party of the Philippines opted not to join the opposition, ordering its followers to boycott the election—a decision that most observers believe cost the communist insurgency.

The story of the February 1986 peaceful ouster of Marcos was at the time extensively told in such books as "Four Days of Courage," "The Miracle of the EDSA Revolution," and "People Power: The Greatest Democracy Ever Told." The election campaign was violent and contentious. NAMFREL, which included a number of prominent business and civil society leaders, was initially a citizen-led electoral monitoring organization in the

1984 Batasang Pambansa (National Legislature) election. For the 1986 election, the organization mobilized some 500,000 volunteers nationwide. Print media had opened up considerably by the mid-1980s, but broadcast media were still dominated by the Marcos administration. International attention was intense, and the global media descended on the country.

Vote counting after the February 7 election was slow and marked by the walkout of thirty-five computer encoders, who alleged that they were being fed doctored data. The Commission on Elections announced that Marcos had won by 1.5 million votes, while NAMFREL's partial parallel count of 69 percent of precincts showed Corazon C. Aquino ahead by half a million votes. The Batasang Pambansa officially canvassed the votes, and over the objection of opposition members, proclaimed Ferdinand Marcos the winner on February 15. The International Observer Mission concluded that the election was not free and fair and pronounced the Batasang Pambansa proclamation invalid.

Civil unrest and protests continued, largely but not exclusively in Metro Manila. The Catholic station Radio Veritas coordinated some protests through its evening broadcasts. The station had a large audience because it had broadcast Ninoy Aquino's return to the Philippines live, which turned into coverage of his assassination. Thereafter, Radio Veritas was one of the few media outlets that covered protests and anti-administration news. Cory Aquino and opposition leaders used the station to explain what steps needed to be taken in a civil disobedience campaign while Marcos continued to be in power.

However, on the evening of February 22 it was not opposition leaders but Defense Chief Juan Ponce Enrile and Deputy Chief of Staff Fidel V. Ramos who were on the radio, announcing their withdrawal of support from Marcos. Later it was revealed that a elements in the military had plotted to establish a junta to replace Marcos. But Marcos learned of the coup and started arresting the plotters from the Reform the Armed Forces

Movement (RAM) associated with Enrile and Ramos. They retreated to Armed Forces Headquarters in Camp Aguinaldo
and held their press conference. Ramos went across Epifanio
de los Santos Avenue (EDSA) to police headquarters at Camp
Crame. As word got out, Agapito "Butz" Aquino, Ninoy's
brother, announced that civil society was going to EDSA to
protect these two camps. Then Archbishop Jaime Cardinal Sin
went on Radio Veritas to urge ordinary citizens to action: "If
any of you could be around at Camp Aguinaldo to show your
solidarity and your support in this very crucial period when
our two good friends have shown their idealism, I would be
very happy. . . . Please come."

Crowds gathered for days, filled the highway, prevented
tanks from approaching the camps, prayed and fraternized
with the soldiers, and warily watched circling helicopters. The
nation held its breath, but in the end, elements of the military
loyal to Marcos did not attack, so there was no bloodbath.
The reaction was frantic but diplomatic. Marcos involved the
United States, including calling Senator Paul Laxalt, who acted
as go-between between Marcos and President Ronald Reagan.
Laxalt advised Marcos to "cut and cut cleanly." On the morning
of February 25, Corazon Aquino took her oath of office as president, and at noon in the Presidential Palace, Marcos took his
own oath, citing the proclamation by the Batasang Pambansa,
though the live TV coverage was cut off when rebels destroyed
the transmitters. At 9:00 that night, Marcos boarded a heli-
copter to be flown to the US facility at Clark Air Base, then on
to Hawai'i.

What is the Marcos legacy?

The legacy of Marcos is one of the most hotly contested
questions in the Philippines since the family departed the
Philippines on February 25, 1986.

Hawai'i is home to a large number of Ilocanos, Marcos's
ethnic group, who first migrated there in 1906 to work on

sugar plantations. He received aid from some were supporters, including with finding a residence in Hawai'i after he left the Philippines. However, he was not granted any legal immunity, so the Aquino administration and private individuals immediately began to file lawsuits against him. Marcos succumbed to his ailments in 1989. The rest of the family were allowed back to the Philippines in 1991, and by 1992 they were back in politics. Imelda ran for president under the political party Kilusang Bagong Lipunan, although she came in fourth in a field of seven, with some 10 percent of the vote, while Bongbong successfully ran for Congress from Ilocos Norte, their bailiwick.

Most recently, Imelda Marcos continued to serve as member of Congress (1995–1998; 2010–2019) until the end of her term in 2019, despite her November 2018 conviction by the anti-graft court, and her children Imee and Ferdinand "Bongbong" Marcos Jr. have sought national offices (Bongbong unsuccessfully ran for vice president in 2016 after six years in the Senate; Imee was elected to the Senate in 2019). Imee controversially said it was time to "move on" from disputes about martial law, and Bongbong agreed: "The frustration is that you have been asked this question over and over again. It has been decided. The government fell. The cases against us were filed. The cases came to a decision."[6]

The remains of Ferdinand Marcos were carefully preserved and were repatriated in 1993, but burial was not initially allowed in Libingan ng mga Bayani (Heroes' Cemetery), so the family laid him to rest in a refrigerated glass crypt in Ilocos Norte. In 2016 President Duterte, who often expresses admiration for the strongman rule of Ferdinand, allowed Marcos's burial in the cemetery, causing an uproar. The legacy question is indeed a live one.

One focus of debate is on human rights. According to Amnesty International, about 70,000 people were imprisoned, 34,000 were tortured, and 3,240 were killed from 1972 to 1981. In 2013, a law was passed providing reparations for victims of human rights violations, with ten billion pesos ($190 million) of funds coming from recovered ill-gotten wealth of the Marcoses. The Human Rights Victims' Claims Board received over 75,000 applications in one year (May 2015) and approved some 11,103 claims by August 2018. A legacy of this law will be a memorial complex; documentation of all the claims is seen as a way of settling some of the historical controversies.

The funds for this effort, like funds for agrarian reform, are supposed to be sourced from the "plunder" of the Marcoses. Estimates of this ill-gotten wealth vary enormously—an oft-cited amount is US$5 to $10 billion, as referenced by Transparency International. An American estimate at the time was a total of roughly 10 percent of gross national product, which would be somewhere between $3 and $4 billion. The Presidential Commission on Good Government (PCGG), set up after the "People Power" Revolution, has recovered about $4 billion worth of cash, shares, real estate, paintings, and jewels, with lawsuits aiming at recovering another $1 billion.

Imelda Marcos has been convicted by the Sandiganbayan (a specialized anti-corruption court) of graft involving about $200 million in Swiss bank accounts in the name of several foundations. The case was filed in 1991, went to trial in 2000, and was finally decided in 2018. She immediately posted the $3,000 bail and will appeal. The decision needs to be decided with finality by the Supreme Court.

After twenty-five years, Filipino public opinion is evenly split about whether Marcos is worthy of being buried in the Heroes' Cemetery. A narrative has grown over the years, fiercely resisted by opponents of Marcos, that there was a golden age under his leadership. More schools and other infrastructure were built, and the vigorous support of hybrid rice doubled the yields and briefly made the Philippines a net exporter of rice, a rare feat in Philippine history. The political turmoil of the early 1970s calmed down, and economic growth boomed.

Critics derided Imelda for having an "edifice complex," but many of the signature projects are still prominently providing benefits; The Cultural Center of the Philippines continues to be one of the centers of performing arts in the country. Several specialty health centers were built—the Philippine Heart Center, the National Kidney and Transplant Institute, the National Lung Center, and the Philippine Children's Medical Center—that provided world-class care without having to leave the country.

A failed initiative was the Bataan Nuclear Power Plant, which was nearly complete in 1984 but never commissioned. After the 1986 Chernobyl disaster in the Ukraine, post-Marcos governments refused to contemplate operating it. The Cory Aquino government agreed to honor the debt of $2.3 billion, which was only paid off in April 2007. In fact, the post-revolution government agreed to honor all contracted debt, which had ballooned to 82 percent of gross domestic product (GDP), over fierce domestic opposition led by the Freedom from Debt Coalition.

This financial toll is a clue to the trajectory of the Marcos administration. During the 1970s, there was a deficit, debt-fueled economic growth, and an infrastructure spree. By the 1980s, with economic distortions caused by monopolies, such as in sugar and coconut (two top exports), and a fragile banking system, the country was easily pushed over the edge into the 1983 crisis after the assassination of Benigno Aquino Jr. Per capita income did not return to 1982 levels until 1992 or even the early 2000s, depending on how it is measured. In short, the end of the Marcos authoritarian interlude was a blow to the Philippine economy.

What was the immediate post-Marcos restoration?

After Marcos, the Philippines strove for continuity, or more precisely, for preventing further disruption. The country chose not to demonetize existing currency, for instance, despite the large stashes of cash available to the former president, who took twenty-two boxes full of money on the plane when he retreated to Hawai'i. Bureaucratic continuity was also evident, as only 27,500 government officials (2.1 percent of the total) lost their jobs due to reorganization of agencies. Corazon Aquino ruled by decree, enacting a "Freedom Constitution" as an interim measure and appointing a fifty-member constitutional commission. The commission began its work in June 1986 and finished a draft of its constitution—the present one—in October 1986. It was ratified in February 1987 and is generally called the 1987 Constitution.

Elections were held in May 1987 for both the nationally elected Senate and the district-elected House of Representatives. In January 1988, elections were held for all local government positions, which had since the February 1986 revolution been held by officers-in-charge (OIC) appointed by the secretary of interior. Many of these OICs were able to get their first foothold in local power at this election and managed to perpetuate their clans in their bailiwicks. Duterte was appointed OIC-vice mayor of Davao, then successfully ran for mayor in January 1988, beginning his long period of dominance in the city's politics. Jejomar Binay began as OIC-mayor of Makati in 1986, and his family still controls the city's politics. His daughter is a nationally elected senator, and he rose to be elected vice president in 2010 and was an unsuccessful candidate for president in 2016.

Aside from the restoration of electoral democracy, four things stand out in Cory Aquino's term: military coup attempts (see "What is the Season of Coups?" in this chapter), peace talks with insurgents, economic doldrums, and decentralization to reinforce democracy.

At the beginning of her term in office, Aquino's government reached out to many groups that had rebelled against the Marcos administration. She released political prisoners and entered into negotiations with communist insurgents. Such talks were controversial among the military elements of the coalition that had overthrown Marcos. In any case, the rebels suspended the talks after the January 1987 "Mendiola massacre," in which security forces fired upon peasants demonstrating to demand land reform and thirteen were killed. It is worth noting that little progress has been made in negotiations with the Communist Party of the Philippines/New People's Army/ National Democratic Front (CPP, NPA, and NDF, or CNN in the military abbreviation) in the thirty years since.

President Aquino personally reached out to indigenous peoples in the Cordillera Mountains of Northern Luzon and the Moros in Muslim Mindanao. She met with Conrado Balweg at Mount Data in September 1996 to enter into a *sipat* (a traditional cessation of hostilities). Balweg was the most prominent leader of the NPA in the Cordillera, but his Cordillera People's Liberation Army (CPLA) split from them and began negotiating separately with the government. (Balweg was eventually killed by the NPA in 1999.) Cory Aquino also went to Sulu to meet with Moro National Liberation Front (MNLF) chair Nur Misuari, and Misuari was allowed to travel freely around Mindanao to consult his followers. The 1987 Constitution had a provision for two autonomous regions, one for the Cordillera and one for Muslim Mindanao. Yet the one for the Cordillera has not been established, despite two attempts, while the autonomous region in Muslim Mindanao was established in 1989 without the participation of the MNLF.

Corazon Aquino inherited an economy that had been in trouble since the assassination of her husband Ninoy in 1983. The economy stopped falling in 1986, but it was more than a decade before per capita income recovered. In the meantime, her decision to honor the foreign debts that Marcos had run up, a choice supported by orthodox economists, meant that as much as 10 percent of GDP was devoted to debt service. Over the years this ratio has steadily declined, so that it is no longer a constraint on government spending, but government flexibility in the immediate post-Marcos period was constrained. Attempts by the PCGG to recover assets alleged to have been stolen by the Marcoses bore some fruit, but were very slow.

Finally, the Corazon Aquino administration can be said to have been plagued by terrible luck. Aside from an El Niño event causing droughts, a massive earthquake in 1990 in Northern Luzon devastated the cities of Baguio and Dagupan, as well as much of the Cordillera mountain region. Then in 1991, the twentieth century's second most powerful volcanic eruption, of Mount Pinatubo, turned much of central Luzon into a lahar-covered wasteland. Internationally, the 1990–1991 Gulf War crisis raised the price of oil. In the face of all this, it is not surprising that economic growth faltered.

As part of Aquino's basic mandate to restore democracy to the Philippines, a new Local Government Code was passed in 1991. It devolved more power from the national government to municipalities, cities, and provinces and encouraged participatory local governance. Finally, although it was not entirely clear whether the one-term limit on presidents in the 1987 Constitution applied to her since she was not elected under that constitution, she insisted on stepping down at the end of her term in 1992. At that point, the stage was set for the next quarter of a century of electoral democracy, capitalist economics, political struggle, and slow developmental progress.

Is the Philippines a "cacique democracy"?

In 1988, noted comparative politics scholar Benedict Anderson wrote in the New Left Review "Cacique Democracy in the Philippines: Origins and Dreams." He crafted this work during the aftermath of the 1986 "People Power" Revolution, the peaceful though nerve-wracking ouster of Marcos that was hailed as a "miracle." President Aquino was seen as an icon of democracy as the Philippines became part of "Democracy's Third Wave." In the article, Anderson wrote skeptically about the influence of an elite group of families, which he repeatedly called "caciques," without defining the word, perhaps assuming its Latin American origins as a term for local leader was sufficiently well-known. Notably, he pointed out that President Corazon Aquino's family, the Cojuangcos, were part of the Chinese mestizo elite that arose in the mid-nineteenth century.

In 2010, Corazon's son, Benigno S. "Noynoy" Aquino III, won the election for president. He was at the time a senator and is the son of Senator Benigno S. Aquino Jr. ("Ninoy"), Corazon's husband, who was assassinated during the authoritarian interlude upon return from exile in 1983. Noynoy's grandfather was Benigno "Igno" Aquino, also a senator before World War II, who became speaker of the House of Representatives in the Japanese-sponsored "second Philippine republic" toward the end of the war. Noynoy's great-grandfather was Servillano "Mianong" Aquino, who was a general in the anti-colonial revolution, fighting successively at the turn of the twentieth century against Spain and the United States, and who served in the revolutionary government's Congress. Noynoy's great-great-grandfather was Don Braulio Aquino, who belonged to the landed aristocracy and lived 150 years before his great-great-grandson announced a run for the presidency.

Such stories could be endlessly repeated. Lacking institutionalized political parties, politics centers on personality and is often organized by clan. But lest we overstate the solidity of family lineages, we can remember that the Philippines has also been characterized by Alfred McCoy as "An Anarchy of Families." Noynoy is the second cousin of one of the candidates he defeated in 2010, former defense secretary Gilberto "Gibo" Teodoro. Noynoy's mother, Corazon Cojuangco Aquino, is a cousin of Teodoro's mother, Mercedes Cojuangco Teodoro. The two wings of the Cojuangco clan have been feuding for decades; Gibo's father was administrator of the Social Security System during the authoritarian rule of Ferdinand Marcos, under which Noynoy's father suffered.

But there are weaknesses in a focus on "cacique democracy" that go beyond competition among or within clans. For one, the image of the Philippines being continually ruled by "Forty Families" misses the churning of power among political families. Considerable research has gone into the existence and malign effects of "fat" clans dominating provincial politics. When one family holds many different positions— member of the House of Representatives, governor, mayor, and so on—it is characterized as "fat." Many of these "fat" clans share a particular recent origin, however. In the aftermath of the 1986 ouster of President Marcos, the revolutionary government headed by Corazon Aquino appointed members of these families as OICs of their localities. Many managed to use those almost accidental political resources to win elections to local posts in the first local elections in 1988. From then on, they were able to solidify their hold on local political power—either through legitimate personalist politics and name recognition or through more irregular extractive means.

Perhaps a more fundamental problem with the cacique analysis is that its focus on clan connections fails to appreciate the nuances of personalist politics. Certainly kinship is the idiom of social organization in the Philippines, but how kinship is defined can be quite complex. And kinship is not the only force that motivates political activity. After all, while kinship ties were prominent in the struggle for independence from Spain, it was the idea of the Filipino nation and cultural resonances among islands that allowed broad cooperation to that end. Idioms that go beyond kinship are increasingly important in the technological age, as not only does the circulation of ideas speed up, but the impact of memes and social media allows new forms of organization to emerge.

President Duterte, elected in 2016, illustrates the complexity of all these factors. His father was a politician in Cebu Province in the 1940s but then immigrated to Davao after

Rodrigo's birth in the late 1940s. From 1959 to 1965, the father was governor of the province of Davao, and then from 1965 until his death in 1968 he served in the pre–martial law cabinet of Ferdinand Marcos. Duterte's mother, Soledad, became prominent in the anti-Marcos opposition in Davao City. After the 1986 ouster of Marcos, she was approached to be appointed as OIC but demurred, suggesting her son—who was at the time a public prosecutor—in her stead, and he was appointed OIC-vice mayor. In the first post-revolution local elections in 1988, he parlayed that appointment into a successful run for mayor and subsequently served continuously as mayor or vice mayor (to his daughter) when he ran up against term limits, except for one term (1998–2001) when he was a congressman, again because of term limits. In late 2014, he began seriously testing the waters for the presidency, as a somewhat famous but little-known candidate, with a nationwide tour. He spoke about changing the Philippine unitary state into a federal one since he had long chafed at the dominance of Manila. His candidacy only pulled within striking distance, however, when the first-ever series of televised national debates gave him nationwide media exposure in 2016. Shrewd use of social media added to this boost. While Duterte does not tweet, he has Diehard Duterte Supporters (DDS; a play on the Davao Death Squads alleged to operate under his watch), who have millions of followers on social media. Ultimately, he won decisively with a plurality of 39 percent in a field of five candidates.

In short, Duterte's father, a migrant lawyer, pursued a provincial political career. Twenty years after his death, his son was appointed to a political post based on his mother's endorsement after a political upheaval and managed to build a clan dynasty. Duterte's daughter Sara was elected mayor, and because of her temperament and political skills—not to mention her sometimes problematic relation with her father—became a nationally influential person, as in the 2019 elections. All this developed in a time of rapid change, including both mass and social media, and is hardly the picture painted by the term "cacique democracy."

The dynamics of rise and fall of families belies the "cacique" label but nonetheless emphasizes the role of family ties and kinship as an organizing principle.

What is the liberal-reform arc of four presidential terms (1992–2016)?

Corazon Aquino sealed the transition from the 1972–1986 authoritarian interlude by stepping down in 1992, at the end of her six-year term. Some of her supporters speculated that she could have run for election since she had been elected prior to the 1987 Constitution, which stipulates a single elected term for president. Twenty-four years later her son, Benigno S. "Noynoy" Aquino III, stepped down at the end of his six-year term, yielding the office to Duterte, the tough-talking mayor of Davao City who was already labeled a populist and whose strongman style of rule is now feared to herald a return to authoritarianism. In retrospect, the run of administrations from 1992 to 2016 can be seen as the playing out of a particular liberal reform agenda. But that same trend of liberalization seems to have finally been rejected by the electorate, seeing that voters handed Duterte a convincing victory (39 percent in a five-candidate race, 15 percent ahead of second-place Mar Roxas).

The 1992 presidential election was much closer; Fidel V. Ramos, Cory Aquino's chosen successor, won with only 23.6 percent of the vote in a six-candidate race. He was less than 4 percent ahead of Miriam Defensor-Santiago, who maintained until her death in 2016 that she had been cheated in the election. The election confirmed the irrelevance of political parties in vote contests. The party Laban ng Demokratikong Pilipino (Fight of Democratic Filipinos), which had been formed in 1988, held a convention that chose Speaker of the House Ramon Mitra over Ramos as presidential candidate. Ramos then bolted the party to run and win, and Mitra came in third.

Despite the closeness of the election, Ramos started his term with a two-year honeymoon in public opinion surveys and a legislative majority as both congressmen and senators lined up to support the presidential winner. He signaled his reform thrust early when he insisted on the implementation of the 1991 Local Government Code, which devolved more powers and resources to *barangays* (villages), municipalities, cities, and provinces. In fact, Ramos had an overall strategy to strengthen the Philippine state that he implemented quite thoroughly.

First, he wanted to engage in a peace process with various rebel elements: Muslim separatists, military adventurists, and communist rebels. His efforts resulted in the 1996 peace agreement with the MNLF, amnesties that led to some military coup participants getting elected to office, and partial (ultimately stalled) agreements with communist rebels. A direct anti-poverty agenda of laws that established the National Anti-Poverty Commission and National Commission on Indigenous Peoples complemented his peace-seeking. Finally, to rescue the country from economic doldrums, he pursued economic reform through trade and capital account liberalization, oil price deregulation, electric power generation, and the breakup of the telecommunications monopoly.

As the centennial of the 1898 revolution approached, Ramos touted a vision of "Philippines 2000." Some of his allies attempted to enact constitutional change so that he could continue his reform agenda beyond the mandated end of his term in June 1998, but this never happened. The 1997 Asian financial crisis shook the economy's bright prospects as the country dipped into a mild recession, and widespread opposition, plus a Supreme Court decision, put a halt to those efforts.

The 1998 presidential election went ahead as scheduled, leading to a victory for Vice President Joseph§ "Erap" Estrada,

---

§ Tagolog slang for "buddy" is *pare*, which is made even more colloquial by inverting the syllables to get "Erap." This is a frequent practice in Filipino slang; for example, "idol" becomes "lodi."

a movie star. His was certainly a populist campaign, uncon-nected to any established party and touting "Erap para sa Mahirap" (Erap for the poor). Prominent intellectuals and ac-tivists supported him, partly due to his social network and partly due to his perceived anti-American stance (e.g., his Senate vote against the renewal of the bases agreement). But as his administration spiraled down into personal scandals, in particular profiting by stock manipulation and involve-ment in the illegal numbers game *jueteng* (leading to the term "juetengate"), many reform people left his administration, and he was impeached by the House of Representatives in late 2000. During his impeachment trial in January 2001, the Philippine Senate reached a procedural impasse on live TV, and crowds gathered at the symbolic EDSA site, in what was dubbed "People Power II." In this instance, the military and Supreme Court sided with the crowd, and Estrada was ousted.

His replacement by Vice President Gloria Macapagal-Arroyo in early 2001 seemed to restore the full-blown reformist agenda. Civil society leaders were influential in staffing her administra-tion, and Arroyo's credentials as an economist boded well for continued economic reform. Regulatory reforms laid the basis for the spectacular growth of the business process outsourcing industry. "Crossover" leadership, referring to activists from civil society becoming senior government officials, seemed on the rise. But the reformists split with Arroyo in 2005, after her constitutional yet unfavored decision to run for re-election in 2004 and the "Hello Garci" election scandal, in which a leaked recording exposed her call to election commissioner Virgilio Garcillano seeking to ensure a one-million-vote winning margin. Throughout the rest of her administration, she was unpopular with the public (see figure 5.13), but the institutional powers of the presidency meant that she was able to continue to govern. In this period, the Philippines avoided a recession during the 2007–2008 global financial crisis, and Arroyo made some important changes, such as legalizing roll-on/roll-off interisland shipping, thus driving down the cost of goods and travel nationwide.

When Corazon Aquino passed away in 2009, a wave of nostalgia swept over the country and propelled her son—previously a senator without discernible ambition for the post—into the presidency in May 2010. Again, reform elements were a prominent part of his coalition, running on the slogan *Kung walang corrupt, walang mahirap* (if no corruption, no poverty). Until the very end of his term in 2016, Noynoy Aquino remained quite popular, though some controversies dented his ratings.

In particular, a scandal broke out in 2014 over the long-running practice of pork barrel, whereby senators and congressmen got a budget allocation to specify particular projects. It was alleged, that legislators received kickbacks for favoring individual contractors and recipients; court action was still ongoing five years after the events. The Supreme Court ruled this manner of allocation by legislators unconstitutional, overruling its own previous decisions on the matter. Some months later the court also ruled that a budgetary mechanism used by the Aquino administration, the Disbursement Acceleration Program (DAP), was unconstitutional. This program was a technocratic mechanism used to reallocate funds from slow-spending projects to ones that were moving more quickly; the court ruled that this violated the budgetary powers of Congress. In the public eye, this DAP was conflated with the pork barrel kickbacks.

In any case, the continued popularity of President Noynoy Aquino was insufficient to support his chosen successor, Mar Roxas. Instead, Rodrigo Duterte won in May 2016 with the slogan "Change is Coming," but it is clear that the change President Duterte had in mind was not of the liberal reform variety.

The liberal reform period is perhaps best described by its quantitative indicators. For instance, the World Bank examines many data sets to analyze governance indicators along six dimensions, and for the Philippines, all six peaked as Ramos stepped down from the presidency in 1998, and only recovered (without quite reaching their previous highs) during Noynoy's administration. A similar quantitative index is the share of government revenue of the economy, which spiked in 1997 just before a tax change took place and only started to rise again steadily under Noynoy Aquino. The increase in tax take has continued under Duterte, as did the upward trend in the World Bank's measure of the government's ability to have sound policies to promote private sector development. This is testimony to the quality of Duterte's economic team. But the continuity of economic thrust is out of step with the rest of the administration's actions, which are populist, verging on authoritarian.

Why is populism a recurrent thread in recent Philippine politics?

The Philippines was thrust into the international spotlight in 2016 when Duterte catapulted to the presidency from his post as mayor of Davao City in Mindanao. This was the first time in Philippine history that any local official jumped directly from a local office to the highest office in the land. Estrada had been elected in 1998 and had previously been mayor of San Juan in Metro Manila, but he had a transitional step as a nationally elected senator and then vice president, as well as the advantage of his movie-star fame. President Duterte has come under considerable scrutiny for policy issues, including his international rebalancing, moving away from the alliance with the United States and toward China and Russia. The bulk of the attention has focused on his rough language and the bloody "War on Drugs" that has cost tens of thousands of lives in both police operations and killings of alleged addicts and drug pushers in murky circumstances.

Duterte's victory is often seen as part of a global rise in populism in 2016, in line with the UK's "Brexit" vote to leave the European Union and the election of Donald Trump as the US president. Analysts of the Philippines, however, point to the recurrence of populist strains in Philippine politics going back to Manuel Quezon, president of the Commonwealth from 1935 until his death in 1944. After World War II, Ramon Magsaysay, known for the slogan "Magsaysay is my Guy," operated on populist principles and won the 1953 presidential election. Joseph Estrada utilized a populist campaign, "Erap para sa Mahirap" (Erap for the poor) to win election in 1998, though he was ousted in 2001.

While there are a number of possible characterizations of the populism phenomenon, it is clear that populists are not creatures of political parties, but rather are outside them. Party affiliation among Filipinos has always been weak, and in recent years 90 percent of voters have had no party identification.

Magsaysay was defense minister for President Quirino, a Liberal, but jumped to the Nacionalista Party to win the presidency. Estrada ran in 1998 as the candidate of a loose coalition of three political parties. In 2016, Duterte ran as the candidate of a party, PDP-Laban, that was formed in the early 1980s, but his unsuccessful vice-presidential running mate was from the Nacionalista Party.

Populists work not through either programmatic or clientelistic parties but connect directly to the voter. Quezon succeeded with a "social justice" program during the Commonwealth era, and Magsaysay carefully cultivated his image as the "Champion of the Common Man" and was famous for his quote: "He who has less in life should have more in law." Estrada had his purpose-built movement, the "JEEP (Joseph Ejercito Estrada for President) ni Erap," playing on his cinematic image as a man of the people who was once the driver of a jeepney, a ubiquitous form of cheap mass transportation.

In 2016, Duterte benefited from the first-ever nationally televised presidential debates, which allowed direct communication with voters. His team also mobilized the new social media. The Philippines had almost 30 million Facebook users in 2016, when the total presidential vote turnout was 42 million and Duterte's winning total 16.6 million. Once in office,

Duterte's rhetorical style continued to be down to earth, vulgar, and colloquial, even in set piece speeches such as the State of the Nation Address at the opening of Congress, bolstering his image as a leader who identifies with the average citizen.

Populists do not have a particular set of policies that they carry out. They often employ what are termed "economic populist" policies, labeled as beneficial to the average citizen but often criticized by mainstream economists as counterproductive. Subsidies of many sorts, including free irrigation or college education, and price controls (e.g., oil price controls or floor prices for rice) are judged to distort economic incentives and lead to perverse outcomes. But populists do not have a monopoly on such policies.

One characteristic of populism is an "us versus them" narrative. Crime is so often a theme of these narratives that the term "penal populism" has been coined to describe a situation in which the populist leader is prosecuting the criminal "other" on behalf of the people. This certainly resonates with the Philippine experience; for example, former vice president Estrada reprised his cinematic tough-guy persona when President Ramos named him head of the Presidential Anti-Crime Commission. This boosted his subsequent run for the presidency, but it pales in comparison with the vehement rhetoric of Duterte in the 2016 campaign, when he vowed to fatten the fish in Manila Bay with the bodies of slain drug pushers. Observers pointed out that crime statistics were down and thus it was unlikely to be a winning campaign theme. While the downward trend in crime was real, there had been a rising fear of crime throughout the Aquino administration, providing fertile ground, particularly in urban areas, for a candidate willing to demonize the criminals.

In short, without institutionalized political parties of any sort, the Philippines was prone to populism even before the mid-2010s rise in global populism. This is unlikely to change any time soon.

What is the "Season of Coups"?

The Philippines long had no history of coups by military forces. All that changed in February 1986, when an abortive coup plot against Marcos was discovered, but it led to the peaceful civilian "People Power" Revolution that ousted Marcos. In the eighteen months after the ouster of Ferdinand Marcos, there were seven coup attempts, ranging from aborted to farcical to combative. Then, after a lull of two years, a truly serious attempt lasted more than a week in December 1989.

The July 1986 Manila Hotel incident introduced the nation to a series of coups. Thousands of Marcos "loyalists" and hundreds of soldiers took over the iconic hotel, where Douglas MacArthur had stayed before World War II, and tried to proclaim Arturo Tolentino, Marcos's running mate in the February 1986 election, "acting president." This event ended peacefully with promises that there would be no punishment for soldiers who swore allegiance to the new government, though Armed Forces Chief of Staff Fidel Ramos ordered the military men to each do thirty pushups. In November a conspiracy was uncovered, leading to the firing of Juan Ponce Enrile as defense secretary.

In January 1987, soldiers seized the GMA Network TV station and briefly held a monopoly on TV broadcasting, as they had sabotaged the other networks. There was a short battle in which the station was retaken, with one rebel soldier killed and dozens of civilian coup supporters injured. In April of the same year, a raid on the Philippine Army (AFP) camp at Fort Bonifacio resulted in one rebel killed and lasted less than two days. In July, another plot was uncovered before it could be launched, and there were some resulting court martials. In August 1987, more than two thousand soldiers launched a coup attempt, including a direct assault on the Presidential Palace (Malacañang). There were considerable casualties: fifty-three dead and two hundred wounded, including President Cory's son, Noynoy, who would go on to be elected president in 2010. Casualties were so high because the rebel soldiers actually fired on civilian onlookers who were jeering at them.

The December 1989 event was the most serious of the coup attempts, not least because the rebels took over two air force bases, Sangley near Manila and Mactan near Cebu, and conducted air strikes on the morning of December 1. American jets from Clark Air Base, north of Manila, conducted "persuasion flights" over rebel positions to demonstrate US support for Aquino, but all air action against the rebels on December 1 and 2 was carried out by Philippine government aircraft. On December 2, the rebels retreated from Fort Bonifacio and took over a section of the financial district of Makati. They agreed by December 7 to march back to their barracks, and on December 9 the rebels in Mactan surrendered, ending this attempt, in which 570 were wounded and 99 died, 50 of them civilians.

A complete list of coups would include two localized incidents outside of Metro Manila that were after-effects of the December 1989 attempt, in Northern Luzon (March 1990) and Mindanao (October 1990). Some lists include the January 2001 ouster of President Estrada as a coup, but in reality it was a civilian-led effort that Defense Secretary Orlando Mercado and Armed Forces Chief of Staff Angelo Reyes joined by withdrawing their support from Estrada.

In 2003, there was a one-day takeover on July 27 of a luxury hotel in the heart of the financial district of Makati, the Oakwood (since renamed the Ascott). Over three hundred junior officers and soldiers peacefully entered the hotel in the early morning, planted mines in its surroundings, and stationed snipers on the roof. This attempt was supported by civilian elements, including former colonel and then senator Gregorio "Gringo" Honasan—who had been part of Enrile's group in the late 1980s attempts—and supporters of recently ousted President Estrada. Known as the "Magdalo" group, recalling one of the factions during the Philippine Revolution, the military men had grievances—outdated equipment, poor healthcare, corruption—and felt that they were not getting a hearing from President Macapagal-Arroyo. Their civilian supporters were prevented from amassing near the hotel, and there was no sympathetic response from the rest of the military, so they surrendered peacefully just before midnight.

A fact-finding commission, while not sympathetic to the political aims of the coup attempt, did find that the complaints and grievances used to recruit soldiers and officers into the conspiracy were "to a substantial degree real, and not merely fictitious." (See "What is the state of the military?" in chapter 5.)

In November 2007, some of the Magdalo group simply walked out of the court where they were being tried for the 2003 mutiny and marched to yet another luxury hotel in Makati, the Peninsula. They were joined by some soldiers and civilians, including former vice president Teofisto Guingona Jr. (2001–2004), as they took over one of the ballrooms, Security forces rushed the hotel, and an armored personnel carrier shot up the lobby, but no one was hurt. The entire incident, covered prominently by the media, lasted about six hours before the group gave up once again.

One of the Magdalo group, Antonio Trillanes, successfully ran for senator in the May 2007 election by using the social networking service Friendster from his jail cell. But he was unable to take up his duties until after the next president, Noynoy Aquino, issued an amnesty proclamation in November 2010 for those involved in the anti-Arroyo coup activities. In 2013 and 2016, another junior officer, Gary Alejano, was elected to Congress as a representative of the Magdalo Party List, though he failed in his 2019 attempt to succeed Trillanes in the Senate.

The amnesty impulse goes all the way back to the beginning of the series of coups, when the July 1986 Manila Hotel occupation ended with a punishment of thirty pushups. In March 1994, President Ramos issued an amnesty proclamation for those who had taken part in the "Season of Coups." This allowed, for instance, retired Philippine Army officer Gringo Honasan to serve multiple terms in the Senate.

The military's adventurous genie was let out of the bottle at the end of the Marcos authoritarian interlude and continued for almost twenty years because fundamental problems in the Armed Forces were not sufficiently addressed. Since 2003, the genie has gradually been stuffed back into the bottle, but some of those involved—including Trillanes, Alejano, and Honasan—are still candidates and have been elected senators.

What are the roots of the Muslim separatist insurgency?

What has been termed the "orthodoxy" about Muslims in the Philippines is quite straightforward. Muslims had their own systems of government in the sultanates when the Spanish arrived. For almost three hundred years they successfully resisted incorporation into the colonial state, which labeled them "Moros," until the overwhelming might of the new American colonial power managed to bloodily conquer them. Despite their protests, Muslims were included in the Philippine Commonwealth in 1935, and thus their territory was part of the new Philippine Republic at independence in 1946. The mainstream Philippine government tried to "integrate" Muslims by eradicating their culture and by sponsoring large scale migration to Mindanao by Christian settlers, making Muslims a minority in their own land. Increasing conflict and a number of atrocities galvanized Muslim opposition, which appropriated "Moro" as a term of pride. Opposition flared into open warfare with the 1972 martial law declaration by President Marcos. Any long-term peaceful settlement in Muslim Mindanao must address these injustices and provide Philippine Muslims increased control over their own destiny within a Christian-dominated country.

As with any compelling narrative, there is considerable truth embedded in it, but historians can critique the orthodoxy. For instance, the three largest Muslim ethnic groups—Maguindanao, Maranao, and Tausug—were never united in one political unit and often fought against each other. Still, the narrative has the power to inspire political action and provides the basis for the search for solutions.

Moros initially declined to join the resistance to American occupation undertaken by Christians in Luzon and the Visayas. In 1899, the sultan of Sulu signed a treaty with General John Bates; the Tausug version says "the support, aid, and protection of the Jolo Island and Archipelago are in the American nation" while the English version reads, "The Sovereignty of the United States over the whole Archipelago of Jolo and its dependencies is declared and acknowledged." In any case, the United States unilaterally abrogated the Bates Treaty in 1904, and in 1915 the sultan of Sulu signed an agreement with Governor Frank Carpenter stating his "recognition of the sovereignty of United States of America."

Although hostilities in Luzon died down after 1902, the Moro Wars erupted in Mindanao as the Americans extended their authority in the south. From 1903 to 1914, the "Moro Province" was governed by US military officers rather than civilians, and its area covered Jolo, Zamboanga, Cotabato, Lanao, and Davao. The capital was Zamboanga City, leading some Muslims to advocate the inclusion of the city in Muslim Mindanao, despite the fact that the city had been the linchpin of the Spanish presence continuously since 1718.

Notorious incidents in the Moro Wars include the 1906 massacre at Bud Dajo, an extinct volcano near Jolo, occupied by several hundred people who were beyond American authority and had been raiding nearby communities. In the battle itself, twenty-one Americans were killed and almost a thousand women, children, and men were killed among the Tausugs. The casualties caused an uproar in the United States, and over a century later Philippine president Duterte politicized the incident again in 2016 by mentioning it in one of his anti-American outbursts. A similar conflict took place in 1913 at Bud Bagsak, also situated near Jolo, where a combined force of Philippine Scouts—Maguindanaos, Maranaos, Ilocanos, and

Tagalogs, along with US cavalry—overcame several hundred Tausug men.

In 1914, the Moro Province was changed to the Department of Mindanao and Sulu and the colonial bureaucracy was Filipinized, the beginning of a long, complex history of relations between Muslims in the south and the government in Manila. The colonial government appointed Muslims to government positions, including as senators, and some Muslims were elected to the 1934 Constitutional Convention that drafted the basic law for the Commonwealth. On the other hand, in 1935, 150 sultans and *datus* from Lanao asked to be excluded from the grant of independence to Luzon and the Visayas; orthodox narratives often cite this "Dansalan Declaration" as an early separatist initiative.

Upon the establishment of the Commonwealth, most Muslim leaders reached accommodation with this national political settlement and the postwar independent republic. In the meantime, Mindanao was filling up with Christian settlers, and Cebuano became the lingua franca on mainland Mindanao. While the orthodox narrative points to various government land laws that discriminated against Muslims and government schemes that encouraged migration, the vast majority of migrants were spontaneous, including from northern and central Luzon. In fact, they were welcomed by Muslim elected leaders to help develop the economy of the region.

It was often the non-Islamized indigenous people, now called collectively the Lumad, who were displaced from their sparsely settled territories (the areas in figure 2.4 labeled Infieles, or infidels). The solid green areas, labeled "Moro," roughly correspond to the area of the current Bangsamoro Autonomous Region in Muslim Mindanao—except for the coastal areas around mainland Mindanao, where Muslims still reside in villages but are outnumbered by in-migrants at the provincial level.

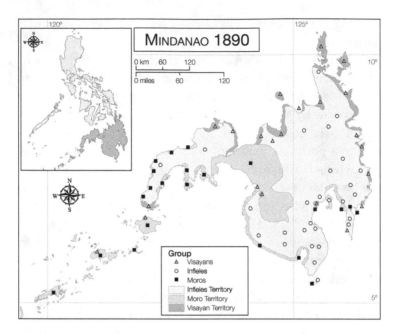

Figure 2.4 Ethnographic distribution in Mindanao, 1890
Source: Sabino G. Padilla Jr.

By the late 1960s, as empty lands had largely been filled up, Muslim and Christian communities began to clash, particularly in central Mindanao. The area had long been awash in weapons, and communal violence broke out, with a Christian militia known as the Ilaga (rat) opposed to the Muslim "Black Shirts." The Philippine state also began to intrude more into local arrangements, dividing the "Empire Province of Cotabato" into smaller units and reducing the scope of Muslim political dominance.

Two incidents are generally cited as triggers for Muslim resistance in recent Filipino history. In March 1968, Tausug recruits to the Armed Forces of the Philippines supposedly destined for an Operation Merdeka (Freedom) to recover Sabah from Malaysia were massacred during training, allegedly after they mutinied. No convictions followed, causing considerable protest over the Jabidah massacre (the name of the Tausug unit). Following this, in May 1968, former Cotabato governor Udtog Matalam announced the formation of the Muslim Independence Movement (MIM); many have attributed this to his reaction to the Jabidah massacre, but the roots were more likely in local politics, as President Marcos had backed a political rival of Matalam for office. Just five months after issuing this call, Matalam met with Marcos, who designated Matalam as his adviser on Muslim affairs, but the MIM continued to resonate with disaffected Muslims and even merited a few paragraphs in the 1972 declaration of martial law.

What is the course of fighting and numerous peace settlements with Muslim separatist fronts?

The increasing unrest in Mindanao, the encroachments on the political power of traditional Muslim officials, and the political ferment in Manila formed the backdrop for the organization of the MNLF by a group that selected Nur Misuari, a Tausug, as chair. Misuari was educated at the University of the Philippines and influenced by Marxist organizing in the mid-1960s during his membership in the Kabataang Makabayan youth organization, but by 1971 he was organizing exclusively among Muslims. A group of ninety men went to Malaysia for military training in 1969; known as the "Top 90," they returned in 1971. Throughout the early 1970s, Muslim countries, including Libya and Pakistan, provided support for the Muslim rebellion.

In October 1972, a group of young students briefly seized parts of Marawi City. Fighting spread in Mindanao in 1973, culminating in the MNLF seizure of Jolo, the capital of Sulu, in February 1974. The Philippine military retook the city with the use of heavy artillery, including naval bombardment, in the Battle of Jolo. While the true casualty figures are unknown, estimates range up to twenty thousand.

Under martial law conditions of media censorship, it was impossible to get accurate accounts of battles, atrocities, or effects on local communities. One of the most notorious atrocities took place in September 1974 at Malisbong, Palimbang, on the coast of Sultan Kudarat province; the military killed hundreds of Muslims, raped women, and burned houses en masse. This is among the human rights violations that, beginning in 2014, the Philippines recognized through its Commission on Human Rights and the Human Rights Victims' Claims Board.

There was international support for the insurgency, but also continuous involvement in the search for a negotiated solution. In 1972, the Islamic Conference of Foreign Ministers expressed concern for the Moro issue, and the Organization of the Islamic Conference (OIC) has since that time been involved in reaching settlements with the MNLF. In 1973, the OIC formed a commission that included Libya, and in July 1974, after diplomacy by the Philippines, the Fifth Islamic Conference of Foreign Ministers in Malaysia called for "a just solution to the plight of Filipino Muslims within the framework of the national sovereignty and territorial integrity of the Philippines." With this bottom line emphasized, the Philippine government accepted international involvement in negotiations, which included a diplomatic turn by Imelda Marcos. In 1976, the Tripoli Agreement called for an autonomous region covering thirteen provinces, including Palawan. When Ferdinand Marcos regained the initiative in the domestic implementation of this agreement, he set up two different "autonomous regions" covering only ten provinces.

This decision set a pattern for the next four decades: the government failed to implement an agreement, the MNLF refused to accept Marcos's faulty implementation, a new movement sprang up, and sporadic fighting occurred, sometimes displacing hundreds of thousands of people. The new movement was the Moro Islamic Liberation Front (MILF), headed by Hashim Salamat, an Islamic scholar from Al Azhar University who had been vice chair of the MNLF. Both the MILF and

MNLF were central in the search for agreements, including the following developments:

- The 1987 Jeddah Accords, in which the post-revolution Aquino government reached an agreement with the MNLF but then went ahead with the autonomy process that was mandated in the new 1987 Constitution (without the participation of the MNLF).
- The 1996 "Final Peace Agreement" reached with the MNLF with Indonesia heading the OIC effort. The MNLF rejected the subsequent 2001 revision of the autonomy law, and Nur Misuari, who had been governor of the Autonomous Region in Muslim Mindanao since 1996, led a brief rebellion and was then jailed. Arguments over the implementation of this agreement went on until January 2016 in "tripartite" meetings of the MNLF, the OIC, and the Philippine government. The Abu Sayyaf group was formed in the late 1980s over discontent that the MNLF was negotiating with the government.
- The 2008 Memorandum of Agreement on Ancestral Domain (MOA-AD) reached with the MILF after more than a decade of peace talks was declared unconstitutional by the Philippine Supreme Court. The resulting upsurge of fighting caused 780,000 displaced persons. When the MILF returned to the negotiations, the Bangsamoro Islamic Freedom Fighters (BIFF) broke away.
- The 2014 Comprehensive Agreement on the Bangsamoro with the MILF was supposed to have been implemented by a law, but Congress did not pass it in the wake of a botched police operation in Mamasapano that resulted in forty-four deaths among the Philippine National Police (as well as MILF, BIFF, and civilian casualties).

Throughout the period under discussion, the Philippine government also practiced a policy of attraction, to varying degrees. For instance, Marcos enticed many of the "Top 90" to join the two autonomous governments, Regions IX and XII, set up after the 1976 Tripoli Agreement. In 1977, Marcos issued a decree establishing the Code of Muslim Personal Laws of the Philippines. In the last decade, two Muslim holidays have been officially declared for national observance, Eid'l Fitr and Eid'l Adha.

Today, the elected officialdom of Muslim areas of Mindanao and local governments is overwhelmingly Muslim. The quality of governance can be quite low, and the region is one of the least developed in the country, with decades of conflict exacerbating poverty. Peace and development remain a hope for the future. However, in early 2019 the implementation of the 2014 Comprehensive Agreement on the Bangsamoro finally moved forward with the ratification of the Bangsamoro Organic Law and the institution in March of the Bangsamoro Autonomous Region in Muslim Mindanao (BARMM).

What lies behind the long-running communist insurgency and failure to reach a peace agreement?

On November 30, 1964, the anniversary of the birth of Andrés Bonifacio, the Kabataang Makabayan (KM; Nationalist Youth) was established. To the dismay of the old-style Partido Komunista ng Pilipinas (PKP), the KM was influenced by Maoism, and in 1966 José María "Joma" Sison of the KM wrote a critique of the history of the PKP. He and his supporters were expelled from the party, and duly founded the Communist Party of the Philippines (CPP)[**] on December 26, 1968, based on "Marxism-Leninism-Mao Zedong Thought." In March 1969, several dozen fighters launched the New People's Army (NPA). In 1970, Sison's most famous book, *Philippine Society and Revolution*, was published; it analyzed "U.S. imperialism,

---

[**] Throughout this volume, PKP is used to refer to the communist party that was founded in 1930 and CPP to the party that was founded in 1968.

feudalism and bureaucrat capitalism now regnant in the present semi-colonial and semi-feudal society" of the country.

In the unrest that led up to Marcos's authoritarian interlude (see "How did the authoritarian interlude (1972–1986) unfold?" in this chapter), the CPP was organizing both in the cities, especially in colleges and universities, and in the countryside. The agrarian conditions that had provided the seedbed for the earlier Huk rebellion had not been decisively addressed, so the notion of a protracted people's war that would surround the cities from rural havens seemed feasible. The declaration of martial law in 1972 dealt a blow to communist organizing because public figures were arrested and many organizers went underground. Still, throughout the 1970s, the insurgency regained its footing and started to spread, especially in mountainous areas and in Mindanao, where the Armed Forces of the Philippines had their hands full with the Moro separatist rebellion.

The rising crises of the mid-1980s allowed the communist insurgents to spread throughout the country, except in areas populated by Muslims. Their estimated armed strength rose to twenty-five thousand, and travel after dark became dangerous in many areas. Some elements of the movement came to believe that a protracted people's war could be short-circuited by urban insurrectionary uprisings, and Davao City was the laboratory for this approach, resulting in the Agdao district of the city being dubbed in the early 1980s "Nicaragdao."

The communists interacted with the open protest movement that mobilized after the assassination of Ninoy Aquino on August 21, 1983, but the noncommunist Left (social democrats and Christian democrats) cooperated most closely with the elite political opposition. When the 1986 snap presidential election was called, and all elements of the legal opposition coalesced behind Corazon Aquino, Ninoy's widow, the CPP called for a boycott of the election, which it regarded as a sham. Thus, when the aftermath of the election eventuated in the February 1986 "People Power" ouster of Marcos, the CPP was completely marginal.

Still, the new government released all political prisoners and entered into preliminary negotiations with the communists, as it did with other forces, including the Cordillera People's Liberation Army and the MNLF. For a while, the CPP could operate openly. Military elements of Cory Aquino's government were leery of legitimizing communist organizing, while leftists were pressing the advantage of the democratic space for organizing. This unstable equilibrium came to an end on January 22, 1987, when a march organized by various "nat dem"[7] groups approaching the Presidential Palace was fired upon; dubbed the "Mendiola massacre," this attack resulted in thirteen deaths and the end of peace talks.

The insurgency reached a low point in the early 1990s due to a combination of international and domestic changes. Internationally, the movement of China under Deng Xiaoping away from Maoism and the collapse of the Soviet Union undermined the ideological credibility of the communists' analysis. Domestically, the economy started to climb back and electoral politics were once again engrossing. Congress passed land reform, although the bill was not as strong as advocates had hoped. In the face of internal debates and purges in the insurgency, Joma Sison issued a paper reaffirming basic Maoist principles in 1992, thus causing a split between the "reaffirmists" and the "rejectionists."

As part of an overall attempt to solve insurgencies, the Ramos government repealed the "anti-subversion law" that had outlawed the communist party. The 1992 repeal made it legal to openly espouse communist principles. The government reached agreements with several of the "rejectionist" factions. And progress was made in talks with the Communist Party of the Philippines-New People's Army-National Democratic Front (CPP-NPA-NDF; which the Philippine military further shortens to CNN). In March 1998, the Comprehensive Agreement on Respect for Human Rights and International Humanitarian Law (CARHRIHL) was signed.

This has been the last major agreement, and the joint monitoring committee on the implementation of the CARHRIHL has never been operationalized. In subsequent administrations— Estrada, Arroyo, and Aquino—there was generally initial optimism about peace talks like those hosted by Norway. But such aspirations broke down during what both sides alleged were violations of their existing agreements, and the government once again vowed to crush the insurgency.

The pattern has been repeated in President Duterte's term. Unlike their stance with regard to the Muslim separatist insurgency, the Armed Forces of the Philippines tend to be fiercely anti-communist and suspicious of all peace talks. In those periods when talks at the national level break down, there is generally discussion of localized peace talks, but the CPP-NPA-NDF regards these as merely efforts to split the movement into smaller segments or to solicit surrender without resolving what it views as the structural problems facing the country.

In the past decade, the general estimate of the armed strength of the NPA has been roughly four thousand. About half of that strength is in Mindanao, in particular among the indigenous peoples. Major driving forces for mobilization include poor governance and neglect, as "nat dem" organizations provide services where the government does not. One academic study showed that when government did attempt to expand its services, the insurgency shifted to adjacent localities, since the effort was not comprehensive. Countryside poverty remains a problem, and agrarian issues have not been resolved after thirty years of agrarian reform.

3

ECONOMY

At the turn of the millennium, a team of economists from the Australian National University and the University of the Philippines published *The Philippine Economy: Development, Policies, and Challenges*, in which they declared, "The Philippines is one of the world's major development puzzles. . . . [I]ts development outcomes have been disappointing by any yardstick."[1] Fifteen years later a similar group published a far more optimistic report, *The Philippine Economy: No Longer the East Asia Exception?* Clearly, considerable change has occurred in recent years, but the question mark in the title indicates some doubts remain about future prospects.

It should be noted that there is vigorous dissent from the general conclusions of professional economists that intrudes into debates on economic policy in the Philippines. At one extreme of this dissent is the well-documented Maoist analysis by the National Democratic Front of the Philippines, which calls for "national industrialization" and liberation from imperialist domination. This point of view resonates in many quarters of the intelligentsia. On the other end of the scale are politicians who are inclined to provide free services such as college education or irrigation, disregarding what economists would call skewed incentives and outcomes. For instance, it is widely reported that President Ramon Magsaysay wanted to "repeal the law of supply and demand"—though he was probably joking when he said this. In the middle of the debate are those suspicious of foreigners in the Philippine economy, globalization, and liberalization. These views are embodied, to an excessive degree in the view of most economists, in the protectionist clauses of the 1987 Constitution.

What has been the experience in economic growth since independence?

A common statement about the Philippines is that, after Japan, it was the second most developed country in Asia in the 1950s but was a laggard by the 1990s. Actually, in 1950 the Philippines was third, behind Japan and Malaysia, but indeed economic prospects looked good. The country withstood the communist Huk rebellion and had stable politics with two-party alternation in power. Economic growth of the import-substitution variety seemed to be working well, and growth rates were above those of its Southeast Asian neighbors. Growth slowed in the 1960s but picked up again in the 1970s. While overall the neighboring countries grew somewhat faster, and more steadily, the Philippines's growth was respectable.

However, a recurrent weakness was lurking that plagued the country for many years: crises in foreign exchange. At independence in 1946, the peso was pegged to the US dollar at two pesos to a dollar. Imports were controlled and foreign exchange was rationed as exports were limited. Aside from its effects on the wider economy, this arrangement yielded a continual flow of scandals because permits and licenses were the subject of favoritism and corruption. In 1959, legislation was introduced to give the executive branch the power to change the exchange rate and import regime. President Diosdado Macapagal fully implemented this change at the beginning of his term in 1962; the peso dropped to roughly four to the dollar and tariffs were raised. The peso stayed at that level until 1970, when it fell to six to a dollar in the wake of government deficits in President Ferdinand Marcos's first term, a wildly expensive re-election campaign in 1969, and the political unrest that was unfolding in the "First Quarter Storm." The "managed float" continued slowly downward until the economic crisis of 1983–1985, when the peso/dollar rate dropped from eight to approximately twenty.

While the 1983–1985 crisis was the most profound, each of these episodes repeated roughly the same narrative. Economic growth stimulated demand for imports (e.g., to supply the import substitution industries), terms of trade (agricultural exports for manufactured imports) were moving against the Philippines, and there were external shocks (oil price increases), all of which made for a shortage of foreign exchange. Balance of payments crises were periodic. Thus, the surge in growth under import substitution reached its limits by the end of the 1950s. The debt-fueled growth of the 1970s was imperiled when the price of oil doubled in 1979 in response to the Iranian Revolution. The last round of this cycle was in 1990, when oil prices doubled again in response to Iraq's invasion of Kuwait.

The 1980s were a lost decade—the financial crisis set the country back ten years at a time when the Indonesian and Malaysian economies were growing at more than 6 percent and Thailand's at more than 8 percent. After the mid-decade crisis and the 1986 "People Power" Revolution, recovery was hampered by debt overhang, political uncertainties caused by coup attempts, and natural disasters such as the Baguio earthquake in 1990 and the eruption of Mt. Pinatubo in central Luzon in 1991.

Since 1992, for more than twenty-six years the boom-and-bust cycle has been tamed thanks to some basic reforms in the 1990s (see the section "What economic reforms have led to recent sustained robust growth?" in this chapter). The only time the country went into recession was in 1998 during the Asian financial crisis, when growth dipped slightly into negative territory because of drought induced by an El Niño event. Agriculture contracted sharply enough to drag the growth rate down. Were it not for that weather-related phenomenon, the country would have avoided a recession, as it did in 2009 during the global financial crisis.

In fact, from the turn of the millennium the growth rate averaged over 5 percent, and since 2010 over 6 percent, with the Philippines finally graduating into the "upper-middle income" category. This robust growth is underpinned by success in business process outsourcing (BPO), as well as a steady supply of foreign exchange from overseas Filipino workers (OFWs). What did not happen, however, is a manufacturing transformation of the economy, as occurred elsewhere in the region, or a consequent rapid reduction in poverty rates. In fact, the structural shift was from agriculture to services, rather than to industry.

Services in the Philippines can be seen as composed of two basic types: low skilled, often informal, and highly skilled. Sometimes termed "last resort" jobs, low-skilled jobs include transportation workers such as tricycle or jeepney drivers and petty retail workers such as street peddlers and *sari-sari* (neighborhood sundry) store owners and employees. Even service jobs in the more formal sector, such as department store clerk, can be pretty dismal, with low wages, unsatisfactory work conditions, and short employment contracts allowing the employer to avoid providing the benefits and restrictions that the law requires for permanent employees. On the other hand, highly skilled service jobs such as in the BPO industry have been growing rapidly, with over a million jobs by 2018 and 7 to 10 percent growth. These jobs are high wage by Philippine standards, though still low paid by global standards, and have in recent years spread throughout the country. For families and the economy, one advantage of the outsourcing industry is that services are exported, not people as in the OFW phenomenon.

Industrialization grew in importance from the 1950s, seeming to mirror global trends, until about 1980. The country failed to shift from import substitution when it proved unsustainable due to foreign exchange problems. Critics of mainstream economics say that the decline in industry, which went back to 1950s levels, was due to the reduction in protections for domestic manufacturing, such as quantitative restrictions and high tariffs. The next sections deal with the reforms of the 1990s and the protectionist debate.

What economic reforms have led to recent sustained robust growth?

While recent high rates of growth in the economy are widely recognized, another feature is just how sustained these gains have been. Growth has not paused since 1992, except in 1998 when a drought exacerbated the Asian financial crisis. The global financial crisis slowed growth but did not tip the country into a recession. Inflation has always been in the single digits, peaking only in 1998 and 2008 as the peso exchange rate adjusted to the two international financial crises, making imports, including oil, more expensive.

The most important reform that led to all this was the restructuring of the financial sector. In 1992, most restrictions were lifted on foreign exchange transactions and flows of capital in and out of the country. This was followed in 1993 by the restructuring of the Central Bank of the Philippines, previously weakened by the debt crisis of the 1980s, to form the Bangko Sentral ng Pilipinas (BSP). The independence of the BSP was reinforced, and the BSP focuses on controlling inflation, not trying to manage the exchange rate. This focus has been credited with avoiding balance of payments crises by allowing the peso to depreciate or appreciate. Regulation of the banking system has been sound, with BSP governors repeatedly named "Central Banker of the Year" by *The Banker*, so the cycle of systemic banking crises has been broken.

One widely recognized reform that even critics of mainstream economics can applaud is the breaking up of the telephone monopoly held by the Philippine Long Distance Telephone (PLDT) company. In 1992, former prime minister of Singapore Lee Kuan Yew jibed, "Ninety-eight percent of Filipinos are waiting for a telephone, while the other two percent are waiting for a dial tone."* The solution was a combination of executive-branch initiatives introducing competition in both the cellular and landline markets and exerting pressure on the company to accept these changes without legal challenges. This pressure was possible because at the time the government had elected a majority of PLDT's board members due its ability to vote sequestered shares from the 1986 "People Power" Revolution. Improvement was immediate; the number of landlines doubled in a couple of years. The mobile revolution took over thereafter; currently there are more active mobile phone numbers than people in the country.

More controversial was the oil price deregulation effort that occupied the latter part of the Fidel V. Ramos administration. An oil price stabilization fund had been in place since the 1984 economic crisis and was typically seriously in deficit. Thus governments faced the unpalatable political choice of either using budgetary resources to subsidize the price of oil or ordering a price increase. In pursuit of macroeconomic stability, for instance, the government tried to raise oil prices in 1994 but backed down amid public uproar. Under legislation passed in 1998, deregulation took place at a time when global oil prices were fairly stable. Government finances are no longer strained by subsidizing oil prices, and the process of changing prices is somewhat depoliticized because it is private players who make the adjustments. Governments are still sensitive to oil price surges and sometimes make adjustments such as temporary reductions in import duties or excise taxes, offering fuel discounts to public utility vehicles such as jeepneys, and jawboning the companies into spreading out price increases over a longer period of time.

---

* The author can confirm that by 1992 he had been waiting ten years for telephone service.

Sensible financial reforms and prudent regulations have laid the basis for continued growth and avoided the systemic crises that used to interrupt Philippine growth. Government, however, struggles to raise revenues for programs and projects, including both physical and human capital, that would underpin continued and accelerated growth. Government revenue peaked at 19 percent of gross domestic product (GDP) in 1997, but after tax "reform" that weakened revenue collection it plummeted. In 2005, faced with a spiraling fiscal crisis, an expanded value-added tax (E-VAT) briefly halted the decline and cost the senator who had sponsored the bill, Ralph Recto, his re-election bid. Revenue bottomed out at 13.5 percent of GDP, then began to grow again, particularly due to hard-won increases in "sin taxes" on tobacco and alcohol during the Noynoy Aquino administration (2010–2016). The Rodrigo Duterte administration proposed beginning in 2016 a very comprehensive multiphase set of tax measures, but has struggled to get them through the Philippine Congress. Fiscal space to undertake Duterte's flagship "Build, Build, Build" infrastructure program will depend on success at this endeavor.

Some barriers or limits to growth remain, such as poor transportation infrastructure and weak enforcement of contracts. But one last positive factor can be mentioned here: remittances from OFWs. As deployment increased from the beginnings of this program in the 1970s, the importance of remittances to the economy also grew, from less than 5 percent of GDP in 1990 to over 10 percent now. This steady and in general slowly rising source of foreign exchange helps to keep the balance of payments positive, again reducing the likelihood of an economic crisis.

With over a million employees, the BPO sector currently rivals the deployment of OFWs as a source of foreign exchange. Building on English-language skills, the improved telecommunications situation, and familiarity with Western culture, the Philippines now has the largest number of call centers in the world. In 2000 it was decided that incentives for export processing zones could extend to single buildings for the purpose of hosting call centers, leading to a proliferation of them—first in Metro Manila and then throughout the country.

Beginning during the administration of Noynoy Aquino (2010–2016) and continuing into the Duterte administration, there were signs that the long stagnation of manufacturing was beginning to end. Manufacturing began edging up as a percentage of GDP, and the Department of Trade and Industry launched "industry roadmaps" laying out steps to encourage industry. Growth in manufacturing and construction has also increased the proportion of wage and salary workers, rather than informal sector workers, to almost two-thirds of the workforce. Economy watchers find encouragement in these straws in the wind, but structural transformation of the economy will take time.

What is the role of protectionism in the Philippine economy?

One of the most controversial topics in Philippine public policy discourse is the role of the protectionist provisions of the 1987 Constitution (some of which were first written into the 1935 Constitution) in hindering economic development. The Philippine economy did not shift out of agriculture into manufacturing, but rather into services, and over sixty years of uncertain growth, industry did not change its share of production or employment. Many still argue that this is due to the "liberalization" of the economy and a failure to protect infant industries, but they are mistaken. Real opening of the economy only happened in the 1990s; what are often taken as previous openings did not in fact create openness. For instance, when quantitative restrictions on imports were lifted in 1962 under the Macapagal administration, high tariffs were imposed instead.

Thus, lack of industrialization long predates the reductions in protection that were initiated in the 1990s. The liberalization thrust included, after a vigorous Senate debate and Supreme

Court decision, the Philippines being a founding member of the World Trade Organization when it was instituted in 1995. Critics see the WTO as an instrument of imperialism by the advanced countries and continue to criticize the commitment to openness that it embodies. Criticism of the Association of Southeast Asian Nations (ASEAN) Free Trade Agreement that came into effect in 2015 is considerably less heated. In general, the importance of foreign trade in the Philippine economy is greater than for Indonesia but less than for Thailand.

Despite the openings of the 1990s, the Philippines ranks as one of the most restrictive regulatory regimes in the world for foreign direct investment. Most economists in the Philippines lament the fact that this drives down the inflow of long-term capital. Comparisons are often made with other ASEAN countries. The most vociferous opposition to this line of argument comes from the advocates of "national industrialization" (the national democratic left) since they view foreign capital as exploitative. In the middle are those, like former president Noynoy Aquino, who point out that the Philippines currently enjoys a high rate of growth, and countries such as India and China have high growth rates despite their economies being almost as restrictive as that of the Philippines.

In pursuit of the 1987 constitutional mandate that "the State shall develop a self-reliant and independent national economy effectively controlled by Filipinos," large swaths of the economy are reserved for citizens or corporations with at most 40 percent foreign equity. Some sectors are even more restrictive; mass media, private security agencies, and cockfighting arenas are exclusively for Filipinos, while advertising only allows 30 percent foreign equity. The executive branch periodically issues a foreign investment negative list that is closely watched for signs of liberalization. The October 2018 issuance provided new exemptions for Internet businesses, now classified as distinct from media; foreigners teaching in higher education, except in professional disciplines subject to government exams such as medical, nursing, and legal; and some construction projects, in line with the Duterte administration's infrastructure emphasis. Furthermore, it relaxed the restriction on public utilities from no foreign equity to 40 percent foreign equity.

The intersection of protectionism and ethnic sentiment toward the Chinese is illustrated by the saga of retail trade liberalization. In 1954, after twenty years of advocacy, the Retail Trade Nationalization Act passed, restricting business ownership to Philippine citizens. This was clearly aimed at Chinese, who possessed over 98 percent of all outlets owned by noncitizens. The law was implemented over a period of ten years. But in 1975 Ferdinand Marcos allowed the mass naturalization of Chinese as part of his opening to China, thus vitiating the ethnic aspect of the policy. By 1995, as a part of the general trend toward economic liberalization during the administration of President Ramos, there were moves to once again allow noncitizens and their corporations to operate in the retail trade, leading to the passage of the Retail Trade Liberalization Act in 2000. The most obvious effect of this policy in urban areas is the profusion of foreign-brand stores now found in Filipino malls.

In 2010 another decision relaxed citizenship requirements: aliens were allowed to own gambling establishments. At first this change was associated with the construction of new casino complexes by foreign companies. But with the Duterte administration's opening to China, there has been a flood of Chinese workers because most of the market for offshore gambling is from the mainland. Numbers are murky and record keeping chaotic, but estimates of the number of Chinese casino workers run into the hundreds of thousands. The influx of immigrants comes with knock-on effects on a frothy property market and once again raises nativist fears.

One of the most emotive restrictions is on ownership of land. The average citizen is against allowing foreigners to own property, and most discussions of liberalizing foreign investments avoid disturbing this part of the status quo. In

1999 the Preparatory Commission on Constitutional Reforms under President Joseph Estrada, which focused on possible amendments, went the furthest towards liberalizing land ownership when it proposed that land classified by law as commercial or industrial be opened up to foreign investment; the commission's estimate was that this only covered 1 percent of all land. This attempt at constitutional reform did not make any progress; most foreign involvement in the property sector is in residential condominium projects, where up to 40 percent of the units can be owned by foreigners.

What is the role of agriculture?

During the first part of the twentieth century the Philippines depended to a large extent on the export of agricultural products: sugar, coconut, and abaca (Manila hemp). Over the years there has been a shift, and now the Philippines is only twenty-seventh in the world for sugar exports. Coconut oil is still the highest-value agricultural export, followed by newer commodities: fresh bananas, fresh and canned pineapples, and tuna. Overall, services and electronics have greatly outpaced agriculture.

For 150 years the Philippines has imported its staple food, rice. The country has been the top importer of rice several times in recent years, despite growing a per hectare yield that compares to Thailand's (a major exporter). The price of Philippine rice has traditionally been higher than in its Southeast Asian neighbors, due primarily to the dysfunctional protectionist policy pursued by governments over the decades. This is particularly unfortunate for Philippine consumers, who get almost half of their calories from rice. "Rice self-sufficiency," briefly attained under Ferdinand Marcos after the introduction of "miracle rice," is a rhetorical goal for politicians, one they try to promote with quantitative restrictions on imports and inflated wholesale prices. Given that even rice farmers depend on buying the commodity to feed their families, this policy has hurt the poor the most, as they spend up to 25 percent of their total family budget on rice. It was only at the beginning of 2019 that the Philippines finally legislated the "tariffication" of rice—free importation of rice subject to a 35 percent tariff—which is likely to lead to a 15 to 20 percent reduction in prices.

Changing the rules of the game with respect to such a politically sensitive commodity meant the legislation needed to provide compensation for rice farmers. Thus, the Rice Competitiveness Enhancement Fund is allocated for the Department of Agriculture to enhance rice farmer productivity. But most agricultural economists think that too much of the public agriculture budget is spent on rice and corn—instead of on promotion of higher-value crops (e.g., fruits, vegetables, tree crops) or agro-industrialization utilizing agricultural products as inputs.

The stark fact is that the agriculture sector is one of the weak links in the Philippine economy. Three-fourths of the poor reside in rural areas. Some 25 percent of the Philippine workforce is in agriculture, but only 10 percent of the economy is produced there—meaning productivity is low. A number of reasons can be adduced for this result. As a mountainous archipelago, the Philippines's arable land per capita is much lower than in countries with large plains such as Thailand. Irrigation could be expanded but is frequently starved of operating funds, as the government often offers irrigation water for free but does not subsidize maintenance sufficiently to replace irrigation fees. The Philippines stands out in ASEAN as the only country whose trade balance in food has worsened over the past decades, in part due to poor agricultural policies.

Another factor is the drawn-out process of agrarian reform, decades long and producing considerable uncertainty in land tenure. Agrarian reform policy has been one of the most hotly debated issues in the country for decades. To say it is a matter of large landowners versus landless peasants would be an oversimplification. The 1988 Comprehensive Land Reform Program (CARP) hit many middle-class people throughout the countryside: schoolteachers, doctors, and government employees. Those who had managed to accumulate more than the 5-hectare retention limit had to dispose of the land (they were compensated by the government). Theoretically, CARP beneficiaries can be awarded as much as 3 hectares of land, but the average has been 1.7 hectares each (two-thirds of all Philippine farms are less than 2 hectares in size).

Mainstream economists point out that several features of the agrarian reform regime prevent growth in the agricultural sector. First is how long the process is taking; roughly 10 percent of land still needs to be distributed after thirty years. Second, uncertainty about land tenure has discouraged investment in the sector. Third, CARP lands cannot be leased or sold, deterring agribusiness because a processing plant cannot control its supply. Contract growing is possible, but investors complain about "pole vaulting," when farmers divert contracted output to other buyers offering higher spot prices.

The alternative narrative discounts these barriers to market-led growth and focuses on landlord resistance, the shortfalls of land redistribution, and inadequate support services such as irrigation, subsidized inputs, and agricultural extension. Landlord resistance is exemplified by Hacienda Luisita, a sugar plantation owned by the family of President Cory Aquino, where beneficiaries only received their land in 2018 after years of struggle. A number of studies have quantified a modest improvement in the welfare of beneficiaries of agrarian reform: a decrease in poverty rates in the range of 2 percent.

The coconut sector is a striking example of how poverty is linked to government policy. Coconut growers have high poverty rates of over 50 percent, despite the product's prominence in exports. Over 20 percent of all coconut trees are unproductive because they are at least sixty years old, but farmers are prohibited by law from cutting senile coconut trees unless they replant them. Given their level of poverty, replacement planting is difficult for them to finance themselves, and the government supply of seedlings has been inadequate. Intercropping of coffee and cacao is often touted as a way to boost incomes, but support services from the Philippine Coconut Authority or local governments are lacking. The coconut sector was monopolized during the 1972–1986 authoritarian interlude, and the funds generated, known as the Coconut Levy, have been tied up in legal action for thirty years. Increased funds invested in this sector would have great potential to begin to bring down the high poverty rate.

How important are political considerations in the economy?

One of the general criticisms of the Philippine economy is that weaknesses in contract enforcement and the politicization of business transactions generate much uncertainty. Investing, particularly for the long term, is difficult in this environment. The domestic private sector has learned how to survive in this environment, which gives it an advantage over foreign investors. A clear trace of this is seen in the investment cycle, in which total investment tends to decrease before a presidential election in the face of uncertainty about who will head the next administration, and then accelerate again once it is known who will be in charge for the next six years.

For instance, when President Noynoy Aquino began his administration in 2010, he canceled a number of contracts to undo what were perceived to be the corrupt practices of his predecessor, Gloria Macapagal-Arroyo (GMA). One was with a Belgian company to dredge Laguna Lake, which suffers from siltation that makes flooding in Manila more frequent. The deal was to be one-third funded by a grant from the Belgian government. The Belgian company successfully sued the Philippines in an international tribunal and got an award of $15.3 million. Similarly, Noynoy Aquino canceled 90 percent of the roll-on, roll-off (Ro-Ro) modular ports that were to be added to the network of the Greater Maritime Access port projects. Ro-Ro was a signature policy success of the administration of GMA.

There are also disputes among private entities vying for government favor. Notably, such disagreements held up a major public transportation project for a decade. Progress on the common station that will connect the northern ends of two light rail lines in Manila, currently 1.5 kilometers apart, was stalled by rival mall owners. In 1999, after negotiations, the owners of one large mall, SM North, paid the government $3.8 million to locate the station near their mall. After the change of administration, in 2004 the government decided to locate it near a neighboring mall, TriNoma. Lawsuits followed, and it fell to the succeeding administration of President Duterte to broker a deal that allowed construction to finally begin in 2017. The station will be above the main road across which the two malls face each other.

The SM malls are owned by Henry Sy, an immigrant from China who won big on his retail expansion in the late 1980s and was the richest man in the Philippines[†] before his death in early 2019. TriNoma Mall is owned by the Ayalas, whose head is ranked fourth richest man in the country. A Spanish-Filipino family prominent since the mid-1800s, the Zobel de Ayalas are most famous for owning most of the land in the financial district of Makati City. These two families, the Ayalas and the Sys, are among those who do not get involved directly in politics; others do.

The venerable Nacionalista Party is headed by Manuel Villar, a real estate tycoon who is the second richest man in the country. The National Unity Party is associated with Enrique Razon (the fifth richest man in the country), while the Nationalist People's Coalition has 1992 presidential candidate Eduardo Cojuangco Jr. (the fourteenth richest man) and Ramon Ang of San Miguel Corporation (the eighth richest man). Among them, these three business-linked political blocs

---

† Wealth rankings vary, of course, from year to year. These in the text are from Forbes 2018 listing: https://www.forbes.com/philippines-billionaires/list/.

held 85 seats in the 297-member House of Representatives in 2018. The House facilitates the granting of congressional franchises for public utilities such as telecommunications, ports, and tollways.

It is difficult to generalize about the connection between local politics and the local economy, given the great diversity of the country. Some localities, particularly highly urbanized ones with complex economies, are basically arenas in which many clashing interests—business, labor, advocacy groups, and homeowners' associations—compete for the favor of local governments. In other parts of the Philippines, one interest might dominate, such as a transportation firm owned by the local governor or a chain of filling stations that refuse to sell to the opposition during election time.

An interesting example is the Isabela Province, where, despite being illegal, logging is still as important as it used to be in many other places in the country. One family has dominated politics for fifty years—with one exception from 2004 to 2010, when a reform-minded woman, journalist Grace Padaca, was governor. She had the enthusiastic support of national civil society organizations, which advocated for good governance and protection of the environment, and under her leadership the provincial government cracked down on illegal logging. When Governor Padaca failed to be re-elected in 2010 (despite the national victory of her Liberal Party mate, Noynoy Aquino), it was the municipalities in which illegal logging was suppressed that gave her opponent, Faustino "Bojie" Dy III—grandson of the original clan patriarch—his margin of victory.

The fact that the Philippines has eighty-one provinces makes statistical analysis possible for some particular problems. Provinces in which clans are stronger ("fatter," in the jargon) because they have multiple members in various positions, such as governor, mayors, and members of Congress, tend to be poorer. The direction of causation is uncertain and probably mutually reinforcing. Poorer, less-developed economies tend to produce fewer viable candidates, and a dominant clan can discourage political and economic competition.

The same dynamic holds for the country as a whole. Seven companies that belong to family-controlled groups make up more than half the market capitalization of the Philippine Stock Market index. The reason the groups are family controlled is that networks of trust predominate within the family conglomerates, as they do within Philippine society as a whole. Protectionist legal restrictions often require foreigners to partner with local businesses, but even if the law did not require it, most foreign investors would be well-advised to do so. In aligning themselves with Philippine family networks, investors can avoid the problem of weak contract enforcement, doing business the Filipino way. And though the Philippines ranked 151 of 190 economies in the World Bank's 2019 rankings of contract enforcement as a factor in their "Ease of Doing Business" report, there are opportunities for growth.

4

SOCIETY, CULTURE, AND RELIGION

In late 1987, American journalist James Fallows caused a stir with his article "A Damaged Culture" in *The Atlantic*, in which he took a pessimistic view of the Philippines. He argued against euphoria in the wake of the peaceful ouster of Ferdinand Marcos, which was followed by the restoration of electoral democracy. He felt that looking at the Philippines as a success story was unrealistic, and that Filipino culture was "the main barrier to development" in the country. In short, he attributed the dismal prospects of the Philippines to a damaged culture, a "feeble sense of nationalism and a contempt for the public good."

Trying to understand the culture of a country as diverse as the Philippines can be a daunting task, particularly when the bewildering variety of Asian, Western, Latin, and Middle Eastern influences is taken into account. "Authentic Filipino" in contemporary discourse often refers to indigenous peoples, those who by the twentieth century had not been Islamized or Hispanized, and this leads to questions about what the mainstream culture is, if not "authentic." The colorful kaleidoscope of Philippine religions, media, cuisine, social arrangements, and more is endlessly fascinating, and amply repays attention to nuance.

What are Filipino values?

Fallows's article resonated with readers in the Philippines, though many were offended that an outsider, an American, was the one to make the observation. The Philippines is nonetheless interested in assessing its national values. In a September 1992 executive order, President Fidel Ramos institutionalized a "Moral Recovery Program," following an academic study of the strengths and weaknesses of the Filipino character. To this day, Filipinos still cite the Fallows article and academic work on character, and various entities from provincial governments to civil society organizations continue to launch projects called "Moral Recovery Programs."

In writing about the Philippines, Fallows admitted that "outside this culture [Filipino immigrants] thrive," something that has become obvious over decades in the diaspora of overseas Filipino workers (OFWs). It seems unlikely that persons who have been socialized in a "damaged culture" would suddenly act differently when they migrate as adults.

Instead of "culture," differences in how people act can be explained by rules, incentives, and punishments. Filipinos "thrive" outside the Philippines because institutions allow them to advance according to merit instead of personal connections. Inside the Philippines, behavior changes when institutions do. For example, Subic Bay Metropolitan Authority was famous for enforcing traffic rules in the 1990s, so Filipinos drove more carefully there than in other, less-regulated areas. Today, Davao City enforces its traffic rules, so driving is more orderly there.

Most Filipinos encounter discussion of values as they are taught in schools. Elementary and high school texts discuss roughly the same number of positive and negative "values." These texts characterize close family ties and respect for elders as "extreme family-centeredness." The ability to get along with others, *pakikisama* (getting along with others) is connected with the dysfunctional behavior of groups such as fraternities. They also see "colonial mentality," debated for over a century, in the preference for imported goods or the valuing of experience, education, and achievement abroad. But educational texts also link it to justified pride in the hard work and achievements of Filipinos abroad—such as performance in West End or Broadway theatrical productions, as chefs, or as academics.

Another attempt to provide insights into Filipino character, amid a mass of contradictory assertions, is Sikolohiyang Pilipino (Filipino psychology; the term is universally cited in its Filipino form). Virgilio Enriquez pioneered this academic stream in the late 1970s. He used concepts in Tagalog-based Filipino to inject a Filipino perspective into psychological discourse, which at the time was largely conducted in English and utilized Western models. For instance, from a traditional Western perspective, the Filipino phrase *bahala na* (it's up to god) is often seen as "fatalism" and a barrier to taking initiative. Instead, Sikolohiyang Pilipino suggests that this phrase can be a spur to action, as in the statement, "I'm not certain I can do this, but *bahala na!*" conveying a sense of "I'll try it anyway." Likewise, *pakikisama* (which American sociologists defined as "smooth interpersonal relations") connects to Sikolohiyang Pilipino's core concept of *kapwa* (shared identity). The compound *pakikipagkapwa* thus means treating others as *kapwa* (qua fellow human beings); this notion has been deployed in gender discourse to describe respect for women's personhood.

Discussions of Filipino values tend to accentuate the negative: what Filipinos are lacking or what's wrong with a particular pattern of behavior. Taking another look at how Filipino values are interpreted, however, can provide an alternative narrative and lead to a deeper understanding. For instance, "lack of discipline" is often mentioned as a negative value, illustrated by terrible traffic and problems with littering. These behaviors are seen to reflect a Filipino attitude toward public space, the tendency to feel the right to occupy any space that is not private. For example, drivers may feel that if a maneuver is physically possible, it can be tried. Buses and jeepneys are notorious for this, and private vehicles will fill up the oncoming lane to try to get around a traffic jam, thus exacerbating the problem.

The process of "informal settlement" is another example of attitudes to space: first sleeping outside, then setting up a lean-to, and gradually constructing a more robust shack. Settlement replicates indigenous peoples' views of property: that the mountains and forest belong to everybody in the community. Upkeep determines ownership; agricultural land such as orchards or swidden fields belongs to the clan, and house lots and rice paddies or vegetable farms are the private property of the family that invests labor and effort in them. So informal settlements tend to accumulate along public easements where waterways flood during storms or in vacant lots, whether publicly or privately owned, unless there is clear evidence of somebody owning them (e.g., a person keeping watch on shack housing). The obverse of this "privatizing" of public areas is a lack of regard for truly public space (e.g., as long as one's yard is clean, garbage elsewhere is not a problem). Littering is an oft-cited example, with media covering how much trash is left after large events.

However, the "tragedy of the commons" is a universal human phenomenon; resources without any institution regulating them tend to be overexploited. Filipinos recognize this and often yearn for a strong leader to impose more order. Davao City under Mayor Rodrigo Duterte brought littering, traffic, and uncontrolled fireworks under control; airline passengers are warned upon touchdown in Davao about the strictness of enforcement. This tough reputation was a key part of Duterte's successful run for the presidency. Of course, reliance on a particular individual rather than an institution is in line with the personalism that permeates the Philippines. But "softer" methods also work. For instance, the Iglesia ni Cristo (Church of Christ) encourages its members to tithe, to vote as a block, and to respect their space, and after its mass events litter is minimal. Similarly, the massive anti-pork barrel demonstrations of 2013 left very little litter behind; because participants were advocating for civic virtue, they were socially conscious of their space.

What is the basic social structure?

In continuity with precolonial society and culture, the family is the basic unit of society. "Family" is used here in a broader sense than the nuclear family of one set of parents and their children; extended kinship is important. The Philippines, like most societies throughout archipelagic Southeast Asia, has a bilateral kinship structure, meaning that one is equally related to the mother's and father's sides of the family. Furthermore, in Philippine languages the terms for children and siblings are not gender-specific; to say "son" or "daughter" one must say "male child" or "female child." The lack of gendered terms does not apply when speaking of elders; not only are there separate terms for "father" and "mother," "grandfather," and "grandmother," there are specific terms for "older brother" and "older sister," which were adopted from Hokkien in pre-Spanish times. All these terms can be utilized generically for older people or as a respectful form of address (e.g., to drivers on public transportation or in interactions in stores or markets).

In general, kinship is the way social organization and relations are expressed. In pre-Spanish times, intermarriage was a way that families, villages, and rulers could relate to each other. When Miguel López de Legazpi established a permanent presence in Cebu in 1565, the last pre-Hispanic ruler in Cebu, Rajah Tupas, offered him a niece. The explorer turned her over to the friars for instruction, baptism—the first by this expedition, and in which Legazpi was the godfather—and marriage to one of his men. Legazpi's refusal of an alliance by marriage angered Rajah Tupas, but it was natural to the colonizers given the Spanish Catholic focus on monogamy and prohibition on divorce. In fact, another institution accomplishes roughly the same end: *compadrazgo*, the Spanish practice of becoming "co-parents" at special ritual occasions, baptism and marriage in particular. Thus, Legazpi stood as "sponsor" or "godparent" when Rajah Tupas was eventually baptized.

In the Philippines, parents reach out to social equals and superiors to be godparents at their child's baptism to extend kinship-like ties to greater networks. Tradition holds that godparents are supposed to have special relationships with their *inaanak* ("who has become one's child"), often reinforced during the extended Christmas holidays, when children hope to get some money from their godparents. More realistically, the exchanges within these "fictive kinship" networks are social and symbolic: favors granted, birthdays remembered, political support (politicians tend to have a large number of such contacts), and expressions of affection and concern.

Both blood and fictive kinship ties tend to generate very amorphous groups of people with relationships that are in theory equally important. Thus there tends to be an implicit or explicit negotiation process about levels of interaction and allegiance. In the Philippines, if everything is personal, the personal is open for renegotiation; groups expand and contract, split and re-form.

Educational experience also tends to generate groups to which Filipinos feel close—often high school classmates, the "Band of Brothers" who graduate from the Philippine Military Academy in a particular year, and fraternities and sororities. The latter are active in secondary schools as well as colleges, despite school authorities' best efforts to regulate these organizations. The fraternities' and to a lesser extent sororities' harsh "hazing rituals" are meant to form intense connections but can result in injuries and even death. Since 1991, there have been more than twenty deaths due to fraternity "rumbles" that disrupted campuses and caused casualties.

In contrast with these social groups, formal organizations tend to be fragile. A cynical take is that the result of an election in an organization is often two organizations, as the losing party withdraws to form its own. One of the Philippines's most robust non-governmental organizations is Philippine Business for Social Progress. But with fewer than six hundred regular and project-based staff members in 2016, their numbers pale in comparison to those of Bangladesh's BRAC, which employees tens of thousands.

In short, social interaction uses kinship as a template, which provides assurance of compassion and assistance.

What are the situations of and special challenges for indigenous peoples?

The discourse about "indigenous peoples" is sometimes controversial among mainstream Filipinos, who regard themselves as "indigenous" in the sense that their ancestors were in the Philippines before colonizers came. After all, the Philippines is not a "settler" country; during colonial times, relatively few Spanish or Americans settled permanently in the archipelago. The 1987 Indigenous Peoples' Rights Act (IPRA) refers to those "who have, through resistance to political, social and cultural inroads of colonization, non-indigenous religions and cultures, became historically differentiated from the majority of Filipinos." This means that the legally indigenous population is made up of those who were not Hispanized or Islamized. This definition can be problematic, since most of the indigenous peoples were by the end of the twentieth century Christian, either Catholic or Protestant. Also, the IPRA connects ancestral domain as a legal term to the legal definition of indigenous people while the Moros occasionally use the term "ancestral domain" to describe the territorial limits of the influence of their sultanates over the centuries.

Making up some 10 percent of the population, though that estimate is controversial, the main indigenous groups are the inhabitants of the northern Luzon Cordillera mountain range and the Lumad in Mindanao, both of which are comprised of many ethnolinguistic groups. They face special challenges from economic development—pressures from both migration into the areas near them and particular large-scale developments such as logging or mining.

In addition, the long-running communist and Muslim separatist struggles impinge on their autonomy. In Mindanao, a high proportion of New People's Army (NPA) recruits are Lumad, unsurprising given the government's neglect of their remote locales. National Philippine security forces also recruit their paramilitary allies from among the Lumads, so the indigenous communities are very often riven by conflict among their members. Muslim separatists, on the other hand, tend not to recruit Lumad, believing that their struggle for control of their traditional territory overshadows Lumad claims. Still, the Bangsamoro Organic Law, as ratified in January 2019, does include provisions aimed at protecting Lumad rights.

The National Commission on Indigenous People is in place to implement the provisions of the IPRA. In particular, titles to ancestral domain are to be issued to groups in an indigenous community, and certificates of ancestral land titles are to be issued to individuals. The distinction is observed by the community; ancestral domain is the general boundary for the community, whereas ancestral lands are those that traditionally belong to a particular family or individual (e.g., irrigated rice paddies). The commission is supposed to assist in the formation of ancestral domain management plans and supervise the process of obtaining "free and prior informed consent" for projects and enterprises that wish to operate inside an ancestral domain.

Administrative processing of these issuances can be long and arduous, particularly given difficulties in geographic mapping and obtaining consensus among an often divided community. Enterprises engaged in extractive enterprises such as logging or mining, politicians looking for political support, and the contending armed parties in an insurgency all have enormous incentives to influence the outcomes of community discussions. Given that these all take place in remote areas, it is often difficult to judge the quality of any particular awarding of claims or permission, much less the hundreds scattered throughout the archipelago.

The indigenous peoples of northern Luzon tend to be in the best condition among those in the country. They received special attention from the Americans, retained control of their demography and most of their natural resources in the Cordillera, and had their first college graduates before World War II. Lumads in Mindanao, on the other hand, were treated as vassals by Muslim overlords into the twentieth century, were displaced by in-migrants from the rest of the Philippines, and have only been graduating from college in significant numbers in the current millennium.

Among the most marginalized of indigenous peoples are the Negritos, including Aetas and Agtas, who previously lived on the margins of mainstream Austronesian populations. They adopted Austronesian languages, but their shifting cultivation/hunter-gatherer economy was preserved until recently, when population pressure and government policies restricted their range. Similarly situated are the Badjao, the sea nomads, of the Sulu Archipelago. They prefer to live on the water and are very mobile. Their general reaction to oppression, whether by Tausugs or Christians, is to move away. Their education levels are very low, though schools on boats are being tried to remedy this. In recent years, many have migrated in increasing numbers to Metro Manila to eke out a living, mostly begging on the street. The IPRA is of little use to the Negritos, though some ancestral domain claim attempts have been made, and of no use at all to the Badjao, since they have no traditional land-based community.

A particularly controversial group is the Tasaday from southern Mindanao. In 1971, they became world-famous as a "lost tribe" from the Stone Age, living in isolation in the rainforest. Television specials and *National Geographic* covered them. The head of PANAMIN (Presidential Assistant on

National Minorities) was a crony of Ferdinand Marcos and persuaded Marcos to declare a reservation for the Tasaday to isolate them from outside pressures. Thus, they dropped out of public view until 1986, after Marcos fled to Hawai'i, when journalists and some academics branded the Tasaday as fakes because they were seen in T-shirts and jeans instead of the leaf garments they had worn in 1971. Subsequent investigations by other anthropologists and linguists have concluded that the Tasaday were genuine, having fled into the forest to escape violence or a plague so long ago that their language became distinct from that of their Manobo ancestors. Some of the original objectors still believe the Tasaday were a Marcos-era hoax, and many in the Philippines only remember the post-Marcos furor.

What are some ethnic variations among "Hispanized" Filipinos?

To the outside eye, the inhabitants of the Philippines are basically all ethnically "Malay"; aside from the Negritos, who are of different ancestry, there is little variation in appearance. Generally, "ethnolinguistic group" is the term used to refer to specific peoples within the Philippines, since it is language that marks differentiation.

One of the drivers of resentment against "Imperial Manila" is the privileging of the national capital region and the Tagalog ethnolinguistic group in Manila. Tagalog language privilege dates back to at least the early twentieth century, when the 1935 Commonwealth Constitution mandated "a common national language" be based on one of the existing native languages. After a study by the Institute of National Language, the government decided that the basis of the national language would be Tagalog. For some time, the putative national language was known as "Pilipino," but "Filipino" became the preferred term to reduce the perceived dominance of Tagalog, which has no "F" while other languages do have it. Under the 1987 Constitution, the Komisyon sa Wikang Filipino (KWF; Commission on the Filipino Language) was established, and societal trends such as the centralization of broadcast media and cinema production in Manila led to the widespread understanding of this language. In turn, in-migration to the metropolis has diluted the influence of "deep Tagalog" from the native Tagalog-speaking central Luzon provinces such as Bulacan or Batangas; the simplified Manila version is easier for those with different mother tongues to understand.

The use of the Filipino language may make it appear as though the Philippines is homogenizing, but that would be a false representation of its multiplicity of cultures. One difference among ethnolinguistic groups is evident in discussion of the alleged decline of respect and civility, when discussants ask, "Why don't people use 'po' anymore." Po and its variants are used in Tagalog to express respect for the elderly or individuals of higher social rank and can be used to sound more polite in general. However, many Philippine languages do not have this "respect" syllable. Instead, many use pluralized pronouns to denote respect in general, such that plural second-person pronouns are used in daily speech. Even more respectful is the third person plural; one way of politely asking on the phone "Who is calling?" can be translated as "Who are they?"

Other language groups have resisted the dominance of Tagalog-based Filipino in various ways. Cebuano is the lingua franca in much of the southern Philippines. For decades, those in Cebu City insisted on singing the English version of the national anthem rather than the Filipino version. The original Spanish was translated into English in the American period, and a Pilipino version was composed in the 1950s. Recently, with the rise to the presidency of Rodrigo Roa Duterte from Cebuano-speaking Davao City, interest in the language has spiked.

Similarly, Ilocano is the common language throughout northern Luzon, though even in that region the Pangasinan speakers resent the growing influence of Ilocano. As with Cebuano, much of the language usage is due to immigration, as Ilocanos left their rugged Ilocos region with its narrow coastal plain for the broader reaches of the Cagayan Valley on the other side of the Cordillera Mountains. The highland ethnolinguistic groups traded with the Ilocano-speaking lowlanders who surrounded them, adopting Ilocano as a common language, spoken even among themselves.

Ilocanos have a reputation for being frugal and hard working, known for consuming a simple, low-meat cuisine and for looking far and wide for work, whether as agriculturalists in Mindanao or *sacada* plantation workers in Hawai'i. Closer to Manila are the Kapampangan, whose language is quite different from both Ilocano and Tagalog. They have a reputation for being warriors; they were part of the colonial army—the Macabebes—during Spanish times and the center of gravity of the mid-twentieth-century Huk rebellion. It is generally conceded that they have the richest cuisine in the country. South of Manila is the long Bicol peninsula of southern Luzon. Bicolanos have some of the spiciest food in the Philippines— most ethnic cuisines are mild—and they are proud of their linguistic, literary, and artistic achievements.

Ilonggos (Hiligaynons) in western Visayas, in central Philippines, are among those who feel put upon by the dominance of Cebuano. The eastern half of Negros Island speaks Cebuano, in contrast to the western half, which shares Ilonggo with Iloilo, across the Guimaras straits. Ilonggos have a reputation for extravagance, but this is based on the sugar-planting *hacendero* elite and those who imitate them. In the eastern Visayas are the Waray of Leyte and Samar, generally regarded as fierce—for instance, the famous Balangiga clash was in Samar—and they are known for magnificent woven *banig* mats of *tikog* (a grass).

Perhaps the most important effect of ethnolinguistic differentiation is on elections. Given that kinship is the basic idiom of politics and organization, it makes sense for ethnic solidarity to emerge in national elections. Bicolanos, the sixth largest group in the country, have a record of solidly voting for Bicolano candidates. Ilocanos are the third largest after

Tagalogs and Cebuanos, and have managed to elect five presidents since independence.

When it comes to other aspects of culture, the variations are immense. Detailed customs related to birth, marriage, death, and the like are disputed even within particular ethnolinguistic groups. Part of the reason lists of "you know you are Filipino if . . ." are so amusing is that Filipinos will recognize some as almost universal, such as the widespread use of nicknames, whereas other are quite particular, such as the practice of some Christians of not bathing on Good Friday. As the book by David L. Steinberg puts it, the Philippines is "a singular and a plural place."[1]

What is contemporary popular culture like?

Stereotypically, Filipinos are musical. Aside from being lounge and cruise singers worldwide, Filipinos have been major contenders in various reality singing competitions across the globe. They have starred in London West End musicals and those on Broadway. More prosaically, karaoke is a feature of most gatherings, leading stereotypically to loud singing and disputes over song choice.

Original Pinoy music (OPM) emerged in the 1970s, and Western music and K-pop have large followings in the country as well, with international acts visiting the Philippines and aspiring Filipinos constantly producing covers of foreign songs. Filipino sentimentality makes balladeers, belters, and crooners indispensable, but hip-hop or rap mainstreamed in the 1990s, with subjects ranging from partying to social issues such as traffic, the plight of OFWs, and the struggles of a gay person.

Artists performing in various genres are active in commercial and independent music scenes. Many artists are influenced by global pop trends; others, they strive for authenticity and indigeneity by playing gong-chimes, which Filipinos share with other Southeast Asian cultures. Muslim Mindanao is known for particularly elaborate music that utilizes the Kulintang, a set of graduated knobbed kettle gongs; the Cordillera has the *gangsa* (a single hand-held smooth-surfaced gong), and these instruments frequently accompany traditional dance performances.

Sports are also a popular form of entertainment in the Philippines. Basketball is the most beloved, followed by boxing. Every village has its own basketball court and half-courts and makeshift courts can usually be found throughout the neighborhoods. Collegiate and professional competitions are followed closely, often leavened by a regulated number of "imports" to boost the games, while the National Basketball Association in the United States is continually followed by both newspapers and broadcast media. The popularity of boxing is boosted by the weight classifications that allow small Filipinos to be competitive on an international level, and by outstanding achievements by individual Filipinos. Manny Pacquiao's boxing fights are watched by so many people that crime rates go down during his matches. Billiards is among the favorite sports, thanks to world champion Efren "Bata" Reyes, and many boys and men can be found in billiard halls, whether sophisticated or makeshift, when they are not on the basketball courts. Football (soccer) and volleyball, particularly women's, are growing in popularity but do not yet rival basketball and boxing. Cockfighting is universal across the country, in both urban and rural areas, with largely a male following and a twenty-four-hour cable channel devoted to it.

Beauty pageants for women, men, and children are ubiquitous, from the national down to the village level, and in schools and other institutions. Almost every noontime, a broadcast TV show hosts its own beauty contest as a segment, and OFWs have them on their days off. The Philippines is now a powerhouse of international beauty pageants, producing titlists in major competitions, and aspirants from other countries now look to Filipino costume designers and coaches for help.

Popular broadcast TV shows are generally in Filipino, including the nightly news, which used to be in English, and some foreign shows are dubbed into Tagalog. Cable channels are the refuge of English shows. Teledramas, both local *teleseryes* and foreign series, dominate afternoon and evening primetime broadcasts, with some running for several years. Filipino *Teleseryes* are now exported to other Southeast Asian countries, Africa, and Eastern Europe as well.

Despite Filipinos' reputation for fluency in English, many still fear speaking the language because they fear being ridiculed for making mistakes. In the media, fellow Filipinos jeer at beauty queens and even at Manny Pacquiao when they struggle with English during interviews. That said, English words frequently enter colloquial speech. Taglish, Tagalog and English code-switching, is heavily used in Tagalog-speaking areas, while Bislish, which could be any Visayan language such as Cebuano or Hiligaynon combined with English, is widely used by educated younger generations in Visayas and Mindanao, and by President Duterte.

In 2018, the Philippines ranked twelfth in a list of the top twenty Internet-using countries in the world, despite the nation's slow Internet speeds. Filipinos spend an average of almost four hours daily on social media sites, particularly Facebook. This is due to a partnership between Facebook and the two cellular providers, whereby use of the "Lite" version of Facebook does not incur data charges.

In the realm of cosmetics, both men and women purchase skin-whitening products and services because fair skin is highly regarded and associated with looking well-groomed and rich. Fair-skinned mestizos often land lead roles in TV and film media and, with dark body makeup on, they even portray brown-skinned characters. This was the case in the 2018 historical fiction drama series *Bagani*, which did receive backlash for not casting "pure" Filipinos as leads. The privileging of mixed-race appearance is reflected in the international beauty queen realm as well, as the Filipinas who win often have one European parent.

Except for Muslims and some isolated indigenous peoples, Filipinos mainly follow Western fashion. "Filipiniana" generally refers to the styles of the late Spanish colonial era (though recently Moro and indigenous influences have crept in) and is sometimes specified as the dress for formal receptions. Terno dresses and the Barong Tagalog are worn on formal occasions, such as the yearly State of the Nation Address by the president. There is a widespread myth that colonial authorities forbade Filipino males from wearing shirts tucked into their trousers, thus leading to the loose-hanging design of the Barong Tagalog. In fact, there was no such decree; the loose, comfortable cut was always preferred.

Unsurprisingly for a tropical country with a consumption-driven economy, the Philippines is a nation of mall goers. New air conditioned malls keep opening all over the country, and three of the world's ten largest malls are in the Philippines. Philippine malls are a one-stop location for retail, food, entertainment, fitness, and government services; as public institutions go, they are a convenient substitute for parks and museums. Many hold regular Sunday religious services, particularly for Catholics, and some set aside prayer rooms for Muslims.

What are some of the themes and creatures in Philippine folklore?

As might be expected in a land that had an incredible variety of an animist peoples, who then absorbed and adapted elements of Islam and Christianity, there is wide variety in Philippine folklore. There is no one pantheon of gods, spirits, or magical objects and places, but rather different enumerations, of which some are widely known.

"Malakas at Maganda" (Strong and Beautiful) is a creation myth, originating among Tagalogs but known throughout the archipelago due to its inclusion in the educational curriculum. In the story, a bird pecked at a bamboo and it cracked open, revealing the first man (Malakas), who asked that another bamboo be opened, which revealed the first woman (Maganda). During the authoritarian interlude, paintings were commissioned showing Ferdinand and Imelda Marcos emerging from bamboo as Malakas and Maganda, the parents of the Filipino people.

In 1885, José Rizal famously illustrated and analyzed the children's animal tale "Monkey and the Tortoise," in which the clever tortoise eventually gets the better of the mischievous monkey, who tries to eat all the bananas on a tree. His was the Tagalog version, which ends with the tortoise tricking the monkey, as opposed to the Ilocano version, which ends with the tortoise cooking the monkey and feeding him to other monkeys.

Given the dominance of Manila in Philippine history, and latterly in governance and culture, it is perhaps inevitable that Tagalog versions are often accepted as typically "Filipino." Tagalogs called their supreme god Bathala, derived, as is Batara Guru in Indonesia, from the Sanskrit *bhattara*, or noble lord. Nowadays, *bahala na* (it's up to god) is commonly heard throughout the country. Some Filipino mythologies and supernatural phenomena are shared with other Southeast Asian cultures. A particular variety of vampire, the *manananggal* (detached), also features in folk culture in Indonesia. The creature is said to be "detached" because her upper torso flies at night, looking for victims, and only needs to return to the bottom half by daylight. Likewise, what Filipinos call deadly nightmares, or *bangungot*, have been documented among Thai and Hmong as well as Filipinos. Known in English as "sudden unexplained nocturnal death syndrome," this is said to overwhelmingly affect young men who are apparently healthy, causing them to die in their sleep.

There are many mythical creatures, often malign, that populate the Filipino imagination. The Aswang Project (*aswang* is a general term for evil spirits) lists approximately 250 different creatures, with Luzon mythology highly represented. One term, *duwende*, covers a number of spirits such as elves, dwarves, and goblins, and the term seems to derive from the Spanish *duende* (*duen de casa*), a mischievous spirit that inhabits a house. The Filipino *duwende* are thought to inhabit certain spaces as well. Sometimes, without specifying what type of spirit is being propitiated, Filipinos will ask permission from the spirits when walking in unfamiliar rural areas.

Not all such creatures are malign. The terms *diwata* and *anito* are used nowadays to refer to spirits that live in and protect nature. The nymph Maria Makiling, for instance, is said to protect Mount Makiling (80 kilometers south of Manila). Most environmental landmarks have origin myths, which make for good literature. Some of these places are considered sacred and are visited by many people; Mount Banahaw (110 kilometers southeast of Manila), for instance, is so popular that access is restricted. Mainstream Filipinos find Mount Banahaw a peaceful place for rejuvenation and meditation, while Rizalistas, who believe that José Rizal was divine, are concentrated around the mountain.

A variety of traditional medicine and protective processes echo the mythologies and religions of the Philippines, from the animist past to the world religions introduced into the archipelago. Many mainstream Catholics wear or carry religious medallions; more syncretic versions called *anting-anting* or *agimat* (amulets) are said to protect the wearer. The most famous of such *anting-anting* were worn during the revolution against Spain; the most notorious are utilized by paramilitary groups such as the Ilaga (anti-Muslim militia in Mindanao). Such amulets are supposed to make the wearer impervious to harm (e.g., bulletproof). Often but not always, the symbols derive from Christianity. A common *anting-anting* is a bullet, and these are carried often enough that in 2015 airport screeners credibly executed a scam of planting, and then accusing passengers of carrying, a bullet in their luggage (soliciting a bribe to let the passenger go).

Traditional medicine includes a variety of herbal remedies, which are widely available and sometimes sold by women who provide advice about how each remedy works. Some remedies discreetly include herbs that will "induce menstruation," serving as abortifacients in a country where abortion is illegal. A specialist is called an *arbolaryo* (herbalist), the English translation of which is often rendered as "quack doctor." A related practice is *hilot* (therapeutic massage). Ordinary massage is widely performed by trained massage therapists, but curative massage is accomplished by a *manghihilot* (one who does *hilot*). Herbal treatment and *hilot* are often combined to address various ailments or to assist with childbirth if a formally licensed midwife or doctor is not present.

The far end of the traditional medicine spectrum is occupied by faith healers. There are mainstream Christian versions, both Catholic and Protestant, as well as Muslim practitioners, who often embrace elements of Sufism; prayers are believed to cure, and particular priests, pastors, and imams are held to be specialists. But there are also idiosyncratic faith healers with a wide following, often beyond the country's borders, the most spectacular of which are "psychic surgeons" who perform surgery without the use of scalpels or other instruments. Their clients believe that these men, and sometimes women, can remove diseased parts of their bodies with their psychic powers.

Generally speaking, most Filipinos believe in spirits of some sort and take care not to upset them. They trust in the restorative powers of their religion and the advice of their religious leaders, and some carry medallions or *anting-anting*. The efficacy of herbs is generally accepted, massage is felt to be healing and healthy, but most are skeptical of psychic surgery.

What are the annual holidays in the Philippines?

The year typically starts off with a bang on New Year's Eve— literally, as all sorts of fireworks, generally locally made in a thriving industry, are set off by individuals and families. YouTube videos can give an idea of the extent of this exuberance, with everything from vast aerial displays launched from affluent neighborhoods to small rockets and strings of firecrackers set off by families and kids in the street. The

celebration reaches a crescendo at midnight, causing considerable though short-lived air pollution. A more pressing public
health problem is injuries due to fireworks, and the Department
of Health has developed a robust monitoring system among
fifty hospitals that keep detailed records from December 21 to
January 5. For years the annual casualty numbers ranged from
850 to 1,000, but the ascent of Rodrigo Duterte to the presidency changed that. To general astonishment, he effectively
banned individual fireworks in Davao while he was mayor,
and he has reduced firework injuries nationwide as president.
In the Philippines as a whole in the 2017 holiday season, only
630 injuries were reported, and the decline continued into 2018
and 2019, with 463 and 319, respectively.

February brings Chinese New Year, which most Filipinos
welcome as a day off, and many retail stores are decorated for
the event. Actual celebrations, complete with dragon dancing,
tend to be concentrated in Chinatowns across the nation and
in businesses owned by Chinoys or Chinese. February 14,
Valentine's Day, is an informal holiday. In Metro Manila, it is
marked by extremely heavy traffic as many folks go out, but
it is largely uneventful in the rest of the country. The anniversary of the 1986 "People Power" Revolution at Epifanio de
los Santos Avenue (EDSA, a major highway through Metro
Manila) is observed on February 25 and generates controversy
between those who feel it is worth celebrating the demonstrations and those who think it is time to "move on" from the
controversies of the Marcos era.

Late March or April includes Holy Week for Christians;
Maundy Thursday (the day of the Last Supper) and Good
Friday (the crucifixion of Jesus) are holidays, and the country
shuts down almost completely during the latter half of the
week; for example, newspapers do not publish on Friday or
Saturday. While this was originally a solemn time for Catholics,
who make up approximately 80 percent of the population, the
commemoration has become more relaxed in recent years.

Many families go on vacation during Holy Week, and notably, Metro Manila seems deserted, with little vehicular traffic.

April brings Araw ng Kagitingan (Day of Valor); this is the anniversary of the fall of Bataan during World War II, but the holiday was restyled in 1987 so that it would not seem to celebrate a defeat. "National Heroes Day" in August was originally the anniversary of the "Cry of Pugad Lawin," when the Katipunan initiated their armed insurrection in 1896. It has since been generalized to honor many heroes, but August 21 remains focused on the 1983 assassination of Benigno S. "Ninoy" Aquino Jr.

Other national holidays include Labor Day on May 1 and Independence Day on June 12. The date of Independence Day was changed in 1962 to recognize the anniversary of the 1898 Declaration of Independence from Spain, rather than July 4, 1946, the anniversary of when the United States granted independence to its colony.

Christmas season begins September 1—when morning talk shows are already decorated with holiday decor—and by mid-December the frenzy is on; thus, many Filipinos proudly claim to have the "longest Christmas season in the world." November 1 sees a mass movement of people for All Saints Day, as families visit their deceased loved ones in cemeteries, often in their hometowns, and it is the single heaviest travel event of the year. Police, traffic authorities, and other government authorities deploy thousands of personnel along major routes and in transport terminals to assist travelers.

In 2017, the Philippines added another Catholic holiday, the Feast of the Immaculate Conception, on December 8. After the turn of the millennium, the Philippines made two Muslim holidays official: Eid'l Fitr (the end of Ramadan) and Eid'l Adha (the Feast of the Sacrifice). Based on the lunar calendar, the days of these two celebrations process through the year, and the exact dates are declared by the National Commission on Muslim Filipinos.

Finally, the birth of Andrés Bonifacio, leader of the Katipunan, on November 30 is a holiday, as is December 30, the anniversary of the execution of José Rizal. At least with respect to official historical commemoration, these two figures are currently equal.

How can religious diversity be characterized?

The Philippines has long been styled "the only Christian country in Asia," a characterization that became outdated when East Timor gained its independence in 1999. The Philippines has the third largest Roman Catholic population in the world (after Brazil and Mexico), with some 80 percent of the population identifying as Roman Catholic, but there are important religious minorities.

Perhaps most consequential for both Philippine history and contemporary affairs is the Muslim population, estimated at 6 percent of the population. Over 90 percent of Filipino Muslims reside in Mindanao, though communities are now spread throughout the country.

There are also non-Catholic Christians. At the beginning of the American period, President William McKinley was speaking to a group of Protestant pastors when he avowed an intention to "Christianize" the Philippines. Many Spanish friars had fled during the anti-Spanish Philippine Revolution, and American Protestants wanted to fill the perceived void. Approximately one hundred missionaries had arrived before hostilities ceased. In 1901, most Protestant denominations reached an agreement about dividing up the country geographically to avoid undue competition, an arrangement similar to the one entered into by the Spanish religious orders three hundred years earlier. The Methodists and Seventh Day Adventists did not join the agreement, however, wishing to work freely throughout the islands.

Much like the secular American civilian government, these missionaries established educational and medical facilities, some of which thrive to this day. Their more successful efforts were among the un-Hispanized Filipinos—indigenous people in the highlands of the Cordillera and un-Islamized indigenous peoples in Mindanao who are collectively known as "Lumad." As a result, some of the highest concentrations of Protestants and missionaries are found in Baguio City and the Cordillera region. Evangelicals have grown in strength in the region, as they have done worldwide. They present an interesting "prosperity" angle by discouraging lavish feasting. While traditional Cordillera feasting involves slaughtering and eating animals ritually, evangelical doctrines prohibit consuming blood and meat that has been sacrificed to idols. Thus, Christianized families and clans can opt out of the ritual expenditure of resources and invest them instead.

Evangelicals have been successful elsewhere in the Philippines, totaling some 2.4 percent of the population in 2015. Two of the ten largest evangelical congregations in the world are based in Manila—Victory Church, with an estimated weekly attendance of sixty-five thousand, and Christ Christian Fellowship, with fifty-five thousand. They both began in 1984 and have expanded overseas. A larger movement, which is also spreading globally, is the Jesus is Lord (JIL) Bible-based church, which claims five million members. The head, Brother Eddie Villanueva, ran for president twice, receiving almost two million votes in 2004 and over one million in 2010, though in both races he came in fifth of five candidates. His son, Joel, served as a party-list congressman for the JIL-linked Citizens Battle Against Corruption (CIBAC) party, then as head of the national Technical Education and Skills Development Authority under President Noynoy Aquino for five years (2010–2015), and was elected senator in 2016. Furthermore, Joel Villanueva reaped the second-largest sum of votes in the national senatorial elections, with more than eighteen million votes.

The Church of Jesus Christ of Latter Day Saints has been steadily growing in the Philippines and now has an estimated 700,000 members. Its missionary activity had been ongoing for years, at the beginning tapping young Americans and more recently utilizing Filipino missionaries. Yet the Book of Mormon was only translated into Tagalog in 1987, and it has since been translated into other Philippine languages. Mormons have gained general acceptance in the Philippines as well. Even Filipinos who don't agree with the beliefs of this church admire its members' discipline, healthy lifestyles, and solidarity.

Philippine-specific versions of mainline Christian dominations have emerged. Perhaps most prominent is Iglesia Filipina Independiente, often called Aglipayan after its first head, Gregorio Aglipay. Iglesia Filipina Independiente split from the Catholic Church at the beginning of the twentieth century, and since 1960, it has been in full communion with the Episcopal Church. Notably, Iglesia cites abuses by Spanish friars and the execution of José Rizal as its reasons for denouncing Catholicism. This uniquely Filipino church has always had a nationalist streak; Aglipay represented Ilocos Norte in the revolutionary Malolos Congress and ran unsuccessfully for president in 1935, and the church continues to be active in progressive causes. Aglipayan supreme bishop Alberto Ramento was killed in 2006, in the midst of an upsurge of counterinsurgency extrajudicial killings, and Bishop Carlos Morales was arrested at a Mindanao checkpoint in May 2017 along with a "consultant" of the National Democratic Front of the Philippines.

The Iglesia ni Cristo (INC; Church of Christ) is visible throughout the Philippines, with more than five thousand of its distinctive structures (see figure 4.1) scattered throughout the archipelago. This genuinely Filipino church was registered in 1914 and founded by Felix Manalo. After leaving Catholicism as a teenager, Manalo worked to find a new reading of the Bible. Catholics and Protestants alike find his version heretical because it claims that while Christ is a mediator between God and humanity, he is not divine, and there is no trinity. Besides its doctrine, the INC emphasizes discipline, tithing, and twice-a-week religious services. In 2014, the INC opened the world's largest multipurpose indoor arena. The church also provides medical and social service outreach to the general population, and hundreds of thousands of people flock to its charitable events. The INC's growth exploded in the unsettled situation after World War II and was not halted by the succession of Felix Manalo's son, Eraño G. Manalo, or by that of his grandson, Eduardo V. Manalo. Though there was some division in the Manalo family in 2015, the INC seems unshaken. 2015 census data list the INC as the third largest religion at 2.6 percent of the population, behind Catholicism (79.5 percent) and Islam (6 percent). Like other dynamic religions in the Philippines, the INC has aggressively expanded overseas, adding "Church of Christ" in English or the local language as part of the title of the church. Within the Philippines, the INC is especially visible at election time because it admonishes its congregation to vote as a bloc. (See figure 4.1.)

A religious strain that is particular to the Philippines is the group known as the Rizalistas, who believe that José Rizal

Figure 4.1 Typical Iglesia ni Cristo (Church of Christ) building
Source: © iStock/yullz

was another coming of Jesus Christ, or some variation on that theme. They claim that Rizal was sacrificed for the Filipino nation, as Jesus was for Israel at about the same age, thirty-five years old. While there are a number of groups around the country, most gather in Calamba in Laguna Province, where Rizal was born, or at Mt. Banahaw, which many Filipinos believe is a spiritual place. While the number of Filipinos who are Rizalistas is small, the prestige of Rizal is so widely recognized that they are treated with respect.

Is the Philippines a Catholic country?

To call the Philippines a "Catholic country" is an oversimplification. The constitution of the Philippines mandates the separation of church and state, and while the Catholic Church is perceived to have played a central role in the 1986 ouster of President Marcos, it has lost influence recently (e.g., with the 2012 passage of the Reproductive Health Act, and by criticizing President Duterte's "War on Drugs"). In this technically secular state, divorce is outlawed (the Vatican is the only other jurisdiction where this is still true), but the average Catholic often does not agree with the stance of the Church.

From the beginning of the interaction between missionary friars and the Philippines, the Catholic religion has been adapted, in a process technically called "enculturation," so that there is a difference between ecclesiastical or scriptural Catholicism and the lived version. When Legazpi's expedition burned Cebu and discovered a small statue of the Santo Niño (Holy Child) in the ashes in 1565, the locals clearly felt it was an *anito* (spirit). In fact, Magellan had given the statue to Rajah Humabon's wife in 1521. Nevertheless, the friars had no difficulty promoting devotion to the Santo Niño, interpreted in catechism as the young Jesus Christ. Today, Catholic Filipinos show devotion to the Santo Niño; the original statue remains in a shrine in Cebu City. There is a Philippine-specific Catholic feast day in January, and people keep statues in their homes and public or private offices, sometimes dressing them in various occupational costumes, as fishermen, firemen, bakers, farmers, and so on.

In the modern day, Filipino takes on Catholic rituals draw large crowds. The procession of the statue of Black Nazarene, which depicts Christ carrying a cross, is celebrated on January 9. The march goes from Manila's Luneta Park to its home cathedral in Quiapo, traveling 6 kilometers over the course of twenty-two hours. Roughly five million devotees crowd the route, trying to touch the statue or its transport vehicle. The image is considered miraculous, and many devotees return each year to fulfill a vow of thanks for the favors they receive. Other localities around the country host a similar event with replicas.

The most extreme display of fulfilling vows despite hardship is the crucifixion of devotees on Good Friday. The penitents, who are predominantly though not exclusively male, spend a few painful minutes on the cross before receiving medical care—all watched by thousands of spectators.

Marian devotion, to the mother of Jesus, is common among Catholics and can be seen both as the closest Christian equivalent to precolonial female religious shamanism and as a reflection of the importance that Filipinos ascribe to the family. "Mama Mary" is seen as the hope of her children, the faithful. In 1942, the Catholic Church declared Mary, under the title of "Immaculate Conception," the principal patroness of the Philippines. Recently, the Feast of the Immaculate Conception, on December 8, was made a regular holiday in the Philippines. Globally, Filipinos are connected to, and exporting, other Marian devotions (e.g., in Medjugorje, Herzegovina).

Some Catholic leaders in the Philippines are worried about the erosion in their flock, as the observant population dropped from 85 percent of Filipinos in 1970 to 79.5 percent in 2015, and point to the growth in evangelical Protestants as one of the causes. The Church has responded by offering evangelical experiences and solace via the largest Catholic lay organization in the world, El Shaddai. Begun in 1984 as an informal gathering at a radio station owned by businessman Mike Velarde, El Shaddai is a prominent Catholic movement. It uses media to magnify its reach, broadcasting gatherings live and then rebroadcasting them. Estimates of El Shaddai's reach are imprecise, though the organization claims millions of devotees, and its weekly gatherings do draw hundreds of thousands. In some ways, the gatherings resemble Protestant prosperity gospel preaching, since participants hold up envelopes with petitions for divine favor and "prayer offerings." It should be emphasized that despite its resemblance to non-Catholic Pentecostal or charismatic movements, El Shaddai is recognized as a Catholic lay organization by the hierarchy, has bishops and priests as spiritual advisers, and always includes a complete mass as part of the four-hour-long weekly gathering.

The Catholic Church in the Philippines is not under the shadow of an existential threat such as the Church seems to be facing elsewhere. For instance, many sources note declining crowds for papal visits (e.g., to Ireland), but when Pope Francis visited the Philippines in 2015, an estimated six million people attended his trip's final mass, a larger crowd than the five million who attended a mass officiated by Pope John Paul II in 1996. The overall generational change is also muted; in survey data there is no correlation between age and attendance at church services. Thus, young adults are as likely as older adults to attend, though overall church attendance has been declining over the past twenty-five years.

In particular, child abuse accusations, investigations, and the attendant global turmoil in the Church have not thus far roiled the Catholic Church in the Philippines. There are indications of problems; Filipino priests in the United States are included in lists of alleged abusers. Additionally, Rodrigo Duterte said during the presidential campaign that he had been abused by an American Jesuit; the priest he named was the subject of a 2007 settlement in California over accusations of abuse before his death in 1975. And an American priest has been criminally charged in the Philippines. But even a 2013 book devoted to reportage of scandals, *Altar of Secrets: Sex, Politics, and Money in the Philippine Catholic Church*, concluded that such "infractions of Filipino clergymen have been isolated cases at most, unlike in the US, for instance."[2]

The scandals related in the book are encapsulated in the subtitle: *Sex, Politics, and Money*, and these have long been issues in the Philippines. The sex in question is priests having consensual relationships, and offspring, with women—and this has been a reality since the beginning of the Spanish colonial era. Offspring of friars tended to be absorbed into Indio (indigenous) society, and it is often said that many families have friars among their ancestors. As for politics and money, these have been part of the story of the Catholic Church from the beginning, as friars administered local affairs and worked with the local *principalia* (the local ruling class).

Scandals about sex, politics, and money provide ammunition for Duterte when he attacks clergy who criticize his violent "War on Drugs." To that end, he even distributes copies of *Altar of Secrets*. But these realities do not threaten the institution of the Church, since the average parishioner knows full well that such anomalies are present, yet continues to believe.

What is the role of women?

The Philippines has one of the smallest measured gender disparities in the world. The gender gap has been closed in both health and education; throughout the country, women outlive and have higher academic achievement than men. Women are prominent in the professions, such as medicine and law, and almost half of all new lawyers are female. The country has had two female presidents—Corazon Aquino from 1986 to 1992 and Gloria Macapagal-Arroyo from 2001 to 2010—and had its first woman Supreme Court justice, Cecilia Muñoz Palma, in 1973, before the United States had one (Sandra Day O'Connor, in 1981).

As is common throughout insular Southeast Asia, the pre-colonial status of women was relatively high. Kinship was reckoned through the mother's as well as the father's side, for instance, and women played a prominent role in rituals. Though the terminology differed among languages, such ritual specialists were called *katalonan* or *babaylan* (with the latter term more recognized currently). The introduction of two major world religions—Islam and Catholicism—did make a difference, displacing women from ritual roles and privileging men in other social roles.

But in economic and social realms, equality is almost the norm. The fact that the domestic sphere is a woman's domain often means that the family budget is controlled by the wife. Moreover, girls receive more education because it is more compatible with female gender stereotypes. Parents may consider girls' education to be a better investment, because a responsible girl who accepts authority would be more willing to use her success to care for her elders in their old age. Boys, it might be said, are discriminated against in the education system, as rambunctiousness is discouraged, and for males getting a job at an early age is a socially acceptable alternative to finishing school.

The greatest gender gap in statistical analysis is in the realm of political power. Among members of the Philippine House of Representatives elected in 2016, some 29 percent are female, and this represents a considerable increase over the past fifteen years. For local government executives, the proportion is lower—23 percent for provincial governors in 2016, for example. Political office is often acquired through connection to males in the clan, and wives frequently replace husbands who reach term limits for elective office (or die in office) or run in auxiliary races to help the clan acquire a broader array of offices. For instance, Corazon Aquino was the widow of Ninoy Aquino, who was assassinated in 1983 upon his return to the Philippines, and Gloria Macapagal-Arroyo is the daughter of Diosdado Macapagal, Philippine president from 1961 to 1965.

Other institutions in the public and private sector replicate this gendered power dynamic. Despite parity among male and female faculty at the University of the Philippines, only one of the twenty-one presidents of the university has been female.

There are certainly persistent "macho" elements in Philippine culture. The Spanish colonial experience is often blamed for this, though polygamy and easy divorce were widespread in traditional societies in the archipelago before Catholic missionaries strove to eliminate the practices. Extramarital relations are more common for males than for females. And in a 2018 survey on family roles, 79 percent of adult respondents agreed that "a husband's job is to earn money; a wife's job is to look after the home and family." There was no statistical difference between responses from men and from women.

Estimates of the incidence of sexual harassment are scanty. One survey of Quezon City estimated that 60 percent of women had experienced sexual harassment in public, largely unwanted verbal remarks or catcalling (wolf whistling), and one-third had had experiences that went beyond the verbal, such as groping or exhibition. Since 1995, there has been a national law on the books against sexual harassment in the workplace or in educational environments, and a growing number of cities, including Quezon City and Manila, ban harassment in public spaces. The impact of these legal strictures is probably limited, however. Arguably, even President Duterte himself violates Davao City's anti-harassment ordinance with his treatment of female reporters and critics.

In 2017, the National Demographic and Health Survey measured the prevalence of physical, sexual, or emotional violence against women as roughly 25 percent, which represents a small decrease from previous years. The Anti-Violence Against Women and Their Children Act was passed in 2004, and both government and non-government organizations try a number of different tactics to tackle the issue. Community-based interventions seem to make the most difference, but these are difficult to sustain.

The sex industry is an unfortunate reality, with estimates that there are 400,000 to 800,000 sex workers in the country, mostly female. While sex work is technically illegal and thus subject to mulcting by law enforcement officials, local health offices often provide care and a clean bill of health to sex workers who opt to receive these services. Only a fraction of sex workers seek care, however. There have been initial discussions but no movement on legalizing sex work to provide more protection for the workers. However, legal protection and law enforcement are increasing in the realm of international human trafficking; this is particularly important for women, given the feminization (and potential sexualization) of overseas work. Within the Philippines, the sex trade districts that are most publicized are those frequented by foreigners—near the former US Clark Air Base in Angeles, in downtown Manila, and in similar locations in other cities—but the vast majority of clients are locals.

A growing issue is online sexual abuse, particularly of children. The widespread availability of the Internet, including on mobile devices, has allowed such crimes to spread, and the Philippines is now one of the global centers for child pornography. The legal system—with its outdated evidentiary rules, constraints on wiretapping, and agonizingly prolonged court cases, which often discourage witnesses—is struggling to cope with this development.

Has the Philippines made progress on lesbian, gay, bisexual, and transgender (LGBT) and intersex rights?

In Asia, the Philippines ranks first in positive responses to an international survey question, "Should Society accept Homosexuality?" It is ahead of the United States in this regard, and is on a similar level with European countries and Australia. Globally, the Philippines is unique in combining strong religiosity with tolerance of homosexuality. In figure 4.2,

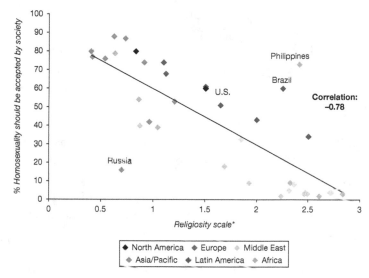

*Religiosity is measured using a three-item index ranging from 0–3, with "3" representing the most religious position. Respondents were coded as "1" if they believe faith in God is necessary for morality; "1" if they say religion is very important in their lives; and "1" if they pray at least once a day. The mean score for each country is used in this analysis. Religiosity scores for the U.S., Britain, France, Germany, Spain and Japan are from the Spring 2011 global Attitudes Survey.

Figure 4.2 Philippines both very religious and very tolerant

Source: Pew Research Center, "The Global Divide on Homosexuality" (June 4, 2013), https://www.pewresearch.org/global/2013/06/04/the-global-divide-on-homosexuality/ (accessed June 26, 2019)

the distinctiveness of this pairing is indicated by the country's position far above the trend line.

Philippine-specific data from a Social Weather Stations survey in 2013 show 85 percent of adult respondents agreeing that "Just like me gays and lesbians also have the right to be protected against any form of discrimination." However, on the same survey, 59 percent of Filipinos still agree that "If there are gay or lesbian members of my family, I would like them to change and become straight men or women." Clearly, a distinction can be drawn between tolerance of and acceptance of LGBT persons. There are occasional hate crimes against transgender women and feminine-presenting men, including murder—so the picture is not entirely rosy.

While LGBT identities are not illegal in the Philippines, specialized legal protection is sparse. Quezon City does have an enforceable ordinance banning discrimination on the basis of gender orientation, but it is rarely invoked. At the national level, an anti-discrimination Sexual Orientation and Gender Identity and Expression (SOGIE) Equality Bill passed the House of Representatives in September 2017, but it made no progress in the Senate before the June 2019 adjournment. Same-sex marriage seems remote since even divorce is not legal. However, in 2008 the Supreme Court ruled that intersex individuals could have their birth certificate changed to reflect their preferred name and sex.

In the past, a party-list organization, *Ladlad* (to come out), ran for Congress to support LGBT rights. The Commission on Elections initially refused to accredit the organization but was ordered to do so in 2010 by the Supreme Court. However, *Ladlad* subsequently lost its accreditation for receiving insufficient votes in repeated elections. In 2016, the Philippines elected its first transgender member of House of Representatives, Geraldine Roman. Her victory probably is attributable to the fact that she comes from a prominent political family in her home province of Bataan. The media noted her identity at election time and she sponsored the SOGIE anti-discrimination bill that passed the House of Representatives in 2017 but died in the Senate. Interestingly, most coverage of her work in Congress has not made a story of her pioneering status but rather covered her just as it would cover any other member of the Congress (e.g., as Chair of the House Committee on Disaster Management).

In certain ways the LGBT community is quite prominent in Philippine culture. For instance, the Filipino mania for beauty pageants throughout the country and the diaspora includes "Miss Gay Philippines"—where any geographic location, event, or organization may replace the word "Philippines"— and Mr.

Gay Philippines. The *bakla*, a term accepted as meaning "gay" by most Filipinos but which has a more varied usage within the LGBT community, are most noticeable in popular culture. The social category *bakla* is often traced back to the pre-Hispanic babaylan, a type of shaman. The historic babaylan included women and, sometimes, femininized men (or, more precisely, "persons who were considered male at birth, but present characteristics considered feminine"). This latter category is very similar to one modern-day usage of *bakla*. The most immediately visible aspect of *bakla* identity is effeminacy in flamboyant mannerisms and dress, sometimes but not always including cross-dressing. *Bakla* are also stereotypically expected to confine themselves to certain professional arenas that welcome them, such as fashion houses or hair and nail salons. "Tomboy" is a counterpart, though less prominent in popular culture: a person considered female at birth but dresses and acts in stereotypical ways.

In the traditional classification of effeminate *bakla* and masculine men, or masculine tomboys and feminine women, there is little room for the idea of a non-effeminate homosexual man or a feminine homosexual woman. However, urban areas increasingly come into contact with Western ideas of gender and sexuality, and the "Idol Philippines" televised singing contest had in 2019 several gay men, a lesbian, and a trans woman among the finalists. The Philippine LGBT community today contains both people who identify as *bakla* or tomboy, as well as those who identify more closely with the Western conception of gay, lesbian, transgender, etc.[3] Public figures have been coming out as "gay," as non-effeminate homosexual men, and there are more public discussions of the issues and discrimination faced by lesbians, who were previously been somewhat overshadowed by issues concerning *bakla*. In urban areas, modern work places such as large organizations and BPO call centers are more open to different experiences and expressions of gender as well. In the end, activists continue to chafe against remaining restrictions and fight discrimination.

Of course the vast majority of the population, while tolerant and perhaps becoming more accepting of the LGBT community, is utterly ignorant of the multiplying distinctions that help persons deal with their experience and identity. The best advice is not to initiate the use of any of these labels to describe any people until the people themselves do so, and indicate that it is fine for others to do so.

What is the progress of social media in the Philippines?

Once the Philippines began improving telecommunications infrastructure in the middle 1990s, social media started to take off. After decades of excruciatingly long waits for a landline, competition from mobile network providers was introduced in 1993. Soon, mobile lines vastly outnumbered landlines. By the end of the 1990s, the Philippines was the "texting (SMS) capital of the world," sending more messages than all of the European Union combined. Texting was much cheaper than making phone calls and fit right into the Filipino cultural preference for a large social network.

In 2001, the "People Power II" ouster of Joseph Estrada was the first "text" revolution. When the televised impeachment trial of President Estrada abruptly adjourned one evening as the Senate deadlocked over consideration of evidence, text messages spread, instructing "Go to EDSA." By midnight, an enormous crowd had taken over the vital intersection in a conscious reprise of the original "People Power" Revolution of 1986, and they stayed until Gloria Macapagal-Arroyo was sworn in as Estrada's successor four days later when the military, led by Chief of Staff Angelo Reyes withdrew their support from Estrada.

Texting remained dominant for most of the rest of the decade, but there was a brief florescence of Friendster as a social networking site. The Philippines, along with Indonesia, became the center of gravity of this service before it faded away beginning in 2009. By now, Facebook is the dominant social media site by a wide margin. It is reported that when Mark Zuckerberg was told that 97 percent of Filipinos on the Internet use Facebook, he asked "What are the other 3 percent doing?" The Philippines has repeatedly been dubbed the social media usage capital of the world; clearly these new platforms fit Filipino interpersonal interaction styles.

There is more to this situation, however. First of all, there are now more mobile phone lines than people in the Philippines, and an increasing number of them are smartphones. Perhaps more important, Facebook offers its free mode (Facebook Lite) on both mobile providers, Smart and Globe. The importance of this is that when users access the Internet through the free application, it is without charge. This is why almost all adults are on Facebook. For keeping up with family and friends, this is clearly a boon.

However, many analysts have concluded that this experiment by Facebook exacerbates the proliferation of "fake news" and the weaponization of social media in political and social disputes. In the Free mode, users see news headlines and photo captions, but not the text of the news articles or the pictures themselves. To access these things a user has to incur data charges, and since most mobile phone subscribers are in prepaid plans, the majority do not. The reasoning is that without the full articles, users are hard-pressed to separate fake from genuine news.

In the 2016 election campaign, the team of Rodrigo Duterte took the utmost advantage of this new technology. By the end of the campaign in April, he was the subject of 64 percent of all Facebook conversations about the Philippine election. This aggressive use continued after his inauguration, with Diehard Duterte Supporters (DDS—taking off from the alleged Davao Death Squads during Duterte's rule of Davao City) using social media tactics against his critics. While there were accounts of paid "trolls" and certainly instances of automated bots being involved, much of the rhetoric and venom on both sides seems to have been ideological.

Globally, Facebook has enlisted the assistance of "fact checkers," including[4] the online news site Rappler, which has incurred the wrath of President Duterte for its coverage of his administration, including the bloody "War on Drugs." He has banned Rappler's correspondents, its corporate registration has been challenged, and CEO Maria Ressa was charged with tax evasion. In recognition, Ressa was included as one of the journalists listed as a *Time* Person of the Year in 2018. For his part, Duterte brushed off this accolade: "You can have it."

A technical limit to the usage of social media is the poor mobile Internet speeds in the country, regularly rated as among the worst in the world. Partly this is blamed on a duopoly; Smart and Globe successfully absorbed all smaller competitors, so competition is limited. More stark is the limited number of cell phone towers; the Philippines has less than half as many as Thailand, which has roughly the same land area but only two-thirds of the population of the Philippines. As 2018 came to a close, the Duterte administration moved to address both of these problems by authorizing a third mobile provider and issuing regulations for independent companies to set up towers, which they could lease to mobile providers.

What is the current state of traditional media?

The Philippine press is generally described as one of the most freewheeling in the world; it is rambunctious and licentious, despite the facts that libel is a criminal offense in the Philippines and "false news" was added to the Revised Penal Code in 2017. The media avidly follow every political scandal—at least for a brief period before going on to the next story. Media practitioners tend to repeat the maxim that their job is to "comfort the afflicted and afflict the comfortable." In fact, most major media outlets have institutional charitable arms that help indigents or raise funds in times of calamity, becoming social service adjuncts in governance. The ABS-CBN Network, for example, claims to be "In the Service of the

Filipino Worldwide," while rival GMA News touts *Serbisyong Totoo* (true service). Some media personalities have made their names helping people via a popular type of call-in radio show.

The three leading English-language newspapers all circulate mainly in Greater Manila, with some copies shipped to other major cities. The *Manila Bulletin* is the most staid, the *Philippine Star* leans somewhat to the right, and the *Philippine Daily Inquirer* leans somewhat to the left. There are business dailies and newspapers serving the Chinese community, as well as several dozen local newspapers across the archipelago. There are also glossy periodicals covering society and other topics, largely in English and focused on Manila. There is a thriving print newspaper industry in Tagalog and Taglish (a mixture of Tagalog and English). These tend to have higher circulation than English publications but do less in-depth reporting.

The leading newspapers still claim to be profitable, though they can be vulnerable to economic pressure. President Estrada initiated an advertising boycott against the *Philippine Daily Inquirer* as coverage of his scandals increased, and President Noynoy Aquino rhetorically raised the prospect of a similar boycott. President Duterte has repeatedly attacked the broader interests in real estate and food service of the holding company that controls the *Inquirer* because the newspaper persisted in its negative coverage of his "War on Drugs."

The headquarters of the broadcast media tend to be in the Manila area, and the main TV news shows are anchored from there. The largest networks have affiliates that not only host local reporters but have news broadcasts in the regional lingua franca, generally Cebuano or Ilocano. Cable news networks tend to predominantly use English; ABS-CBN News Channel (ANC) is a prominent example. Radio networks combine centrally produced material, generally but not exclusively in Tagalog-based Filipino, with local language materials.

To deal with the language dilemma, one of the practices in the print media is to switch between English and Filipino in the stories themselves. The market doesn't support up-scale Filipino media—a twenty-four-hour news channel and a broadsheet using Filipino have both gone under in the past—and there is an influential and important foreign audience, particularly in Manila, so English tends to be the language of the main story. But much of the discourse from political leaders or citizens quoted in stories tends to be in Tagalog-based Filipino or even in other languages. To capture the nuances of a quote, the practice has developed of delivering the quotation in the original language with a parenthetical translation into English immediately following. A variant is to just run with the quotation in the English-language story, assuming the reader understands Filipino, and to run an English translation if the quotation is not in Tagalog, such as President Duterte's remarks in Cebuano.

Aside from economic pressures on media owners, there are some constraints on media freedom. In the Philippines, "libel" has been a criminal offense for decades. While prominent journalists typically avoid conviction for this crime—often after considerable defense efforts over several years—ordinary journalists, especially those far from Manila, can be intimidated. Violence against journalists is a more direct threat; the Philippines is often named one of the most dangerous countries in the world in which to be a journalist. From the end of the Marcos authoritarian interlude to 2018, the Center for Media Freedom and Responsibility (CMFR) recorded 164 murders of journalists in the Philippines.

The worst incident was the November 2009 "Maguindanao massacre." Elements of the Ampatuan clan in Maguindanao Province halted a convoy that was going to register the candidacy of Esmael Mangudadatu, a politician from a rival clan. Journalists were involved because Mangudadatu promised them money in exchange for accompanying the political convoy on this journey—5,000 to 10,000 pesos ($100 to $200). Mangudadatu knew about the danger of registering candidacy and sent his wife, two sisters, and others in his place in the vain hope that women would be safer. Ultimately, fifty-eight persons were killed, including thirty-two journalists and the members of Mangudadatu's family. The trial of the suspects is still ongoing.

Low pay, and thus vulnerability to influence, is one of the realities of Philippine journalism in the countryside. Often, journalists need to hold a second job or find other means of earning a living. Promotional content can be more lucrative but also garners the wrong kind of attention. The single largest category of victims of media killings is radio broadcasters, "block timers," who buy a block of time from the radio station and recoup their expenses by selling advertising. Sensationalism, including accusations of local corruption, seems to sell products and increase audiences for these broadcasters. Sometimes these block timers are also political candidates—whether potential or previously unsuccessful ones—with a motive to impugn the authorities, and this also makes them targets for violence. Given the level of impunity in the country, with so many violent deaths not being followed by convictions, offended parties seem more likely to kill journalists than to sue them for libel.

What characterizes Filipino cuisine?

The most important element of Filipino cuisine is rice; the Philippines ranks sixth globally in terms of per capita rice consumption. Nutritionally, rice makes up some 40 percent of calories in the diet, and many companies include "rice subsidies" as a benefit to their employees. Eating cannot be called a "meal" unless rice is included; no matter how much food is involved, anything without rice is a "snack." This applies to breakfast as well; fried rice is a favorite breakfast dish that can be made from the previous night's leftover boiled rice. There is also, to be sure, a glorious variety of rice-based cakes and sweets for snacks and deserts.

Wheat-based baked products became more available during the American colonial period, due to cheap imports of American wheat. Thus, the *pan de sal* (salt bread) became the iconic roll to have with coffee at breakfast. It is part of a colloquial saying, "There is no hard *pan del sal* in hot coffee," which implies that ardent romantic pursuit is certain to be successful.

Seafood used to be incredibly abundant in this archipelago and still makes up 60 to 70 percent of the average Filipino's animal protein intake. Seafood is traditionally preserved by smoking or drying and salting, which produces a strongly flavored result. Fish sauce (*patis*) and fermented fish or shrimp paste also have robust and salty flavors.

Chickens are widely kept by individual households and are also raised industrially. Most meat fowl and egg-laying hens can be found in the countryside. In urban areas, the live fowl are mostly fighting cocks and are not eaten unless they lose in a cockfight.

Traditional Filipino cooking combines many influences. Southeast Asian cuisine is a big part of the mix; dishes that are considered quintessentially Filipino, such as *balut* (duck embryo boiled in the shell), are also found in mainland Southeast Asia. Elements of Chinese cooking can be seen in the wide variety of noodles known as *pancit* (a Hokkien term); there are more than three dozen varieties in the Philippines. The Spanish influence was lasting, though the food was often transmitted via Mexico, since the Philippines was ruled by the viceroy of New Spain. New World plants abound in Philippine cuisine: squash, corn (maize/*mais*), *sayote, camote* (sweet potato), pineapple, and occasionally chili peppers. Spanish-inspired dishes, such as tomato-based meat stews like *caldereta, menudo, afritada,* and *mechado,* and stuffed meat such as *relleno, morcon,* and *embutido,* are very common at fiestas, parties, and special occasions.

There is much regional variation, but vinegar, coconut, and pork (except among Muslims) are core ingredients. Vinegar has been used since ancient times since it helps preserve meat.

It is the central ingredient in what is often thought to be the country's signature dish, *adobo* (pork, chicken, or both cooked in a vinegar mixture of some sort). This is sometimes mistaken as a derivative of the Spanish *adobo/adobar*, but the dish existed before the colonial experience, and the Spanish just referred to it as the "adobo of the natives" (later just "adobo"). Coconuts have many uses, but it is generally the "milk" derived from pressing grated fresh coconut that is used in stews, particularly of vegetables. Pork is the most popular meat but also a prestige item, since both fish and chicken are cheaper sources of protein. Beef is even more expensive than pork and hence is less frequently consumed by Filipinos.

Seafood is sometimes only marinated in vinegar, a process that can be applied to almost any fresh ingredient. Another sour taste is that of *sinigang* soup, which is popular in Luzon. Meat, such as pork, beef, fish, shrimp, and sometimes chicken, is cooked in a *pampaasim* or souring agent such as tamarind (the most traditional option), *calamansi* (native lime), or guava, along with vegetables, which typically include okra, *kangkong* (water cress), *sitaw* (string beans), and *labanos* (daikon radish).

There is a variety of fruits available, many of which were introduced to the islands during the colonial administration. Apples are a favorite of Filipinos, particularly at Christmas time, but they are almost all imported. The varieties of bananas and pineapples in supermarkets are bred to stand up to handling and shipping, as the Philippines is a leading exporter. There are many other varieties of locally grown bananas or pineapples available from open-air markets or from vendors who push carts through neighborhoods. The Philippines vies with other countries for bragging rights about the best mangoes. Previously, the mango supply was quite seasonal, peaking in "summer" between March and June, but horticulture management has improved so that yield is plentiful year-round. Filipino opinion is divided, as it is everywhere, about durian, which "smells like hell, tastes like heaven."

Until the turn of the millennium, Filipino restaurant cuisine was essentially the same as home cooking, though often the latter was better. Restaurants were for social occasions, when it was more convenient to eat out than to produce a meal for a large number of people. In the twenty-first century, this has begun to change as new restaurants undertake "fusion" in the conventional contemporary culinary sense of the word, reimagining traditional Filipino cuisine or combining it with other influences. This movement was at first limited to upscale Metro Manila districts and shopping malls. But now experimental Philippine cuisine is present in most urban areas of the country. The food scene has expanded demographically as well. "Food parks," where a number of stalls share an open space and common dining areas, make fusion cuisine affordable for college students and young professionals and offer food that is more adventurous than that found at the "food courts" in malls.

International chain restaurants are often the anchor tenants in the mall food courts, surrounded by many Filipino companies. Under the economic liberalization of the country, chains have thrived. Burgers from chains such as Wendy's and Burger King; pizzas from Pizza Hut and Shakey's (which is thriving in the Philippines while shrinking in the United States); and coffee from Starbucks, Seattle's Best, or Coffee Bean and Tea Leaf are visible signs of fast-food culture spreading throughout the country.

Jollibee is a Filipino fast-food chain that opened in 1978 and survived the 1981 entry of McDonald's into the Philippine market. Currently, Jollibee has almost twice as many stores in the Philippines as does McDonald's, which reformulated its burger into "Burger McDo" in imitation of the flavor that Jollibee offers. In general, in adapting Western fast food, a sweeter taste is brought to spaghetti, pizza, hamburgers, and more. Jollibee Foods Corporation has expanded internationally, with 150 stores overseas, so the Philippines is doing its part for the global fast-food revolution.

5

GOVERNMENT AND GOVERNANCE

How is the national legislature structured?

The bicameral Philippine Congress works in interesting ways. In fact, constitutional designers have been ambivalent about bicameralism in the Philippine state. The revolutionary Malolos Constitution in 1899 was unicameral, the American colonial government was bicameral, and the original 1935 Constitution had a unicameral National Assembly. However, in 1940 amendments established a twenty-four-member Senate that would be elected nationally—partially in reaction to the rise of rural unrest that might propel radicals into the district seats in the House of Representatives. The deliberations of the Constitutional Commission in 1986, after the "People Power" Revolution, began under a unicameral assumption, but a nationally elected Senate was established, with the reform passing by one vote.

The "lower house," the House of Representatives, is rooted in local dynasties because most representatives are elected in single-member plurality districts. Some of the dynasties are of long standing; others have been generated by achieving government office after the restoration of elections in 1987 and are growing in strength. In the past few elections, dynasts have accounted for about three-fourths of members of Congress.

The Senate, the "upper house," is nationally elected and thus relies much more on fame. In 1957, Rogelio de la Rosa, a matinée idol, was the first movie star to be elected senator. Since the 1986 "People Power" Revolution, eight more television and movie entertainment stars have been elected, as well as TV newscasters, two basketball stars, and boxing superstar Manny Pacquiao, in 2016 (he continues to pursue his career in the ring). It must be emphasized that celebrity status does not necessarily reflect on competence. Highly qualified public servants such as Francis Pangilinan and Ralph Recto bring substance to the Senate, but it certainly did not hurt that they are married to movie stars. Another way to get to the Senate is by being a member of the national cabinet, which provides exposure, or for that matter, by leading unsuccessful military coups, as did Gringo Honasan and Antonio Trillanes (who won his first term in 2004, running while in detention).

One of the differences between the houses is the path for acquiring leadership. Senators compete with one another and are highly ambitious, as they may believe they have a shot at being the president. No Senate president has ever served through the full six-year term of his ally, the president, as rivals within the chamber vie for the national media coverage that being head of the Senate affords. Two House speakers have served through a full presidential term, however: Jose de Venecia under President Fidel Ramos and Feliciano Belmonte under President Noynoy Aquino.

The houses are similar in that their members do not owe their election to any party organization or the president, but rather to local roots (for representatives) or national visibility (for senators). There is some internal institutional discipline, in that positions in the congressional structure come with power and resources. But keeping the legislative process moving in an orderly fashion is difficult when the only sanctions involve changing the structure. As the *Economist* described it in June 2018, "The president struggles to push legislation through Congress, not because of determined opposition but because it is a hopeless morass." This was aptly illustrated in July 2018, when former president, then representative Gloria Macapagal-Arroyo mounted a challenge to Speaker Pantaleon Alvarez on live TV, while President Rodrigo Roa Duterte cooled his heels in a nearby room, waiting to give his annual State of the Nation Address. In the end, Alvarez was allowed to preside over the televised speech but was promptly dispatched in the following days.

The legislative process in many countries has been compared to making sausage: if one likes laws, one should not watch them being made. In the Philippines, unpredictability is to be expected of the process. This can have its upside, such as when a determined president forces through a bill, examples being the increase in sin taxes and the reproductive health bill proposed during Noynoy Aquino's administration. It can have its downside, such as when House Speaker Alvarez managed to get a bill through the House in 2017 benefiting a particular tobacco company. (The bill failed in the Senate, after which the tobacco company changed ownership and paid a $400 million fine for tax evasion.) This example illustrates a third possibility: policy stasis. Bills rationalizing tax incentives have been pending for over a decade. Another, perhaps more salubrious, example is President Duterte's initiative to reinstate the death penalty—which was abolished in 2006, allowing over one thousand sentences to be commuted—passing the House in 2017 but failing to get through the Senate.

How strong is the Philippine executive branch?

Beginning in the Commonwealth period, the Philippines adopted a "strong presidential" system of government. An elected president now faces a separation of powers, but typically dominates the other branches. Almost all the constitutions—the 1935 Constitution, the original 1973 martial law Constitution, and the 1987 Constitution—were clear on this point. Under the amended 1973 Constitution, the

Philippines had a prime minister responsible to the parliament, at least on paper. But this only lasted from 1981 to 1986, the end of Marcos's presidency. Of course, there was no doubt that President Marcos was in charge. By virtue of amendment 6 to the constitution, he even had the power to legislate by decree.

Typical constitutional presidencies in the Philippines are not as dominant as they were during Marcos's authoritarian interlude (see "How did the authoritarian interlude (1972–1986) unfold?" in chapter 2). For instance, there is some annual give and take between the president and Congress on the budget. But presidents are by far the most important political player, with wide latitude and many powers. Presidential appointments reach deep into the bureaucracy, down to the directorships of particular bureaus. In sum, the president of the Philippines has more appointments to make than the president of the United States, some eleven thousand compared to nine thousand, despite the fact that the Philippine national government is roughly half the size of the US federal government. While this large number of appointments may make the bureaucracy more responsive to a particular president for that person's term, the capacity of agencies is reduced by having a less-developed permanent civil service management stratum.

The political relationship with the legislature is stacked in the president's favor, as illustrated by the massive party switching that attends the election of a new president. Given the weak party system in the country and a focus on personalities at all levels, no newly elected president has had a majority of party mates in the Congress elected during the May elections. But by the time that Congress convenes in July, legislators aligned with the president dominate Congress. The most extreme example of this occurred in 2016, when Duterte was elected president, running as the candidate of PDP-Laban party. In the House of Representatives, only 3 PDP-Laban candidates were elected among the 292 members, yet one of those three, Pantaleon Alverez, was elected speaker. Likewise,

Koko Pimentel was the only member of the PDP-Laban party in the 24-member Senate, and he became Senate president. Of course, the fractious nature of Congress does mean that there are limits on what the president can get done, even with majority support.

The president is nonetheless afforded extraordinary flexibility, in part because the general tendency of the Philippine electorate is to be generous in their assessments. All elected presidents, with the possible exception of Corazon C. Aquino in 1986, were elected by pluralities, sometimes with quite a small percentage of the vote since there is no provision for a run-off election. To take the most extreme example, Fidel V. Ramos was elected with less than one-fourth of the vote in 1992. Yet at the beginning of his term, more than three-fourths of respondents were satisfied with him (see figure 5.1; note that this is a "net" rating after subtracting those dissatisfied). Such honeymoons are normal for Philippine presidents, as indicated in the figure. Only Gloria Macapagal-Arroyo did not

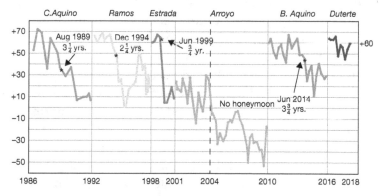

*% Satisfied minus % Dissatisfied correctly rounded. Ignores Don't Know and Refused to Answer responses. Question. Please tell me how satisfied or dissatisfied you are in the performance of [NAME] as President of the Philippines. Are you Very satisfied, Somewhat satisfied, Undecided if satisfied or dissatisfied, Somewhat dissatisfied, Very dissatisfied?

Figure 5.1 Net Satisfaction Ratings of Philippine Presidents, May 1986–December 2018

Source: Social Weather Stations, https://www.sws.org.ph/swsmain/artcldisppage/?artcsyscode=ART-20181228124054 (accessed June 26, 2019)

experience one, as she ascended to the presidency through "People Power II" (the second Epifanio de los Santos Avenue [EDSA] revolution) and thus never quite had the legitimacy of a freshly elected president.

The presidency of Macapagal-Arroyo does teach another lesson: the institutional powers of the president are such that even a deeply unpopular one can maintain a grip on power until the end of her term, if she is careful to avoid an over-whelming coalition such as that which faced Joseph "Erap" Estrada. Arroyo, for instance, differed from Estrada in that she managed to avoid totally alienating the Catholic Church. Her reputation as a devout Catholic who opposed govern-ment support for artificial methods of birth control, for in-stance, strengthened her position. Estrada, on the other hand, was known for flagrant womanizing and lacked the backing of the Church. Deploying patronage resources, Arroyo man-aged to survive many widely publicized scandals of her ad-ministration, avoiding impeachment and taking governance initiatives, from peace talks with the Moro National Liberation Front (MNLF) and the Moro Islamic Liberation Front (MILF) to appointing a Supreme Court chief justice, up through the scheduled end of her term in June 2010.

The abrupt switch from Arroyo to Noynoy Aquino il-lustrates the fundamental weakness of a hyperpresidential system with a limited term. There is considerable policy swing with each ascension into office, and this uncertainty makes ec-onomic development and investment difficult. For instance, when Noynoy Aquino was inaugurated in 2010, his admin-istration voided many of the contracts signed by the previous administration, upsetting private enterprise and even overseas donors.

Additionally, the president appoints Supreme Court just-ices from a list of five names forwarded by the Judicial and Bar Council; no legislative approval is required. Given that there is a mandatory retirement age of seventy in the judiciary, turnover at the court can be quite rapid. By the time Arroyo stepped down after her unusually long tenure (2001–2010), she had appointed fourteen of the fifteen justices on the court. While Noynoy Aquino only appointed five justices during his full six-year term, Rodrigo Duterte is expected to appoint thirteen (based on projections of retirement age) by 2022. In addition to wielding appointive power, the president influences the post-court prospects of those who reach mandatory retirement. The president may appoint former justices to office or help them in political endeavors, so court decisions are often deemed subject to executive influence.

This ability to appoint and otherwise influence judges helps in one of the main tasks presidents face after leaving office: staying out of jail. So far, they have managed it. There were corruption scandals during Ramos's term, but court cases never progressed. Estrada was charged and detained in a hospital and then under house arrest, and he was convicted of plunder, but he was pardoned by President Macapagal-Arroyo within a couple of months. Macapagal-Arroyo was detained in hospital for election offenses and plunder, but the Supreme Court dismissed the charges by July 2016. Since leaving office in 2016, Noynoy Aquino has seen a number of charges filed against him, but no court action has taken place.

In sum, the Philippine executive branch is quite strong in relation to other elements of the political system. But the government structure still limits what presidents can do to effect change in the Philippines.

How do elections unfold?

There are a vast number of offices to fill in a synchronized national election, as citizens need to vote for president, vice president, twelve senators, a district congressman, a party-list congressional choice (the only vote that isn't for an individual), governor, vice governor, provincial board members, mayor and vice mayor, and city/municipal councilors.[1] Midterm elections only reduce the number by two (president and vice president).

Until 2010, voters had to hand-write all names. With an optical marking automated system instituted beginning 2010, voters fill in ovals, but the modern process is still controversial, as opponents do not trust the machines. The voter's job is nonetheless eased, and results are produced quickly instead of being laboriously tabulated for weeks.

Elections tend to be violent, with roughly one hundred deaths of candidates and political workers per election, despite a "gun ban" during every election season. The more rapid announcement of results tends to reduce uncertainty and violence after the election, which is an improvement, but allegations of cheating and fraud still abound. Many voters tend to accept the notion of vote buying. The cleric Jaime Cardinal Sin tried to convince Filipinos to still "vote with their hearts" even after pocketing the money. Some election recounts have been launched, but they are long and tedious, typically being rendered moot as the term of office has expired before a new tally can be produced.

For all these problems, Filipinos love elections. Occasionally there is talk of "No-El" (no election) in particularly fraught times, but public resistance prevents the cancellation of elections. Campaigns can be very festive, with public rallies full of singing, dancing, and bombastic speeches. Posters and banners are supposed to be restricted to certain public areas but tend to spread out as the campaign goes on. T-shirts and hats are popular campaign items since they are useful to the wearer, and there are only restrictions on them on Election Day.

There is a relatively short official campaign period: ninety days for national and forty-five days for local elections. There used to be a theoretical prohibition on "premature campaigning," but in 2009 it was ruled by the Supreme Court that anything that happens outside the campaign period is not "campaigning." Similarly, spending outside the campaign period does not count against spending limits, which are unrealistically low in any case; prices have tripled since the limits were set in 1991, and there is no public financing of political campaigns. Candidates are required to submit statements of their expenses, and some actually do report spending over the limit, but this is rare.

We can begin to assess the impact of national campaigns, but quantitative survey data are rarely available for lower-level electorates such as congressional districts, provinces, cities, or municipalities. Campaigns have some impact, but their influence is moderated by the need to be widely known to win a nationwide election. In 2012 and 2015, the top twelve Senate candidates were included on surveys in December, just before the start of campaigns for the 2013 and 2016 elections. Nine of them won, and all of those rated in the top six succeeded in the May elections. In 2019, ten of the twelve winners were already in the top twelve ranked in December 2018. By far the largest change between December 2012 and May 2013 was when Mary Grace P. Llamanzares shot from twentieth in popularity to number one by dropping her married name. In reverting to "Grace Poe," she made it clear that she is the daughter of Fernando Poe Jr., the undisputed king of Philippine movies and an unsuccessful presidential candidate in the 2004 elections.

The national campaign for president and vice president did seem to have considerable effect in 2016, thanks to broadcast television. At the beginning of the campaign, in December 2015, Duterte was in fourth place in presidential surveys, and Leni Robredo was in a tie for second place with Bongbong Marcos in surveys of the vice presidential race. Duterte went on to win a clear victory, and Robredo edged out Marcos for first place. It was almost unheard of for a local official to go on directly to win a national election. Duterte was the longtime mayor of Davao City, in Mindanao in the southern Philippines; Leni Robredo was a first-term congresswoman from Bicol, at the southern end of Luzon. For all the discussion of the rise of social media, it was broadcast television that made the difference in these elections. For the first time, televised debates were held by the Commission on Elections: three for the presidency and one for the vice presidency. Periodic survey data from two survey organizations make clear that the two "local" candidates (Duterte and Robredo) surged after the debates were aired.

Election Day, the second Monday in May, is a holiday, with campaigning and selling of liquor banned on that day (and the day before). With electronic voting, returns now come in during the night. In 2016, there were almost 45 million votes cast (84 percent turnout); 432,076 overseas absentee ballots were cast in embassies and consulates, while there were only 19,255 local absentee ballots cast by police, soldiers, and media practitioners who would have duty outside their *barangay* (village) of registration.

What is the role of courts and the legal profession?

In the Philippines, the legal profession is prestigious; lawyers are addressed as "attorney" in normal conversation, much as medical doctors are addressed as "doctor." Entry into the profession is very competitive; the passing rate for the bar exam ranges from 18 to 31 percent. All this takes place in a glare of publicity, with front-page newspaper stories covering both when the exam takes place and when the results are released. The Top Ten are always listed publicly, and seven of the eight lawyer presidents were "Top Notchers:" Quezon, Laurel, Roxas, Osmeña, Quirino, Macapagal, and Marcos. Only Attorney Rodrigo Duterte, the first lawyer president since 1986, did not "top the bar"; he has, in fact, always made it clear he was not a top student!

The role of the Supreme Court in the Philippine judicial system is an activist one by institutional design. The roots of its contemporary expanded set of powers go back to the beginning of martial law, when the court ruled in January 1973 that "there is no further judicial obstacle to the new [Marcos-compliant] Constitution being considered in force and effect." Chief Justice Roberto Concepcion dissented and resigned, and later became the chair of the 1986 post-People Power Constitutional Commission and took care to strengthen the court's role, defining it in the 1987 Constitution:

Judicial power includes the duty of the courts of justice to settle actual controversies involving rights which are legally demandable and enforceable, and to determine whether or not there has been a grave abuse of discretion amounting to lack or excess of jurisdiction on the part of any branch or instrumentality of the Government.

Given that this is a "duty," it means the fifteen-member court handles an enormous number of cases per year, always more than ten thousand. In deciding cases, the court theoretically follows precedent, but the rapid turnover in justices due to mandatory retirement at age seventy, along with occasional influence exerted by the president, means that decisions can be quite unpredictable.

Lower courts in the Philippines also have enormous workloads. A number of mundane laws increase the caseload; for instance, writing a check with insufficient funds ("bouncing a check") is a criminal offense, and "unjust vexation" is a misdemeanor crime. The average case takes seven years to complete, and important ones take considerably longer than that. Imelda Marcos was charged in 1991 with offenses arising from the authoritarian interlude, and she was convicted by the specialized anti-graft court, the Sandiganbayan, in 2018, but the decision will not be final until it is ruled upon by the Supreme Court.

A decade-long effort to reduce case backlogs took place under three consecutive Supreme Court chief justices: Hilario Davide Jr. (1998–2005), Artemio Panganiban (2005–2007), and Renato Puno (2007–2010). During that period, the case backload declined by more than 25 percent to just over 500,000. At that point, progress stopped and the numbers started to climb—not coincidentally, as there was turmoil in the Supreme

Court. In May 2010, Renato Corona was controversially appointed chief justice despite a constitutional ban on making appointments during the campaign period. When Benigno S. "Noynoy" Aquino III was inaugurated in June, he did not have the chief justice swear him in, and Noynoy's allies in Congress managed to impeach and convict Corona, removing him from office in May 2012. Noynoy then promoted a junior justice, Maria Lourdes Sereno, to be chief over more senior justices, causing internal turmoil in the court. Sereno herself was removed by a court decision in May 2018, with the clear encouragement of President Duterte. During this period, the case backlog once again began to increase, and the total accelerated past previous highs because of the "War on Drugs" launched by Duterte in 2016.

There is general public recognition that the courts take a very long time to settle disputes and that alternatives are available for reaching a mutually agreeable outcome. Court-annexed mediation, undertaken by a cadre of accredited mediators, now resolves tens of thousands of cases. At the local level, there is the Barangay Justice System, which is mandated to deal with a range of minor and property cases before they reach the courts. The process involves conciliation and appeals to community spirit, kinship, and the like. Citizens tend to find the system satisfying for parties seeking resolution of their cases, though there can be abuses as barangaya officials exercise their informal powers. Of course, lawyers are less convinced of the value of systems that do not involve them, and courts only see cases that the Barangay Justice System was unable to resolve, so judges tend to doubt its efficacy.

Formal and informal justice systems often peacefully coexist; people choose which system to go to for redress of their grievances. Indigenous justice systems, for instance, have stood the test of time in the Philippines and have grown with the indigenous people; they are no less legitimate than the newer formal justice system. The 1987 Philippine Constitution recognizes and promotes the rights of indigenous cultural communities within the framework of national unity and development (article 2, section 22). Additionally, among Muslims, there are special courts under the Code of Muslim Personal Laws but also disputes are also settled under the legitimate persuasion of religious scholars. Even in urban areas, informal methods can arise out of Philippine culture and are utilized within the Barangay Justice System.

What is the state of the military?

The Armed Forces of the Philippines (AFP) were established in 1935, pursuant to Commonwealth Act 1, the first act of the newly elected Philippine government. That said, the Philippine Army likes to trace its roots back to March 22, 1897, when the country established an army to fight the Spanish (Ejercito en la Republica de las Islas Filipinas). The AFP was formed in the shadow of Japanese expansionism and fought in World War II, but since then its primary mission has been internal security and counterinsurgency. During the first phase of independence, the political elite confined themselves to utilizing elections, however dubious or subject to "guns, goons, and gold" these were, as the procedure for selecting government leaders, so an armed forces takeover was never a serious threat. Ferdinand Marcos broke this mould in the 1970s during the authoritarian interlude, using the military for his own purposes. "Marcos's Praetorian Guard"[2] expanded and took on many civilian duties under martial law; military spending hit over 3 percent of GDP in the late 1970s. This collapsed to 1.6 percent of GDP in 1984 during the 1980s economic crisis. The state of the military and its poor performance against the communist insurgency was the spark for the Reform the Armed Forces Movement (RAM) that triggered the 1986 "People Power" Revolution and then the "Season of Coups" that lasted until 2003.

Since 2003, the Armed Forces have tried to professionalize and to increase their ability to defend the country's territory. Particularly in the face of Chinese assertiveness in the South

China/West Philippine Sea, the aim is to establish a "minimal credible defense." However, spending has remained low, declining to just over 1 percent of GDP in 2014 and only rising again in the last few years. The emphasis has been on the army, which makes up some 70 percent of the Armed Forces—a much higher proportion than for advanced countries, but about the same as for Indonesia.

As the United States began to re-engage in military matters after the Visiting Forces Agreement was ratified by the Philippine Senate in 1999, the United States and the Philippines undertook a joint assessment, which led to the Philippine Defense Reform program beginning in 2003. However, the professionalization of the AFP faced serious obstacles during the Arroyo presidency, when a series of scandals harmed the credibility of the institution.

First, in December 2003 the sons of the AFP comptroller, Major General Carlos Garcia, were stopped upon entering the United States with undeclared cash in the amount of $200,000, which was confiscated. Their mother flew to the United States to try to explain the money: "My husband's position in the Armed Forces is one of privilege. The gratitude monies that he receives is common and unsolicited."[3] While a plea bargain was reached with General Garcia, the scandal continued to haunt those involved. Perhaps most affected was Angelo Reyes, the Armed Forces chief of staff who had switched allegiance from Estrada to Arroyo during the People Power II event in 2001, and later was secretary of national defense (under whom the July 2003 Oakwood munity was launched).

During congressional hearings about the Garcia case, it emerged that Reyes had received fifty million pesos as a traditional "send-off" (*pabaon*) when he retired from the chief of staff position in 2001. In 2011, Reyes committed suicide, leaving behind a note: "I did not invent corruption, I walked into it. Perhaps my first fault was in having accepted aspects of it as a fact of life."[4]

Beyond financial improprieties, there continue to be allegations of human rights violations, particularly in connection with counterinsurgency against the communists. Extrajudicial killings and disappearances surged into the hundreds by the mid-2000s, with few perpetrators being convicted. Major General Jovito Palparan is widely considered to be an instigator, and he was finally convicted in 2018 for the 2006 disappearance of two community organizers.

Considerable controversy still exists about the human rights records of the Armed Forces. From 2010 to 2016, there was an Internal Peace and Security Plan, Bayanihan. Proponents said it was based on respect for human rights, but opponents claimed it perpetuated old behaviors. Those sympathetic to the national democratic movement point to military suspicion of schools for the indigenous peoples in Mindanao being run by civil society organizations (rather than the Department of Education). On the other hand, the AFP has responded very positively to the Bangsamoro peace process, with a chief of staff visiting the headquarters of the MILF, and MILF chair Murad visiting the headquarters of the AFP.

Even those sympathetic to improvements in the AFP will point to several obstacles to its thorough professionalization as an effective defender of Philippine sovereignty. First is the force structure, which overemphasizes land forces while there are insufficient air and sea assets to cover an archipelago of over seven thousand islands. Additionally, President Duterte continues to emphasize internal security—the drug war and counterinsurgency—over territorial defense. Another obstacle is the rapid turnover of leadership, given the AFP's mandatory retirement age of fifty-six. In the years since the "People Power" Revolution, the chief of staff has averaged less than a year in office; presidents are loath to violate the military's much-prized seniority, so generals are appointed shortly before retirement. Presidents tend to like generals, since it is perceived that they know how to take orders. Many are highly educated, experienced managers of large bureaucracies, and they are often appointed to civilian jobs after they retire from the military.

There are those who worry about all those retired generals, but the public has a more generous view than many in the policy elite. Some 75 percent of adults say they have "much trust" in the Armed Forces of the Philippines. But it should be clear that, politically speaking, the Philippine military is not an independent actor. The military institutionally has learned the dangers of such an approach, however, and has managed to keep its distance from the Duterte administration's "War on Drugs."

Have the police improved?

Concern has long been expressed about the police in the Philippines, and it has become an international issue in the wake of President Duterte's "War on Drugs." In the 1950s, it was opined that "the deficiencies in the Philippine police systems are numerous."[5] At that time, there were two sorts of police: the national Philippine Constabulary (PC), established by the American colonial regime and a component of the Armed Forces of the Philippines (AFP), and local police recruited and controlled by elected officials in provinces, cities, and municipalities. The PC was most famously used for counterinsurgency, and thus was seen as being on the side of landed elites. The local police were naturally politicized, often acting as enforcers for individual politicians.

In the martial law administration, Ferdinand Marcos brought together the local police, the Integrated National Police, and the PC, forming the PC-INP, which was run by a joint command structure within the AFP. Later, in reaction to this militarized centralization, the post-ESDA 1987 Constitution mandated "one police force, which shall be national in scope and civilian in character, to be administered and controlled by a national police commission." Thus, the Philippine National Police (PNP) was created and the Philippine Constabulary was abolished. That said, those considered for the position of chief of the Philippine National Police are still, given seniority, officers who trained for the PC at the Philippine Military Academy in the 1980s.

Over the years, a steady drumbeat of reports and scandals has harmed the image of the police. For instance, the police get poor ratings from citizens and businesses with respect to corruption, though by no means are they the worst government agency in that respect. Politicization is still a problem, as city and municipal mayors hold "operational supervision and control" over police in their locality. Since local government provides much of the logistical support to make up for underfunding from the national level, police are generally beholden to local power holders.

Police procedures are regularly reported to be violations of human rights, often with creative nicknames:

- *tong*—bribe collected by police
- *hulidap* (from *huli*, "catch," and holdup)—arrest and then release in exchange for money
- *palit-ulo* (exchange-head)—releasing one suspect who helps capture another
- *kama o kulong* (bed or jail)—not arresting a suspect in exchange for sex

Discussions on these violations predate the post-2016 "War on Drugs," but it is this war that has brought the PNP into the international spotlight. In the first two years, the official police count of the number killed in legitimate operations was approximately five thousand. These deaths are generally labeled *nanlaban*, "fought back"—the dead suspects all tend to have a .38-caliber handgun and a couple of small packets of *shabu* (methamphetamine) by their sides. The pattern of incidents tends to be the same as before 2016—the ratio of suspects wounded to suspects killed is very low, as is that of police personnel killed or wounded to suspects killed or wounded—but the frequency has been much higher under the Duterte administration. The Filipino public is divided on whether to believe the police about *nanlaban*, but very much would rather suspects be arrested than summarily killed.

Police personnel reports and research show that they learn the norms of policing on the job rather than in the police academy. Officers report frustration with how long cases take to adjudicate and the tedious process required to convict somebody, and this leads some to believe that summary justice is more effective. Weak administrative sanctions for infractions and impunity for killings spurs an indifference to human rights norms. In November 2018, three policemen were convicted of the murder of a 17 year-old boy, a crime they presented in the guise of a drug bust. But this is the exception that proves the rule; they were unlucky enough to be caught on closed-circuit TV (CCTV), whereas in other incidents CCTV has been mysteriously turned off.

There does not seem to be any gradual change taking place in the character of the police. But the uniformly negative image one might glean from media coverage is not an accurate one. Despite their skepticism about some of the methods being used in the "War on Drugs," the Filipino public express satisfaction with the results in public opinion surveys. Crime incidence, whether self-reported on scientific sample surveys or in official police statistics, has indeed gone down. Expert opinion seems unanimous that the drug epidemic, which is real, should be treated as a public health problem rather than addressed through law enforcement alone, but the public is seeing results.

Nearly two-thirds of Filipinos of all social classes express trust in the police. While this may astonish commentators, there are ways in which the police help the average citizen. Interaction with beat police at their outposts, or on the roads when traffic accidents need documenting, can be pleasant. The police exert considerable effort to create a positive reputation, to "serve and protect." Given general citizen fears of

Figure 5.2 *Balimbing*: Multisided fruit as political metaphor
Source: © sarawut panchawa/Shutterstock

crime, a positive attitude toward police is understandable. It is when the police themselves are criminals, *scalawags* in Filipino English, that their reputation takes the greatest hit.

What political parties are important?

In the Philippines, political parties are notoriously weak, being largely vehicles cobbled together among disparate individuals for the purpose of contesting particular elections. "Turncoatism" refers to switching parties, but a more indigenous term is *balimbing*, named for the Southeast Asian fruit that has many sides (see figure 5.2).

At the beginning of the American period, the Federalists were the first political party, advocating for US statehood for the Philippines. But when elections for the National Assembly were held in 1907, such sentiments were crushed by an alliance of local leaders coalescing into the Nacionalista Party.

The Nacionalista Party was the dominant party throughout the American and Commonwealth periods until 1946, when the Liberal Party was established. Thus began the two-party system in which Nacionalista and Liberal administrations alternated, with politicians switching parties, a norm that prevailed until the declaration of martial law in 1972.

From the beginning, the Nacionalista Party was an arena for personality-driven politics. This can be seen in the political supremacy of Manuel Quezon, the strongman who dominated Philippine politics from 1922 until 1944, when he died in exile during World War II. Quezon prevailed over his rivals, including Sergio Osmeña, until the latter campaigned as Quezon's vice president and eventually succeeded him in the presidency in 1944. The most famous triumph of Quezon was in 1933, when Osmeña and Manuel Roxas came home from a mission to the United States. They returned with the Hare-Hawes-Cutting Act, moving the Philippines toward independence. Quezon split the Nacionalista Party into "Antis" and "Pros" on the issue of Philippine independence. Idealistically, one could say that Quezon felt he could make a better deal with the incoming Democratic administration in the United States. Realistically, one could point out that he did not want Osmeña to get the credit when the fight for self-governance was known as the "OsRox" mission. Quezon's forces won overwhelmingly in the 1934 general election, and both factions of the Nacionalista Party reunited. Thus, Quezon was elected the first Commonwealth president in 1935, with Osmeña as his vice president. Roxas eventually became Senate president, formed the Liberal Party in 1946, and managed to defeat Osmeña in the 1946 presidential election.

The pattern of party switching was set: Defense Secretary Magsaysay left the Liberal administration of President Quirino to run and win as a Nacionalista in 1953. Ferdinand Marcos similarly jumped from being head of the Liberal Party to the Nacionalista Party in order to defeat the Liberal president Diosdado Macapagal in 1965.

In the post-Marcos period, the Nacionalista Party is still in existence, headed by real estate magnate and former senator Manny Villar, who is the second richest man in the Philippines. The Liberal Party remains, having ballooned in 2010 but slimmed down considerably in 2016 as members switched from Noynoy Aquino's party to President Duterte's PDP-Laban. The PDP part of PDP-Laban formed in 1982 as Partido Demokratiko Pilipino while Laban (fight) is from Lakas ng Bayan (the nation's strength) in 1978, both founded in opposition to martial law. They merged in 1986, and so the party has historical depth, but many newcomers signed on after the 2016 elections. Still, the PDP-Laban could only muster a slate of five candidates for the twelve senatorial slots open in the May 2019 elections. Additionally, Davao City mayor Sara Duterte, Rodrigo's daughter, created her own "regional party," Hugpong ng Pagbabago, which endorsed thirteen candidates for twelve open seats, overlapping with the PDP-Laban's slate.

In this welter of names, changes, and the like, there are indeed some parties worth taking seriously. The various Left parties are among the fifty-nine members of the House of Representatives under the party-list system, which is elected nationwide in a restricted proportional system. AKBAYAN, a democratic socialist party, managed to maintain a congressional presence of one to three seats from 1998 to 2019, and occasionally has success getting local officials elected. More to the "national democratic" Left is the Makabayang Koalisiyon ng Mamamayan (Patriotic Coalition of the People [Makabayan]), which consistently has a presence of six to eight members. This group quickly figured out that several parties representing women, youth, workers, and teachers can win seats, so the bloc as a whole gets more than the three-seat maximum imposed under the rules of the party-list elections. This gambit works because the parties are united by ideology, a quality that is absent in the rest of the political system.

The design of the 1987 Constitution is quite explicit: "No votes cast in favor of a political party, organization, or coalition shall be valid, except for those registered under the party-list system." Thus, Philippine political parties have been called "underinstitutionalized," and this may be an understatement. There is, in fact, no evidence that "party" affects vote choice, except with regard to the coalition of national democratic Left parties.

What is the role of religion in politics?

From at least the 1500s onward, when the Spanish clergy played an outsized role in the colonial enterprise in the Philippines, religion has intersected with politics. Part of the lead-up to the 1896 revolution against Spain stemmed from the advocacy of Indio priests. They argued for the Catholic Church to allow native priests to head parishes. The execution of three priests—Gomez, Burgos, and Zamora—in the aftermath of the 1872 Cavite mutiny is generally seen as the curtain raiser for the Philippine Revolution.

In 1986, at the beginning of the "People Power" Revolution that ousted the authoritarian president Ferdinand Marcos, Jaime Cardinal Sin, Archbishop of Manila, called on Filipinos to protect military rebels at EDSA. While there is a Catholic "spin" to memorials of this protest—with nuns, rosaries, and statues of the Virgin Mary taking center state in the pictures— the Church is perhaps given too much credit for the overthrow of Marcos. Overestimation of the Catholic Church's impact on Philippine politics should be avoided in general. Filipinos have elected a Protestant (Fidel Ramos in 1992), a boastful woman-izer (Joseph Estrada in 1998), and a man who cursed the pope (Rodrigo Duterte in 2016).

The Catholic Church, which some 80 percent of Filipinos belong to, is much too amorphous to have a concerted impact. While there is theoretically a hierarchy in the Church, in re-ality, each member of the Catholic Bishops Conference of the Philippines (CBCP) is equal within his own jurisdiction. The CBCP does indeed issue statements on political issues, but they are rarely read in church. In surveys, Filipino Catholics indicate that they do not wish clergy to tell them how to vote, and generally speaking the clergy refrain from doing so. One issue on which the Church campaigned hard was opposition to the Reproductive Health Act of 2012, which provides access to family planning information and care. The faithful had long disagreed with the official policy of the Church opposing artificial means of contraception, but elected officials were sensitive to the Church's opposition or followed their own religious convictions. Local government officials often blocked reproductive health measures in their localities' clinics, and elected members of Congress shied away from making controversial decisions; it took more than ten years to pass the bill.

Smaller, more cohesive religious groups do have a more discernible political impact. Within the Catholic Church, there is El Shaddai, a charismatic congregation said to be the largest Catholic lay organization in the world. El Shaddai is headed by Mike Velarde, whose sons Rene and Mike Jr. have repeatedly been members of the House of Representatives for the Buhay ("life") Party List. On the Protestant side, there is Jesus Is Lord (JIL), headed by Eddie Villanueva, whose son Joel served the maximum three terms as a party-list congressman, was appointed by the Aquino administration to head the Technical Education and Skills Development Authority (TESDA), and then won nationwide election as a senator in 2016. "Brother Eddie" Villanueva himself has run repeatedly for president, though his vote percentage totals are always in the single digits.

It sometimes seems that the greatest religious influence is exercised by the Iglesia ni Cristo). The INC has a tradition of requiring bloc voting from its one million voting members. They supported President Marcos in 1986, Eduardo Cojuangco in 1992, Joseph Estrada in 1998, Gloria Macapagal-Arroyo in 2004, Manny Villar in 2010, and Rodrigo Duterte in 2016. Some of these endorsements have failed, as Cojuangco and Villar both lost, and some were made at the end of the campaign period, when it was clear who would win. Still, candidates troop to the INC compound to seek the "blessing" of its executive minister, and politicians tend to publicly greet the executive minister on his birthday. Iglesia ni Cristo's million votes can certainly swing the tide in a hotly contested election. While the church holds sway in nationwide politics, its votes can also be decisive in particular localities where many of its members live.

Spiritual leaders have long exerted their influence in politics. A current example is Pastor Apollo Quiboloy ("the Appointed Son of God") of the "Kingdom of Jesus Christ, the Name Above Every Name," based in Davao City. While he has been courted by national politicians for a long time, his association with Rodrigo Duterte has increased his influence. Duterte has admitted that Quiboloy gave him property while he was mayor of Davao City, and during the 2016 presidential campaign, Duterte used Quiboloy's private jet.

Another locally powerful group is the Philippine Benevolent Missionaries Association, Inc. (PBMA), founded by "the Divine Master," Ruben Ecleo Sr., in 1967. PBMA dominates the provincial politics of the Dinagat Islands and exerts considerable influence in northern Mindanao. Family divisions among Ruben senior's successors, including the fact that Ruben junior is in hiding to escape a murder conviction, have somewhat weakened their monopoly in local politics. In 2013, for instance, Kaka Bag-ao, who is not affiliated with the family or the church, was elected congressional representative in 2013 and 2016. Still, after the 2016 elections, the Ecleos claimed governor, vice governor, and three of the seven municipal mayor positions in the province but in 2019 Bag-ao won as governor.

The continuing relevance of religion in politics can be seen in the fact that the Philippines prohibits divorce, a distinction it shares only with the Vatican City State. The notable exception is for Muslims, under the Code of Muslim Personal Law of the Philippines. The Catholic Church opposes legalizing divorce despite Catholics' majority opinion in surveys that it should be legalized. The INC shares this anti-divorce position. While a bill to legalize divorce passed the House of Representatives in 2018, its fate is uncertain—not only in the Senate but also with the president. Duterte has repeatedly declared his opposition to divorce, though his marriage was legally annulled—a tedious civil process approved by the Catholic Church—and his current relationship is with a common-law wife.

What is the role of local governments?

The Philippines has long had a decentralized political structure, as factions strove for power in particular localities and national power was acquired by building coalitions among these factions. Given the lack of strong political party organizations (see "What political parties are important?" in this chapter), such coalitions are unstable. Throughout the post-World War II period national elites tried to overcentralize public administration: almost all public works programs at the local level were planned and funded by national government departments, civil servants reported to Manila rather than the elected local governments in which they served, and financial resources for local governance were limited. Public administration specialists decried excessive centralization, while political scientists characterized politics as decentralized.

The issue of decentralization came into greater balance with the 1991 Local Government Code, passed at the end of the administration of Corazon Aquino. President Aquino felt that decentralization was part of her anti-dictatorship mandate and persuaded Congress to pass a law providing more powers and money to levels of local government: the *barangays* (villages), municipalities, cities, and provinces. Local governments retained their existing structure, which consisted of a provincial governor or a municipal/city mayor, a vice governor or vice mayor, and a *sanggunian* (provincial or local council) with directly elected members and indirectly elected representatives of the *Kabataang Barangay* (youth sector) and *barangay* captains.

The major administrative functions that devolved were agriculture, health, environmental protection, and social welfare. Basic education, including secondary schooling, is the largest component of the national government budget and was not devolved. Some prosperous localities do support tertiary institutions out of their own budget, however.

The 1987 Constitution mandates that there be one national police force, civilian in character, and the Philippine National Police (PNP) is to be supervised by the National Police Commission (NAPOLCOM). However, under the PNP reorganization law passed in 1998, provincial governors and the mayors of cities and municipalities are deputies of the NAPOLCOM and have "operational supervision and control" over day-to-day police operations.

In general, along with the staff moved to the localities, considerable new financial resources were sent down, approximately quadrupling as a portion of government spending, so that local government support is one-sixth of the national budget. Fiscal transfers are fixed and calculated by a formula that is based on national government taxes, and the localities know by the middle of the year how much they will receive. As the fiscal year is the calendar, this allows localities to budget for the coming year. The Local Government Code also increased taxing powers of localities—real property taxes, business licensing, and the like. But local elected officials are reluctant to raise taxes on their voters, so locally generated revenues are only significant in cities with greater economic activity. Provinces and municipalities are overwhelmingly dependent on the Internal Revenue Allotment (IRA), as the fiscal transfer is called. The IRA is automatic; the Supreme Court has ruled that past attempts to reduce it (e.g., during the Asian financial crisis) are unconstitutional. So planning has gone from submitting a wish list to national government before the Code, to a possibly rational exercise of spending money under local government control. Nonetheless, there is wishful thinking among local officials about what the national government might support.

The results of the decentralization experience of a quarter of a century are decidedly mixed, as there are different outcomes in different places and service sectors. Local governments complain that national agencies still control the large projects. For instance, the Department of Social Welfare and Development runs its conditional cash transfer project directly and tries to insulate it from local politics. Additionally, the Department of Agriculture undertakes national crop promotion projects, while utilizing local government's extension agents. Expensive services such as healthcare tend to be neglected at the local level, and sometimes hospitals are "renationalized" so that the national Department of Health bears the costs. The extreme fragmentation of local governance—81 provinces, 145 cities, 1,489 municipalities—means economies of scale in service delivery or economic activity, and coverage of an entire ecological unit, such as a watershed, are generally impossible to achieve.

Perhaps most tellingly, the democratic promise of decentralization has not been fulfilled. A number of structures were built into the Code to encourage citizen participation at the local level, but they have not flourished. There are *barangay* assemblies twice a year, local development councils with at least one-fourth of the members from civil society for planning purposes, local health boards or local school boards, and the like. But these often do not work as intended, because organizational density is low in many parts of the country and, more important, because of the influence of locally powerful officials.

Local political families have become more entrenched over the years (see "Is the Philippines a 'cacique democracy'?" in chapter 2) Increased local finances are a resource for clans' election and perpetuation in power, with the term limits in the 1987 Constitution being avoided by having another family member serve for a term or two. The anti-dynasty provision of the Constitution was never implemented, as it lacks congressional legislation. Some localities are lively democracies, while others are under the control of single families, which are sometimes benevolent, but often not. The variation across localities, or among development outcomes, irks those who wish for uniformly good results, but it is to be expected in an extensive archipelago.

What are the roles and limitations of civil society?

The Philippines has a robust civil society, with over a quarter of a million registered organizations that are not overtly political, government, or for-profit. Many of these are primarily self-funded self-help organizations, such as associations of jeepney and tricycle operators and drivers, market vendors, or homeowners. The regulatory environment is quite permissive, requiring minimal reporting to the Securities and Exchange Commission or other government agencies such as the Cooperative Development Authority, the Department of Social Work and Development, the Department of Labor and Employment, or the Housing and Land Use Regulatory Board. It must be noted that contributions or donations to such organizations are generally not tax-deductible for individuals, given the simplified income taxation system. Corporations are allowed to deduct contributions to organizations that the Bureau of Internal Revenue certifies as having "donee" status. The Philippine Council for NGO Certification, an innovative self-regulatory body set up by civil society networks, has certified a few hundred of the more established, larger, non-stock nonprofits.

Many organizations, such as the Philippine Rural Reconstruction Movement, emerged in the 1950s and have a social service orientation. But certain civil society organizations began to acquire a distinctly political edge in the late 1960s and during the authoritarian interlude. Elite members of the corporate establishment in the early 1980s helped to revive the National Movement for Free Elections (NAMFREL) and to establish the Makati Business Club to try to curb political and economic abuses by the administration of Ferdinand Marcos. After the 1986 "People Power" Revolution that ousted President Marcos, "development-oriented non-government organizations" (NGOs) flourished, as restrictions on free speech and the media were loosened. Additionally, both official and unofficial funding came in from overseas as part of the celebration of the global wave of democratization. During this time, civil society work became a reasonable career option for the young educated middle-class in a slow-growth economy.

In 1991, eleven nationwide networks formed the Caucus of Development NGO Networks (CODE-NGO) and encouraged the formation of local equivalents, the largest of which is MinCODE (the Mindanao Coalition of Development NGO Networks). Often, "cause-oriented" NGOs were specialized, supporting "sectors" such as women, children, indigenous peoples, Muslims, and the like. For decades, civil society activity among Muslims was muted by the activism associated with the separatist fronts. But as peace processes progressed and Muslim activists became more involved in politics and governance, Muslim civil society became almost as robust as that among the majority of Filipinos.

Political trends within civil society intensified in the 1990s. The Communist Party's 1992 "reaffirming" of the basic tenets of its Maoist approach to armed revolution from the countryside led to a split in many cause-oriented NGOs in which communists and non-communists had mixed, with the latter being willing to cooperate with the newly democratized government. Thus, there can be pairs of organizations pursuing the same type of advocacy (e.g., human rights) but with differing political goals, and these may collaborate with relevant government institutions or alternatively organize against the government.

At the presidential level, both the Cory Aquino administration (1986–1992) and the Fidel Ramos (1992–1998) administration emphasized democratization. In pursuing peace and fighting poverty, they favored a bottom-up process with institutionalized civic channels in the National Anti-Poverty Commission and the Office of the Presidential Advisor on the Peace Process. Later on, in 1998, many cause-oriented activists supported the candidacy of Joseph Estrada, particularly because of his perceived anti-Americanism. President Estrada won and acknowledged civil society by giving the head of CODE-NGO a cabinet position. His presidency was disappointing, however, and the former leader of CODE-NGO resigned in disgust after slightly more than a year in the face of Estrada's corrupt activities.

Civil society was active in the 2001 "People Power II" overthrow of President Estrada, and the newly installed president Gloria Macapagal-Arroyo welcomed nonprofit professionals into her administration. Again, these "crossover" leaders from NGOs to governmental positions were disillusioned by political machinations and corruption. Such appointees resigned en masse in July 2005 in the wake of evidence of election rigging by President Macapagal-Arroyo as she sought a full term in 2004. Several of these leaders once again entered politics in the 2010–2016 administration of President Benigno S. "Noynoy" Aquino III. They tended to last for Noynoy's entire term, and many are now part of the opposition to the administration of President Duterte.

Civil society actors often have an outsized perception of their importance to politics and governing. Cause-oriented NGOs have considerable experience lobbying the executive or legislative branches about violence against women, human trafficking, violations of human rights such as forced disappearances, reproductive rights, protection of the environment, the rights of children, and more. Keeping issues such as these in the public eye is a valuable service, and policy entrepreneurs can help marshal coalitions to produce executive orders or laws. But in the end, it is politicians and elected officials who enact the rules.

While individual leaders may be active, civil society tends not to involve organizations in politics since direct intervention generally disadvantages an organization. Either the favored politician wins office, in which case organizational support is discounted in comparison with electoral machinery, or the disfavored candidate wins, in which case there can be retaliation against the organization. In short, engaging in politics tends to result in an official who is either an ingrate or an enemy.

On the flip side, getting involved in civil society can be to the advantage of Filipino politicians. Recognizing the post-1986 potential of NGOs, some politicians have set up their own nonprofits, either to capture service delivery funding or to help influence "participatory" democracy. Shell NGOs were at the heart of the "pork barrel" scandal that erupted in 2013, for instance. The organization was established as a mechanism for directing funds, sharing the money between the originators of the scheme and cooperating legislators.

A persistent line of attack is to characterize certain NGOs as "communist fronts." But this reasoning ignores the fact that espousing communism is no longer a crime, as the Anti-Subversion Law was repealed in 1992. It also exposes named organizations to the threat of human rights violations, including assassination, conducted in the course of counterinsurgency against the New People's Army.

What are the roots, extent, and effects of corruption?

The Philippines is almost always in the bottom half of the ranking of countries on Transparency International's Corruption Perception Index. The only exception was in 2014, several years into the administration of President Noynoy Aquino, who won on the slogan "if no corruption, no poverty." Unfortunately, 2014 was also the year when both congressional "pork barrel" spending and innovative executive branch budgetary processes were revealed to the public. After that, the ranking went into yearly decline, reaching the sixty-first percentile in 2017. While Transparency International's global index is based largely on the judgment of non-Filipinos, the

Philippine citizenry tends to agree. Surveys of citizens show dissatisfaction with the anti-corruption efforts of national administrations for decades, until the advent of the Noynoy Aquino administration, but satisfaction flagged after 2014. A divide between the conclusions of the two sources arose during the early part of the Duterte administration. While the Transparency International index continued to decline, Filipinos were satisfied with President Duterte's efforts against corruption because he often abruptly fired officials when they were accused of anomalies.

The problem of corruption is long standing. Most Filipinos know the expression "what are we in power for" to be the attitude of corrupt officials, elected or bureaucratic. This stems from a 1949 report on a meeting involving then Senate president José Avelino and President Carlos Quirino, who were factional rivals in the new Liberal Party. Avelino glibly asked Quirino about investigations into irregularities in the disposal of surplus US war materials: "Why did you have to order an investigation, honourable Mr. President? If you cannot permit abuses, you must at least tolerate them. What are we in power for?" It should be noted that the accuracy of this story has been disputed, but the quote still circulates widely.

Many lay explanations tend to center on the Hispanic or Catholic heritage of the Philippines, suggesting that the Philippines is more like allegedly corrupt countries in Latin America than like those in Asia, especially Singapore. This line of argument suffers from the same sort of weaknesses as the "damaged culture" argument (see the discussion in "What are Filipino Values?" in Chapter 4), ignoring the role of institutional arrangements in shaping behavior. Bribery has not seeped into day-to-day citizen interactions with government; citizens do not have to pay to enroll their children in public schools or to go to the rural health unit. But corruption hurts overall social service delivery as resources are drained from the bureaucracy, harms the business climate, and is a constant feature of political discourse. All sides accuse the others of corruption, often credibly, generating citizen cynicism and failing to address the structural issues.

Over the years, many reform formulas have been tried. Repeatedly, in the Philippines as elsewhere in the world, it has been demonstrated that reducing bureaucratic corruption in particular agencies, or in particular cities, is possible. With the cooperation of the leaders at the top and in partnership with citizens, businesses, and NGOs, change can be made. For instance, during the Noynoy Aquino administration, corruption was reduced in road development projects funded by the national government, since the secretary of the Department of Public Works and Highways focused on squeezing out graft and waste. There was much less improvement in infrastructure funded by local governments, however.

Successes have occurred in the procurement of health supplies or in the provision of school textbooks. But isolated successful reform does not yet seem to touch political corruption, as seen in the continued pervasiveness of money politics and the consequent need to raise funds in illicit ways. The drumbeat of anti-corruption rhetoric continues as each electoral faction uses it against the other, without any sustained improvement occurring or, indeed, any malefactors going to jail.

Analyst Michael Johnston addresses the institutional logic of political corruption involving clans as the political organizing mechanism (rather than, say, institutionalized political parties).[6] This type of corruption process is the most harmful to economic growth because the decisions or policies of one administration can be arbitrarily overturned by a subsequent one. Even within presidential administrations, one faction can take over—for instance, a department or a house of Congress— and use an anti-corruption platform for the next electoral cycle rather than envisioning results-oriented policymaking.

The medium- to long-term prescription is rooted in the need to change the relationship between citizens and their elected officials. Currently voters tend to reward particular favors, from purchased votes to paid health expenses, rather than effective performance in managing government and delivering service. Johnston suggests an "indicator and benchmark" strategy that focuses on services important to people (for example, education or health) develops indicators of good performance, publishes results against benchmarks, and helps citizens hold officials accountable. Johnston proposes to "deepen democracy" in order to empower citizens to hold government accountable against objective measurements. Put this way, reducing both the demand for and supply of corruption could take decades.

6

GEOPOLITICS AND
THE FUTURE

THE PHILIPPINES IN THE WORLD

For the Philippines, it seems that geography is often destiny.
The islands' location, rather than the resources they held, was
what made them attractive to the Spanish imperial enterprise.
While the Spanish tried but failed to get to the Spice Islands,
they ended up more or less controlling the Philippine archipelago and using Manila as an entrepôt for the exchange of
New World silver for Chinese goods. At the end of the nineteenth century, the Philippines' geographic location again
made it attractive, this time to the American imperial project.
During the American period, it became obvious that Japan
would be interested in the archipelago, and after World War II,
the American bases were key installations in the Cold War and
in the shooting war in Vietnam. Currently, the South China Sea
is a prominent zone of contention.

This is the geopolitical context within which we look
to the future, including climate change and the Duterte
administration's domestic agenda.

What is the recent history of military alliances
and shifting alignments?

As the term of President Corazon C. Aquino came to an end,
negotiations with the United States reached completion, and
the Philippines promised ten more years of allowing American

military facilities on the islands. However, in September 1991, the Philippine Senate voted 12–11 not to ratify the agreement, and American forces withdrew from the naval facilities in Subic Bay, having earlier been driven out of Clark Air Base by its total destruction in the June 1991 eruption of Mount Pinatubo.

While this political move was an assertion of Philippine sovereignty, its immediate effect was to deprive the Philippines of military capability for external defense. Without US forces running routine patrols from Subic Naval Base and Clark Air Base, it was Filipino fishermen who alerted authorities to Chinese activities on Mischief Reef in 1995. The Armed Forces of the Philippines were overwhelmingly focused on internal security and lacked air and sea assets for territorial defense. While a modernization program was established—privatization of Fort Bonifacio into Bonifacio Global City began in 1995 to provide some funding—the Philippines remains less equipped than its ASEAN neighbors and the major powers involved in the region: China, the United States, Australia, and Japan.

The alliance structure with the United States began to be revitalized with the Visiting Forces Agreement (VFA), which was duly ratified by the Philippine Senate and entered into force in May 1999. This was followed by the Enhanced Defense Cooperation Agreement in 2014, and in 2016, the Supreme Court ruled that the agreement did not require Senate approval. These agreements govern the rules for US forces in the Philippines—no combat, for instance—and give the United States permission to construct storage facilities on Philippine bases to pre-position supplies for disaster response, training exercises, and rapid deployment. A status of visiting forces agreement (SOVFA) with Australia was ratified by the Senate in 2012. Less formal arrangements have been made with Japan, which used Official Development Assistance to provide ten vessels to the Philippine Coast Guard.

The Philippines gained increased attention from the United States when two American missionaries were among a group kidnapped by the Abu Sayyaf in May 2001. In January 2002, the United States deployed a Joint Special Operations Task Force to help train, assist, and supply the Philippine military for its fight against the Abu Sayyaf on Basilan and Sulu Islands. Approximately six hundred US troops were in country at any given time, on maximum six-month rotation since permanent stationing of troops was not allowed under the VFA. This operation lasted until January 2015, and a similar operation began in late 2017 after militants linked to Islamic State held Marawi City for five months.

The Philippines seemingly became part of the post-9/11 "global war on terror." However, in July 2004, the Philippines withdrew a small contingent of sixty troops sent to Iraq in 2003 as part of the US-led "coalition of the willing." They made this retreat in order to meet the demands of Iraqi insurgents who had kidnapped a Filipino civilian truck driver. This episode illustrates another geopolitical reality for the Philippines; the presence of OFWs in every corner of the globe inevitably affects the foreign policy of the country, as protecting the workers is a formal pillar of Philippine foreign policy.

Territorial tensions between the Philippines and China in the South China Sea brought the United States and the Philippines into closer alliance under the Noynoy Aquino administration. The Philippines acquired surplus US Coast Guard cutters to bolster its maritime activities. The country also pursued its case against China at the Permanent Court of Arbitration (PCA). But just as the PCA announced its ruling in favor of the Philippines, the Duterte administration was inaugurated.

President Duterte presided over what seemed to be an abrupt change in geopolitical stance when he declined to follow up on the arbitral tribunal's decision and instead launched a charm offensive toward China. He also cursed President Barack Obama for remarks he had made about human rights, publicly chided the United States for its counter-insurgency actions at the beginning of the twentieth century, and professed his admiration for Russian president Vladimir Putin.

The Philippine defense establishment disagreed with this change, and Defense Secretary Delfin Lorenzana persuaded the president to allow continued joint military exercises with the United States. Top-level chemistry improved considerably with the inauguration of US president Donald Trump, who in a 2017 phone call praised the "unbelievable" job President Duterte was doing in his bloody "War on Drugs." At the same time, China is wooing the Philippines, promising billions of dollars in loans for infrastructure projects. The discussions raise the prospect of a "debt trap," but in any case the projects have been slow to materialize.

The Philippines is engaged in the classic "hedging" behavior of a small power in the presence of powerful outside actors. The Philippines swung quite far into the American camp under President Noynoy Aquino, but the previous Macapagal-Arroyo administration had attempted to arrange joint resource exploration with China in the West Philippine Sea. These efforts were abandoned in the face of domestic Philippine opposition. Japan remains the Philippines's largest donor of official development assistance, and the United States and Australia retain robust security and development assistance programs. On the other hand, even Defense Secretary Lorenzana, who has called the US alliance the "biggest strength of the Philippines," wondered aloud if the 1951 Mutual Defense Treaty needed to be revisited for its relevance in current conditions.

This multifaceted behavior may exasperate many, but one product is undeniable. After decades of discussion over their status as war trophies, the Bells of Balangiga have been returned to the Philippines (see figure 6.1). Clearly, the United States was motivated to show good faith in what it sees as the long-term partnership between the countries.

What is the situation in the South China Sea?

The South China Sea contains some of the busiest sea lanes in the world, productive fisheries, and proven oil resources. And

Figure 6.1 Balangiga bells returned to the Philippines

Source: Gigi Cruz (ABS-CBN News), https://news.abs-cbn.com/focus/12/16/18/slideshow-the-balangiga-bells-are-home (accessed March 28, 2019)

it is one of the most disputed areas of the sea in the world. The Philippines bases its claims in the area on international law, while China asserts historical rights.

Under the United Nations Convention on the Law of the Sea (UNCLOS), an "island" is a sea feature above water at high tide that is capable of sustaining human life or economic activity; in practice, it must have fresh water. A "rock" is land permanently above water but unable to support life on its own. A "low-tide elevation" is above water only at low tide. These features have differing entitlements to sovereignty, territorial waters, and exclusive economic zones. And artificial islands in the area, which China has constructed by dredging up sand onto coral reefs and then cementing the results, do not count as "islands"; only natural formations count.

However, the claims of China are not based on UNCLOS but on a claim that the area has long been a part of China. The specific version of the claim was first put forward by the

Nationalist Kuomintang government in 1947, with a map showing eleven dashes encompassing the entire South China Sea and labeling these "Chinese Islands in the South China Sea." The new People's Republic of China took up the claim in a slightly revised fashion, issuing a nine-dash line document in 1949. In the overall area, Taiwan and the People's Republic of China agree on the extent of the claim, though the precise coordinates of the lines on the map have never been articulated. But the claim is contested by the Philippines, Malaysia, Indonesia, and Vietnam.

In 2012, the Philippine government began officially calling its exclusive economic zone (EEZ) the "West Philippine Sea" after disputes with China had begun to heat up. Previously, the Philippines protested Chinese structures built on stilts on Mischief Reef (Panganiban Reef), discovered by Filipino fishermen in 1995. Mischief Reef is one of the seven artificial islands built by China in the last few years and is now equipped with an airfield.

The current round of disputes stems from April 2012, when a Philippine Coast Guard vessel found that Chinese fishing vessels at Scarborough Shoal (alternative names: Panatag Shoal and Bajo de Masinloc) had harvested protected species. Chinese vessels then interposed themselves to prevent arrest of the fishermen. Both sides protested diplomatically since both claim the area; they withdrew their protests, and the fishermen were allowed to leave along with their catch. The Philippines objected that Chinese vessels were harassing an archaeological research vessel, while the Chinese objected to Filipino and French researchers diving to a Chinese wreck. With bad weather approaching, the United States used its good offices to negotiate a stand-down, but when the Philippines withdrew, the Chinese did not. The Chinese continue to exert effective control in the area. Since President Duterte launched his effort at rapprochement with China, Filipino fishermen have once again gained access, though stories of harassment continue to surface.

Realizing that its armed forces were no match for the Chinese, and that its treaty ally, the United States, takes no position on sovereignty over islands in the region,[1] the Philippines brought a case before the Permanent Court of Arbitration in 2013. China, for its part, refused to participate. In July 2016, just days after Rodrigo Duterte had been inaugurated as president, the arbitral tribunal issued a ruling stating that under UNCLOS, historical claims do not establish sovereignty or rights over exploitation of resources. There is a provision in UNCLOS about traditional fishing grounds, and the tribunal held that Vietnamese, Chinese, and Filipino fisherfolk were all entitled to exploit Scarborough Shoal.

China rejected the tribunal's ruling as null, and the Duterte administration has decided not to press the advantage afforded by the decision. There has been considerable talk about cooperation between China and the Philippines, and China has been negotiating a code of conduct with ASEAN for the South China Sea, but neither effort has yet borne fruit.

Tensions flare periodically in the area as China objects to other countries treating the South China Sea as international waters. China is particularly incensed by overflights by American aircraft and freedom of navigation operations by the US Navy. In addition, China objects to the Philippines strengthening the nine features that the Philippines occupies in the area, ranging from Pag-asa (Thitu) Island—home to one hundred civilians and forty soldiers—to the BRP (Barko ng Republika ng Pilipinas, ship of the Republic of the Philippines) *Sierra Madre*, grounded in 1999 on Ayungin (Second Thomas Shoal), with a platoon of marines living on it.

Philippine public opinion is firmly against China and opposes how the Duterte administration is approaching the dispute. But perhaps the issue is not very salient; President Duterte's satisfaction ratings remain high. Elements within the Philippine establishment argue vigorously against the Chinese position, asserting that features like Scarborough Shoal have always been part of the Philippines—hence the Spanish name, *Bajo de Masinloc.*

What is the Sabah claim?

One of the long-running difficulties of Philippine foreign relations is the territory of Sabah, which is claimed by both the Philippines and Malaysia. The Philippine government claims Sabah as the successor-in-interest to the sultan of Sulu. Depending on the version of the agreement being used, the dispute dates back to Sabah's lease by or cession to the British North Borneo Company in 1878 by the sultan of Sulu. Since the formation of the Federation of Malaysia to include the state of Sabah, the Malaysian government has been paying 5,300 ringgits (currently $1,270) annually, which the Philippines regards as "rent" while Malaysia regards the payment as "cession money."

When the Spanish arrived in the Philippine archipelago in the mid-sixteenth century, the sultan of Brunei considered the sultan of Sulu a vassal, and had a relative, Rajah Sulayman, in Manila. The Spanish conquered Manila in 1571 and in 1578 attacked Brunei and briefly occupied Jolo, Sulu. The Spanish were not able to establish effective control of the Sulu Archipelago until the latter part of the nineteenth century, and the Sultanate of Sulu flourished as a maritime raiding and trading entity. In 1658, the sultan of Brunei awarded the northeast coast of Sabah to the sultan of Sulu in return for assistance in a civil war.

In 1878, the Sulu sultan entered into an agreement with the British North Borneo Company, around which the dispute centers. The agreement was written in Malay using Jawi script—that is, the Arabic alphabet. Different translators have yielded different results. The version relied upon by the British, and then the Malaysian governments, states "hereby grant and cede of our own free and sovereign will . . . assigns forever and in perpetuity all the rights and powers belonging to us over all the territories," whereas the version relied upon by the Sultanate of Sulu (and subsequently the Philippine government) states "hereby lease of our own free will and satisfaction . . . assigns forever and until the end of time, all rights and powers which we possess over all the territories." In 1962, the sultan of Sulu, having proclaimed the end of the "lease," transferred rights to the Philippine government, which filed a claim with the British government. When the Malaysian federation was formed in 1963, the Philippine government agreed to a UN Commission of Inquiry into the sentiments of the people, but ultimately rejected the commission's findings that a majority wanted to join Malaysia.

Relations between the two countries on this issue reached a low point in 1968, despite a state visit by Ferdinand and Imelda Marcos in January. In the first half of the year, in a scandal known as the Jabidah incident, the Philippine government recruited Tausugs from Sulu in an attempt to destabilize Sabah. However, the training went awry, and the recruits were massacred on Corregidor where they were training. One lived to tell the tale, and the incident was publicized. In September 1968, the Philippines passed Republic Act 5466, declaring Sabah as part of Philippine territory. Malaysia suspended diplomatic relations for over a year, until December 1969.

Since then, there have been occasional but unsuccessful efforts to settle the matter between the two countries, with Malaysia regarding it as a nonissue to be settled among parties on the Philippine side. Efforts have foundered, as there are divisions among the heirs to the Sultanate of Sulu about the terms of agreement—and domestic political opposition to giving up claims to any Philippine territory. In mid-2018, the Consultative Committee established by President Duterte to recommend changes to the 1987 Constitution insisted that the Philippines "has sovereignty over all territories belonging to the Philippines by historic right or legal title," thereby including Sabah.

The issue flared up in violence in 2013 when armed followers of the sultan of Sulu invaded Sabah. Apparently the attack was staged to draw attention to the fact that the claim was not being considered in the peace talks with the Moro Islamic Liberation Front, which were facilitated by Malaysia. This attack resulted in 56 killed and 149 captured by Malaysian security forces. When asked, most Filipinos in Luzon and the Visayas did not believe that the claims by the Sulu sultan were reasonable, but the balance of opinion in Mindanao was favorable.

The practical effects of the dispute are somewhat more prosaic. There are hundreds of thousands of illegal migrants from the Philippines in Sabah, as well as tens of thousands of legal migrants. The Philippines refuses to open a consulate to assist its citizens in Sabah as Malaysians and some Filipinos in Sabah have urged, since a "consulate" implies that Sabah is part of a different country. The distance makes providing services to the Filipinos—and helping when periodic campaigns by Malaysian authorities expel tens of thousands of illegal Filipino workers—difficult for the Philippine embassy in Kuala Lumpur.

How badly would the Philippines be affected by climate change?

Given that the Philippines is disaster prone already, the consensus is that the country would be seriously affected by the storms, droughts, and rising sea levels that climate change is predicted to bring about. Studies rank the Philippines among one of the top five or top three countries to be impacted by global warming. For sea-level rise alone, one study placed the Philippines as the most affected country, in particular due to storm surge. The long coastline and the fact that most municipalities and cities are located on the coast increases vulnerability, as does uncontrolled groundwater extraction—meaning that inhabited coastal areas are sinking.

The effects of climate change, it is often said, are already apparent. In 2013, it was brought to the attention of the Conference of the Parties global climate negotiations that Tacloban City was the scene of terrible devastation when typhoon Haiyan (known locally as Yolanda) killed thousands of people with rain, wind, and a deadly storm surge. The head of the Philippine delegation blamed global warming for the intensity of the storm. It was one of the strongest on record globally, but it must be remembered that twice before, in 1898 and 1912, Tacloban had been hit by storms that caused thousands of deaths. The bathymetry of Leyte Gulf (the contours and depths of the seabed in various places) seems to amplify the magnitude of storm surges, adding to the difficulty of disentangling "weather" and "climate."

The Philippines has the thirteenth largest population in the world, but only the thirty-eighth largest economy in nominal dollars, and twenty-eighth when purchasing power is taken into account. Its contribution to the accumulation of greenhouse gases is only about 0.4 percent of the global total. Still, climate campaigners focus on reducing this amount further, to considerable controversy. Renewable energy, namely wind and solar, is entitled to a fixed tariff when transmitting to the grid, and all electrical consumers pay for the subsidy, which is increasing in amount over time. In contradiction, government plans for increased reliability and reduced cost of electricity involve a considerable increase in coal-fired power plants, making it harder to reach goals of reducing greenhouse gases.

The Philippines ratified the Paris Agreement in early 2017, after some complaints from President Duterte. He opined that the "nationally determined contribution" of a 70 percent reduction from "business as usual" by 2030 (a plan specified by the previous administration) would hamper economic growth. The country was aiming to revise the goal according to the 2020 timetable of the Paris Agreement—with climate campaigners urging more action and those focused on economic growth urging caution.

In any case, the Philippines is focusing on the harmful effects that climate change may bring. The 2013 disaster caused by typhoon Haiyan (Yolanda) highlighted the urgency of action. In 2018, the Philippine Commission on Human Rights began hearings on a complaint filed by Greenpeace against large companies, alleging that their emissions interfere "with the enjoyment of Filipinos' fundamental rights." Later, at the 2018 Conference of the Parties, the Philippine delegation vigorously advocated for "climate justice" for vulnerable countries.

There is a Climate Change Commission, established in 2009, that coordinates the Philippine government response, and the 2017–2022 Philippine Development Plan has climate resiliency and adaptation as considerations throughout the document (such plans are always synchronized with the president's term). Given the decentralized nature of Philippine government under the 1991 Local Government Code, particular emphasis is on assisting localities with adaptation projects. This was mandated in a 2012 law establishing the People's Survival Fund (PSF). In 2018, the PSF began giving grants to localities that would match the funding.

The archipelagic nature of the country, the fragile state of its environment—including the coral reefs, now under increased danger of bleaching due to ocean warming—and deficiencies in disaster preparedness bode ill for the country. Yet many in civil society, government, and the wider policy community are aware of the issues, and steps have been taken. Thus, on balance, the Philippines is probably in the same boat as the rest of the world.

How likely is Duterte to realize his political platform?

As often happens in Philippine politics, the election of the colorful (to put it mildly) Duterte had little to do with political parties or issues. As a populist, Duterte did not have a detailed political campaign platform. He began his initial pre-campaign forays nationwide as an advocate of federalism, but did not have a particular model in mind: "It could be the US Electoral College, or like in France, where only the president is nationally elected and everyone else represents a local or limited territory. Indonesia is a federal parliament, Australia and New Zealand too. Singapore, Japan, and Malaysia are likewise federal parliaments."*

His signature campaign theme became the "War on Drugs" in particular and being tough on crime in general. Though the crime rate in the Philippines had gone down for several years, citizen fear of crime and of drugs increased. Candidate Duterte successfully played up a sense of crisis. His rhetoric dehumanizing drug addicts—claiming that their brains had shrunk and that they did not really have human rights—is a classic populist tactic of designating an enemy of the public and expecting the public to support the strongman who is defending them.

His team put together a "10-point Socioeconomic Agenda" before the June 30, 2016, inauguration. The list was conventional: macroeconomic policies, tax reform, infrastructure spending, agricultural development, promoting science and technology, and social protection. This was duly put into the draft State of the Nation Address for the opening of Congress and then helped give direction to medium-term (i.e., the six-year presidency) development planning process. Eventually, it was noticed that this agenda did not include crime, the one issue that the president did indeed care about. So, the agenda became the "Zero to 10-Point Agenda," in which "zero" was peace and order, the "bedrock that has to be addressed."

In general, President Duterte delegates the substantive running of government to his cabinet secretaries while he focuses most of his rhetorical energy on crime and security issues, as well as political and social opposition entities, including the media. While a legislative agenda is theoretically on offer, not

---

* It is to be noted that of this list, only the United States, Australia, and Malaysia are federal states.

much political capital is expended. A package of tax reforms was designed by the Department of Finance (e.g., simplification and lowering income taxes, raising excise taxes, reducing tax incentives, etc.). But the first tranche was somewhat watered down in 2017, and the subsequent comprehensive follow-up stalled. Even the reinstatement of the death penalty, something to which the president has a strong rhetorical commitment, did not go through the Congress that Duterte supposedly dominates. A number of his cabinet nominees were not approved by Congress, including those who initially had been nominated by the Left and those who angered powerful interests.

Duterte walks and talks a fine line with respect to the bloody "War on Drugs." He promised during the campaign to fatten the fish of Manila Bay with the casualties of the "War on Drugs." But he has tried to maintain some distance from the unofficial estimate that over twenty thousand people had been killed by 2018. His administration points to much lower numbers, but these are still in the thousands. This is also the count that the police admit to, with the rest being classified as "deaths under investigation." Duterte has rejected advice to treat the drug problem as a public health issue rather than a national security issue. Given that the bulk of the effort is directed at small-time drug users, and little at syndicates and big-time protectors, it seems unlikely that he would be able to achieve much progress in stemming the drug epidemic. The effort may not actually be aimed at eliminating drugs but rather at demonstrating prowess and, as political scientists say, the monopoly of the legitimate use of violence.

What Duterte brings to the political scene is not a substantive agenda, but rather a strongman, patriarchal, transgressive style. He bridles at any checks on his freedom of action, demanding the resignation of officials who have security of tenure, lashing out, often in vulgar terms, at both international and domestic actors who criticize him, and bringing the informal action-oriented style of a city mayor to the national stage. A senator was jailed, and a chief justice of the Supreme Court was ousted. Attempts to intimidate the independent media include legal actions such as threats to franchises or tax investigations, but as well as extralegal attacks in social media. His musings about pollution in Boracay tourist resorts or the social effects of men being "half-naked" in poor area communities of Metro Manila translated into six-month closure of the island and police citations issued to tens of thousands of shirtless men going about their daily lives in poor communities.

Some institutions, particularly the police, follow such initiatives with alacrity, while others, such as the military, take a more measured approach, asking for written guidance or undertaking independent analysis of policies. Many citizens are clearly willing to endorse a more authoritarian style, as evidenced by honeymoon levels of public satisfaction with President Duterte throughout the first half of his term and the continued political good fortunes of the Marcos clan, including the near-victory of Ferdinand "Bongbong" Marcos Jr. in the 2016 vice presidential race.

Even before he formally declared for president, Duterte mused in public about declaring a "revolutionary government," and throughout his first year in office he repeatedly floated the notion of invoking martial law. Eventually, insurgents' takeover of Marawi City in May 2017 provoked a declaration of martial law for all of Mindanao, and martial law was renewed even after fighting stopped. Duterte's openly expressed admiration of Marcos's authoritarian interlude and the burial of the late strongman in the Heroes' Cemetery (Libingan ng mga Bayani) has led to widespread suspicion that he has an authoritarian agenda.

Peering into a crystal ball to read the future, authoritarianism seems not to be an agenda in itself. Rather, Duterte is allying with the Marcoses and others to pursue the goal of all presidents once their term is over: to stay out of jail. Duterte's task in this respect is complicated by the fact that the International Criminal Court has opened a preliminary investigation of the situation in the Philippines with respect to the "War on Drugs"—an investigation that will not be halted by the decision by the Duterte administration to withdraw the Philippines from the ICC.

Will there be amendments to the Constitution for federalism or economics?

Since the Malolos Constitution of 1899 at the beginning of Filipino self-rule, constitutionality has been central to the idea of political legitimacy. After the February 1986 "People Power" ouster of Ferdinand Marcos, Corazon Aquino set in motion the writing of a new constitution, which was ratified in a plebiscite in February 1987. The 1987 Constitution was part of her legacy of restoring democracy to the Philippines, and she duly stepped down in 1992 at the end of a six-year term.

In every administration since then there have been initiatives to amend the Constitution, which in the Philippines is often called "Cha-Cha" (for "Charter Change"). Until Corazon Aquino passed away in 2009, she opposed all such efforts. During President Ramos's term there were efforts in 1997 to remove term limits (so he could continue in office) and perhaps shift to a parliamentary form of government; many officials, such as speakers of the House of Representatives, who could not win a national election, like the idea of a head of government being indirectly elected. A protest movement and a Supreme Court challenge stopped this effort. During Joseph Estrada's shortened term, there was talk of loosening the economically restrictive aspects of the constitution, but constitutional reform was overshadowed by the scandals of his administration.

During the long tenure of Gloria Macapagal-Arroyo (2001–2010), there was a serious Cha-Cha effort, complete with a Consultative Commission appointed in 2005. During this decade there was a growth in academic interest in federalism as an accentuation of the decentralization that had already gone to local government units. Despite the presence of some federalism advocates in the 2005 Consultative Commission, the main recommendation was for a parliamentary system. In the end, this idea had no traction, as the public is opposed to indirect election of the head of government; Filipinos prefer to vote directly for the president.

During his term, President Noynoy Aquino (2010–2016) opposed any Cha-Cha. There is an argument put forth both by economists and the international business community that the economic protectionist features of the 1987 Constitution retard growth. There was some discussion of making "surgical" amendments to the constitution by merely inserting the phrase "except as may be provided by law" into several protectionist provisions, but ultimately no change was made.

In late 2014, as the upcoming May 2016 elections were becoming more relevant, Davao City mayor Rodrigo Duterte met with Federal Advocates for a Better Philippines, and by early 2015 a "Listening Tour of Mayor Rodrigo Roa Duterte to Promote Federalism" was launched. As Duterte toured the country, at various events promoting federalism banners started appearing urging him to run for president. When he filed his candidacy at the very last moment, in December 2015, he announced a "federal structure" as his goal. But his threats to carry out a bloody war on crime got much more attention.

In December 2016, after six months in office, Duterte issued an executive order for a consultative commission to review the 1987 Constitution, but it was only in January 2018 that he appointed the members of the commission. They duly worked until July and turned over a draft constitution to President Duterte for consideration. Economic reform advocates were disappointed that the protectionist provisions of the 1987 Constitution were all still in the commission's draft. When the House of Representatives took up the topic in late 2018, both the federalist and the anti-dynasty provisions were watered down, dismaying the political reformers, though some of the economic provisions were tackled. The senators, whose concurrence is needed for any amendments or new draft to be put to a plebiscite, are not interested in the topic. All having won a nationwide election to be in the upper chamber, many their prospects are good in the current setup, with a nationally elected president and a centralized state.

Prospects for constitutional change do not look bright. In the first place, there is absolutely no public demand for it. No matter how pollsters ask the question, voters have more important things on their minds (including jobs, income, or even the drug problem), little knowledge of the issue, and opposition to most of the ideas that have been put forth. Elected officials are those who have prospered under the current situation and would be uncertain about the effects of any change on their prospects (e.g., would a rival clan gain control of a federal state?). Significant economic elites prosper within the current economic provisions of the constitution and would not necessarily welcome more competition from international commerce.

The only reason that this was even a live question was because of the firm and vocal expression of President Duterte's preferences. However, he was never clear about what details would be changed, and his administration made no sustained push to move the policy through the change process. The May 2019 midterm elections are the starting gun for the May 2022 national election, one in which many significant actors will be eying their chances under the current constitution. Amending the constitution will not be a priority.

What is behind the rise of violent extremism in the Philippines?

In the 2018 Global Terrorism Index the Philippines was ranked the tenth most affected country in the world and the worst ranked country in Southeast Asia; Thailand was seventeenth, Myanmar twenty-fourth, and Indonesia forty-second. This was part of a general upswing in Philippine domestic terrorism incidents over the years, at a time when globally terrorism was in fact declining.

In this accounting, 35 percent of the total deaths were due to the New People's Army (NPA), which introduces the first complication. Is the insurgency waged by the NPA at the direction of the National Democratic Front and Communist Party of the Philippines a terrorist endeavor? In terms of legal designation, the answer is "yes," since both the United States and European Union designated the National Democratic Front and the NPA as terrorist organizations in 2002 at the behest of the Philippine government.

However, the vast majority of deaths caused by the NPA are from attacks on military and government targets, as part of their insurgent activities on the "strategic defensive." Use of "land mines" by the NPA, for instance, is restricted to "command detonation devices" as part of complex ambushes, rather than victim-activated devices. They also engage in "revolutionary taxation"—what the government would regard as theft and extortion—on economic activities in their areas of influence. Enforcement of such taxation frequently involves destroying property if businesses do not pay. Civilians also are victims, sometimes as collateral damage in raids or ambushes or as part of enforcement of political control, but this is not a major characteristic of NPA activity.

In December 2017, in a definitive sign of the breakdown in peace talks that had seemed to be making progress at the beginning of President Duterte's term, the government moved for the first time to designate the CPP-NPA-NDF as a terrorist organization under Philippine law.[2] This would partially roll back the effects of the 1992 repeal of the Anti-Subversion Law, which decriminalized membership in the Communist Party.

Most discussions of violent extremism are about groups who believe themselves inspired by Islam. In the Philippines, the Moro National Liberation Front (MLNF) and the Moro Islamic Liberation Front (MILF) have not been listed as terrorist organizations. The Philippines has always asked the international community that they not be. Some have doubts about connections between the mainstream fronts and terrorists—in particular, elements of the Jemaah Islamiyah. This group is mostly composed of Indonesians fighting for a regional caliphate, and they were located in Mindanao for some years, finding refuge and training opportunities. Beginning in 2003, the MILF sought to prove its negotiating bona fides and cooperated with the Philippine government in the Ad Hoc Joint Action Group, operationalized in 2004. Under this cooperation, the Philippine government informed the MILF about ongoing activities against suspected foreign terrorists, kidnappers, and other criminals. In recent years, cooperation has gotten closer as the MILF helped move civilians out of harm's way during Philippine military operations.

The most internationally notorious terrorist organizations in the Philippines are the Abu Sayyaf and the group led by the Maute brothers. The Abu Sayyaf came to international attention in 2000 when it kidnapped Europeans from a Malaysian resort, received large ransoms, and then kidnapped a group from Palawan in 2001. Three Americans were in this latter group; one was beheaded, one was killed in 2002 in a rescue attempt, and Gracia Burnham managed to survive.

Even more spectacularly, in May 2017, the Islamic City of Marawi (see figure 6.2) was seized by a composite group led by two Maute brothers (educated in the Middle East) from the Lanao Region, and Isnilon Hapilon, an Abu Sayyaf commander who had been designated by Islamic State as the "emir" in the Philippines. Urban warfare lasted five months, with a thousand casualties and the devastation of central Marawi.

Mainstream Muslims, including the MILF, object to labeling these kinds of activities "Islamic terrorism" and those who perpetrate them "Islamic terrorists." These kinds of violent activities are not "Islamic," they argue, and labeling them as such makes things worse by alienating Muslims.

The origins of these groups are often tied to politics rather than theological discussions. The Abu Sayyaf was a 1991

Figure 6.2 ISIS in Islamic City of Marawi

Source: AMAQ https://www.dailymail.co.uk/news/article-4540610/ISIS-militants-shoot-nine-Christians-dead-Philippines.html

breakaway from the MNLF over whether to negotiate with the Philippine government. For years, it has maintained itself by profit-oriented kidnappings in the Sulu Archipelago. A group that is less known internationally is the Bangsamoro Islamic Freedom Fighters (BIFF), which broke away from the MILF after the 2008 MOA-AD debacle. It is based in the large and generally inaccessible Liguasan Marsh in Maguindanao and North Cotabato provinces. These two groups tend to recruit from impoverished rural youth, some of whom seek revenge for relatives killed over the decades of separatist combat.

The Maute brothers and their followers represent a new trend: middle-class youth, often recruited initially due to an interest in Islamic discourse or studies. Recruitment begins in colleges and high schools as promising students are approached in order to gauge if they are potential material. Such activities increased with the 2014 declaration of the ISIS caliphate and the pledge of allegiance by several groups in the Philippines. ISIS legitimized Isnilon Hapilon as emir, which helped him to bring diverse groups to work together across ethnic divides and bridge rural and urban differences. ISIS also sent these groups funding and provided advice about urban warfare. Thus, in May 2017 the ISIS-inspired group was already plotting to take over Marawi when a Philippine government attempt to arrest Hapilon set off the uprising.

By the end of the siege in October 2017, the Maute brothers and Isnilon Hapilon were all dead. Others from the city escaped, and recruitment continues. As witnessed by the decades-long persistence in the Sulu Archipelago of the Abu Sayyaf, or the BIFF in central Mindanao, conditions in the area continue to allow "lawless elements," as they are termed in the Philippines, to survive. The region is the least developed in the country. Particularly after decades of conflict, governance is often poor, with high rates of political violence and corruption; other forms of violence such as drug crime and family feuds are rife; and all of this can lead to reactions to a thoroughly unsatisfactory situation. Hope for an end to long-running insurgencies could help reduce the pool of potential recruits to violent extremism.

It is worth noting that much less is known about the violent extremist threat in other regions of the country. Certainly there have been terrorist incidents in Manila, including the 2004 bombing of a ferry in Manila Bay that killed over one hundred persons. In 2017, just before the Marawi siege, there was a bomb attempt on the life of a Shi'ite preacher in Manila that killed the delivery man and the preacher's aide who was accepting the package. In December 2018, an imam who was known for opposing terrorism and violent extremism was assassinated in Baguio City, in north Luzon. Persons perpetrating these acts are unlikely to be swayed even by successful peace and development in Muslim Mindanao.

Are there prospects for peace in long-running insurgencies?

The communist and Muslim separatist rebellions have been underway, at least sporadically, for almost fifty years. Peace talks with the communists last reached signed agreements in 1998, with little progress since. Agreements with the Moros were reached or almost reached in 1976, 1987, 1996, 2008, and 2014, but none have been fully implemented. President Duterte, as a candidate and after assuming office, was rhetorically committed to both processes, but important obstacles have caused talks with the CPP-NPA-NDF to repeatedly be suspended and have restricted the full implementation of agreements with the organized Moro fronts.

At the beginning of his administration, Duterte appointed several leftists acceptable to the communists to cabinet positions that are important to their lines of advocacy: agrarian reform, social welfare, and the second rank in labor and employment. Congress failed to approve the first two appointments, and in October 2018, as part of the general deterioration in relations, Duterte fired the third.

The president had announced a unilateral ceasefire with the communists in July 2016, and his panel held rounds of talks in Norway in August and October and a third round in Rome in January 2017. However, in February first the NPA and then the government called off their respective ceasefires, leading to a termination of the peace talks.

A fourth round of talks was conducted in April, but a May round was canceled after the NPA ordered intensified attacks in response to Duterte's declaration of martial law in Mindanao due to the Marawi siege. Considerable invective was in the air for the rest of the year, so by the end of 2017, Duterte formally ended the peace talks and began the legal process of declaring the CPP-NPA a terrorist organization. Still, backchannel work on a mutual stand-down of forces resulted in a signed document by June 2018, in preparation for a fifth round of talks, but Duterte ordered the cancellation of the planned talks. It seemed the Philippine security forces were not comfortable with the agreements; while the Armed Forces of the Philippines generally accept the negotiated agreements with the Moro fronts, as an institution, they are implacably anti-communist.

There were rumors at the beginning of 2019 of possible backchannels, but there were also continued arrests of "consultants" to the CPP-NPA-NDF, persons who were above ground and helping with the peace process. The long desultory process since the last signed agreements is once again at an impasse, as the government's peace panel has been dissolved. In the meantime, current political unrest seems to be allowing something of a resurgence in NPA activity, despite military claims to the contrary, as it has once again appeared in provinces previously declared insurgent-free, such as Bohol.

Even if the process issues currently plaguing the peace talks (ceasefire, release of detainees, and terrorist designation) are resolved, the obstacles to a substantive agreement seem insuperable. For instance, in January 2017, the two sides exchanged their drafts of the Comprehensive Agreement on Social and Economic Reforms (CASER). The draft by the National Democratic Front is far from the long-standing consensus on the Philippine economy as it proposes to amend or terminate all international trade agreements, impose capital controls, limit retail trade to Filipinos, nationalize (in the sense of state ownership) external trade and public utilities (power, water, mass transportation, telecommunications) and mining, and so on. The government panel, in contrast, proposed to "review, using the criterion of fairness and development impact . . . the country's trade liberalization policy." Granted, there was goodwill between the two panels; the proposals almost agreed on the key issue of agrarian reform. Overall there is still a yawning gap between the two stances. In this regard, it is not only the security forces that object to communism, but also the economic managers that President Duterte has entrusted with his policies.

The prospects for peace with the mainline Muslim insurgent groups look much better. In 2018, the implementing legislation for the 2014 Comprehensive Agreement on the Bangsamoro was finally passed under the administration of Duterte, the first president to hail from Mindanao. Ratified by a plebiscite in January 2019, it replaces the Autonomous Region in Muslim Mindanao with a new Bangsamoro Autonomous Region in Muslim Mindanao (BARMM). This will be led by the MILF (joined by most elements of the MNLF, with the exception of founding chair Misuari) for a three-year transition period before having an elected parliamentary form of government (unique within the Philippines) in 2022.

While the organic law does not follow all the provisions of the Comprehensive Agreement, it increases the powers and resources granted to the autonomous government. The MILF agreed that the process of decommissioning its forces will now begin. It is not envisioned that MILF fighters will be absorbed into the Philippine security forces. Rather, the arms of the fighters will be "put beyond use" under the supervision of an independent decommissioning body made up of international and Philippine members. The fighters themselves are supposed to be assisted to transition to civilian lives through livelihood training and support, and MILF camps are supposed to be developed into civilian communities.

Success in this latest initiative will bring the major Moro fronts into the fold. The pool of recruits for violent extremism will grow smaller, both because the value of nonviolent means has been demonstrated and because it affirms the value of Muslims in the Philippines.

NOTES

Chapter 1

1. Mary Rose C. Posa, Arvin C. Diesmos, Navjot S. Sodhi, and Thomas M. Brooks, "Hope for Threatened Tropical Biodiversity: Lessons from the Philippines," *BioScience* 58, no. 3 (March 2008): 231–240, p. 231.
2. There are also some varieties of "Manila Bay Creole," but these are either extinct or have very few speakers.
3. He was subsequently appointed secretary of interior and local government, but died in a plane crash in 2012.

Chapter 2

1. Vincent J. H. Houben, "Southeast Asia and Islam," *Annals of the American Academy of Political and Social Science* 588 (July 2003): 149–170, p. 153.
2. To be sure, Enrile later retracted this statement.
3. After the return of the Balangiga bells in December 2018, US ambassador to the Philippines Sun Kim wrote that "the unique strength of the Philippine-US relationship lies in the deep, longstanding bonds between our peoples. The human connection between us is unbreakable, linking our two nations' past, present, and future." https://www.rappler.com/thought-leaders/219405-philippines-united-states-friendship-rings-stronger-2018 (accessed December 23, 2018).
4. "Homage to Imelda's Shoes," *BBC News*, February 16, 2001. http://news.bbc.co.uk/2/hi/asia-pacific/1173911.stm accessed 22 June 2019.

5. In 1990, Galman was formally cleared of the crime; in 1991, military personnel were convicted but maintain their innocence to this day.
6. Kristine Joy Patag, "PCGG Corrects Marcos: We're Still Here," *Philippine Star*, August 24, 2018. https://www.philstar.com/headlines/2018/08/24/1845477/pcgg-corrects-marcos-were-still-here (accessed June 22, 2019).
7. "National democrat," as in National Democratic Front, the aggrupation of communist-allied organizations.

Chapter 3

1. Arsenio Balisacan and and Hal Hill (eds.), *The Philippine Economy: Development, Policy, and Challenges* (Quezon City: Ateneo de Manila University Press, 2003), 3, 4.

Chapter 4

1. David Joel Steinberg, *The Philippines: A Singular and a Plural Place* (Boulder, Colo.: Westview Press, 1982; 4th ed., 2000).
2. Aries C. Rufo, *Altar of Secrets: Sex, Politics, and Money in the Philippine Catholic Church* (Pasig City: Journalism for Naationa Building Foundation, 2013), ??.
3. While LGBT is the acronym most used currently in the Philippines, there are those who advocate an expanded version as is evolving elsewhere: lgbtqian+ (Lesbian, Gay, Bisexual, Transgender, Queer, Intersex, Asexual, Nonbinary, + all others). It should be noted that there is neither unanimity on the words (e.g., Q may stand for "questioning") or how detailed to make the acronym.
4. Another Philippine media organization, Vera Files, has been tapped by Facebook, but not attacked so vigorously.

Chapter 5

1. Elections for the 42,209 *barangays* (villages), for the captain, councilors, and Kabataang Barangay (Barangay Youth), are supposed to be nonpartisan, though local politicians strive to have their supporters in these grassroots positions, and they are held separately from the synchronized midterm and presidential elections.
2. Eva-Lotta Hedman, "The Philippines: Not So Military, Not So Civil," in *Coercion and Governance: The Declining Political Role of the*

Military in Asia, edited by Muthiah Alagappa, 165–186 (Stanford, CA: Stanford University Press, 2001), 178.

3. Jarius Bondoc, "More Plunder Admissions from Gen. Garcia's Wife," *Philippine Star,* December 27, 2010. https://www.philstar.com/opinion/2010/12/27/642621/more-plunder-admissions-gen-garcias-wife (accessed June 26, 2019).

4. Malou Mangahas, *The Final Words of Angelo T. Reyes: A Warrior Comes Clean in a Last Battle for Honor* (Philippine Center for Investigative Journalism, February 12, 2011). https://pcij.org/stories/a-warrior-comes-clean-in-last-battle-for-honor/ (accessed June 26, 2019).

5. M. Ladd Thomas, "Philippine Police Systems," *Journal of Criminal Law and Criminology* 46, no. 1 (1955): 116–121, p. 121.

6. Michael Johnston, *Political and Social Foundations for Reform: Anti-Corruption Strategies for the Philippines* (Manila: Hills Program on Governance, Center for Corporate Governance, Asian Institute of Management, Center for Strategic and International Studies, and The Asia Foundation, 2010). https://csis-prod.s3.amazonaws.com/s3fs-public/legacy_files/files/publication/120615_Political_Social_Foundations_for_Reform.pdf (accessed June 26, 2019).

Chapter 6

1. In March 2019, US secretary of state Mike Pompeo confirmed, however, that the Mutual Defense Treaty does apply to Philippine forces in the South China Sea.

2. In fact, only the Abu Sayyaf has been formally designated a terrorist organization under Philippine law.

BIBLIOGRAPHIC ESSAY

If I were to recommend one follow-up book to this volume, it would be *State and Society in the Philippines* by Patricio N. Abinales and Donna J. Armoroso (Maryland: Rowman and Littlefield, 2005 and 2017). The second edition is available in the Philippines from Ateneo de Manila University Press. Written in a roughly chronological fashion at a collegiate level, its four hundred pages end six months into the term of President Duterte.

As work on this book progressed, three volumes came out. *The Philippine Archipelago* by Yves Boquet (Cham, Switzerland: Springer, 2017) is written from a geographer's point of view. At almost 850 pages, it can best be described as magisterial, with copious references covering many different aspects. A more strictly contemporary look is found in Mark R. Thompson and Eric Vincent C. Batalla, eds., *Routledge Handbook of the Contemporary Philippines* (London and New York: Routledge, 2018). Thirty-seven contributions by leading scholars cover in 470 pages domestic politics, foreign relations, economics, society, and culture. A rapidly produced, edited volume is *A Duterte Reader: Critical Essays on Rodrigo Duterte's Early Presidency*, edited by Nicole Curato (Bughaw: Ateneo University Press, 2017).

Among earlier works, easily the most appropriate title is found on David Joel Steinberg's *The Philippines: A Singular and a Plural Place* (Boulder, Colo.: Westview Press, 1982; 4th ed., 2000); the fourth edition was the last of the updates. Two classic works also declare their main thesis in their titles: *A Changeless Land: Continuity and Change in Philippine Politics* by David G. Timberman (New York: M. E. Sharpe, 1991) and *An Anarchy of Families: State and Family in the Philippines*, edited by Alfred McCoy (Madison: University of Wisconsin Press, 1993).

Damon L. Woods, *The Philippines: A Global Studies Handbook* (Santa Barbara, Calif.: ABC-CLIO, Inc., 2006), poses an important dilemma (p. xv): "pressures of writing this book [are] similar to those writing about a close friend or family member. . . . One is delighted to tell others about that friends, but at the same time one wonders . . . what 'good things' to include and what 'bad things' to exclude."

A general resource for public opinion data is the Social Weather Stations (SWS) (www.sws.org.ph). This non-governmental, nonprofit institution has been undertaking scientific sample surveys since 1985. Its flagship survey is the Social Weather Report, a nationwide survey of voting-age adults (generally with a sample size of 1,200); in this book, references to what Filipinos believe come from SWS data unless otherwise specified. There are indeed other survey organizations producing quality work; best known is Pulse Asia (www.pulseasia.ph), which includes in its periodic public releases some details about current events that might influence public opinion.

It is worth reading José Rizal's *Noli me Tangere* (1887) in any edition, as he attempted to depict the state of the Philippines at the end of the Spanish colonial era. Aside from its literary and historical value, all Filipinos read it in one form or another.

INDEX

For the benefit of digital users, indexed terms that span two pages (e.g., 52–53) may, on occasion, appear on only one of those pages.
Figures are indicated by f following the page number